# ECHOES
## OF AN
# ITALIAN
# SUMMER

PAUL GRECH

# ECHOES OF AN ITALIAN SUMMER

## STORIES FROM ITALIA 90

First published by Pitch Publishing, 2023

Pitch Publishing
9 Donnington Park,
85 Birdham Road,
Chichester,
West Sussex,
PO20 7AJ
www.pitchpublishing.co.uk
info@pitchpublishing.co.uk

A CIP catalogue record is available for this book
from the British Library.

ISBN 978 1 80150 454 6

Typesetting and origination by Pitch Publishing
Printed and bound in Great Britain by TJ Books, Padstow

# Contents

Introduction . . . . . . . . . . . . . . . . . .9

The Other Schillaci . . . . . . . . . . . . . 15

Italia 90's Gift to Genoa Resonates Across Time
and Generations . . . . . . . . . . . . . . . 29

Acting Goalkeeper . . . . . . . . . . . . . . 52

In Thy Name . . . . . . . . . . . . . . . . 74

The World Cup that Changed it All . . . . . . 96

Front-Row Seat to Irish History . . . . . . . . 116

Breaking the Curse . . . . . . . . . . . . . . 135

Back-Pass Pain . . . . . . . . . . . . . . . . 152

Scottish Stepping Stone to Glory . . . . . . . 170

The Making of El Maestro . . . . . . . . . . 188

How Milla's Second Act Shaped a Continent . . 209

A Costly Surprise . . . . . . . . . . . . . . . 228

Italy's Wasted Opportunity . . . . . . . . . . 249

Twist of Fate that Disrupted the Magical Nights . 269

Pride of the Nation . . . . . . . . . . . . . . 283

The Soundtrack of Italia 90 . . . . . . . . . . 301

# Dedication

To my loving family, whose unwavering
support made this book possible.

# Introduction

I ALMOST missed the kick-off of Italia 90.

That Friday afternoon I'd attended my first typing lesson; actual typing on a physical typewriter. Not that I'd wanted to but my parents had stubbornly argued that this was something that I'd need if I were to find a suitable job. To make matters worse, the tutor clearly had no interest in football – he told us as much – and kept talking well after the scheduled hour was over, holding us hostage in the process.

Now, if you've never held a typewriter, I can assure you that it's very heavy. Especially the 20-year-old model I'd inherited from my mother. Lugging it across town while trying to walk as quickly as possible wasn't easy, and not being very athletic didn't help my attempt to get home in time.

Yet, somehow, I made it. That memory of cursing under my breath as I made my way home after having to attend the stupid typewriting lesson is for me as integral to my recollections of that World Cup as any goal or action from the competition itself.

Of course, Italia 90 isn't the first World Cup I remember. I'd followed those held in Spain in 1982 as well as Mexico 1986, and have the sticker albums to prove it. Yet rather than memories I have snippets of recollections from those tournaments: someone running out into the street, shouting that Italy were world champions, or echoes of uncles fuming about Diego Maradona's cheating. But 1990 was different. I was 14 years old and as madly in love with the game of football as a teenage boy can be. Pressures from cousins to support Juventus and Italy had been rebuffed three years earlier when I'd caught sight of John Barnes running at two panicking Manchester United defenders, making me a lifelong Liverpool supporter.

An aspect of my fandom that I've retained to this day is that I'd begun reading everything I could about football. The choice wasn't varied but through *World Soccer* and the Italian weekly *Guerin Sportivo* I'd built a decent understanding of the game. When the World Cup kicked off I had a more nuanced appreciation of the various teams' abilities, as well as an admiration for some of the lesser lights. Not that I – like anyone else – wasn't surprised by Cameroon's celebrated win in the opening match, and a little bit delighted, as anyone with no direct emotional involvement tends to be when an underdog succeeds. Surely that victory was destined to herald one of the finest tournaments of all time!

As beliefs go, that one was remarkably wrong. From an entertainment point of view, Italia 90 wasn't good. In fact, it was actually quite bad, with a number of matches ending goalless. In some instances there was barely even a shot! Yet that realisation only came with the passing of time. Remember that this was the first World Cup that I'd followed closely, so I hadn't much to compare it against.

That explains only half the story. Apart from the annoying typing lessons, I had nothing to do during those weeks, so my time was spent swimming, playing computer games and watching football. A lot of football – following not only the matches but every minute of commentary that I could catch either on TV or on radio. Again, and this bears repeating, this was 1990 so there wasn't the wall-to-wall coverage that we've come to expect today. Still, there was plenty.

With a fixation like that at such an impressionable age, I was never going to view Italia 90 through anything other than rose-tinted glasses; a great competition regardless of what anyone else said. That's actually a belief that I can defend to this day. True, Italia 90 was the culmination of the previous two decades' movement towards negative football. It was a tournament teams didn't appear to play to win, more a determined intention to not lose.

Yet there was also a lot to appreciate in that World Cup. Visually, Italia 90 was unlike any other. The stadia looked great, there were some iconic shirts worn and even Ciao the mascot managed to carve a niche in popular culture.

Dig a little deeper, however, and you'll find even more astounding leaps forward made at that World Cup. For instance, for the first time in the tournament's history all accredited journalists had at their disposal the 'FIFA World Cup Database', which was available in five languages. This contained the scorecards of the 2,424 matches played from 13 July 1930 (France 4-1 Mexico) to 19 November 1989 (Tunisia 0-1 Cameroon), the last qualifying match, along with all the statistical information of teams and players. In those pre-internet days, this was simply staggering.

RAI, the Italian national broadcaster, managed to provide a high-definition feed of the matches, which would have been another first, had there been any screens that could show matches at that quality. Another experiment was more successful: the graphics used when matches were being screened on TV. Harnessing the growing computer power, the organisers turned to Italian technology firm Olivetti (who, incidentally, were the manufacturers of the typewriter I was forced to carry around that summer) to provide something new. They did, giving the world a full-screen experience with computerised waving flags of the playing countries that still looks good three decades on. Again, this changed expectations, and fans all over the world could no longer abide the boring, basic graphics that they'd been offered up to that point. It was a lesson that the nascent Sky TV took to heart when it won the rights to screen the Premier League.

Beyond all of this, there were the stories that emerged during the competition. Of Salvatore 'Toto' Schillaci, who became a national hero almost by accident. Or Paul Gascoigne, whose genius with the ball at his feet changed the destiny of English football. It was always these stories that attracted me more than anything else. And they were the kind of stories I always wanted to tell. That came into focus when I heard of Maurizio Schillaci, Toto's cousin, who some regarded as being the better player but for whom fate had a different destiny.

I knew from the start what I did *not* want this book to be: I knew that it wasn't going to be a retelling of what happened during the four weeks of Italia 90. If that's what you're looking for then I'd urge you to check out two great books – Pete Davies's classic *All Played Out* and Simon Hart's equally brilliant *World in Motion* – that do that.

What I wanted to do is dig a little deeper to find those stories that are linked to Italia 90 without being restrained by the competition. Tales like that of Tomáš Skuhravý, who spent a night next to the telephone hoping that his gambit would succeed and he'd be allowed to leave his country to play in Serie A. Or of John Byrne, who went to two major competitions with the Republic of Ireland (playing a pivotal role in reaching one of them) without ever getting on to the pitch. In other words, quirky stories with a heavy human interest.

In researching and writing this book I recalled something of a more personal connection with this World Cup (other than the typewriting incident). I'd actually gone to see a couple of the pre-competition friendlies as both Ireland and Scotland had visited Malta – where I was born and live to this day – as the final stop before they disembarked in Italy.

I must have been excited to see some of my Liverpool heroes play in those fixtures – Ray Houghton, John Aldridge, Ronnie Whelan, Gary Gillespie – but what most stuck in my mind was the behaviour of the fans. The sea of green when Ireland visited (which, local legend has it, was only matched by the sea of beer that they drank afterwards) or the exuberance with which the Scots followed their team.

Many Irish fans used Malta as a base for the first round of the tournament, making the trip to Sardinia ahead of their matches, thus avoiding the draconian Italian policing that was a feature of England's matches.

In that, too, Italia 90 proved to be a pivotal World Cup, for it was during those weeks that the reputation of football fans started on its path to rehabilitation. Not because of the policing tactics adopted but in spite of them. The true heroes were the visionary fans who had formed the Football Supporters' Association and who would go on to play a key role as the sport moved into a more commercialised era. It's not too much of a stretch to argue that the idea for the European Super League and the fan movement that rose up to block it both have their origins in Italy back in 1990.

Those too are stories from Italia 90 that needed to be told, something that I've done my best to do.

As I reflect, I want to acknowledge something else that ties back to that memorable summer – the typing lessons I begrudgingly attended. While I never had the chance to use a typewriter beyond those lessons, the touch-typing skills I acquired during that time have undoubtedly aided me in writing this book a little bit faster. So, to my mother, if you happen to be reading this: you were right.

# The Other Schillaci

THOSE WILD, crazy eyes.

If there's one abiding image from Italia 90, it's of Toto Schillaci's face. It's impossible to think of those nights without recalling the pleading look the Italian striker reserved for referees every time he was touched in the penalty area, a mixture of affront at the injustice that had just taken place while imploring the referee to use his authority and provide retribution.

Of course, Schillaci did more than try to win dubious penalties, and over the six weeks of the World Cup he became a national hero. Thrown in as a late substitute in Italy's opening fixture against Austria – a desperate choice by the under-pressure coach, Azeglio Vicini – Schillaci scored the winning goal. He'd go on to score in all but one of Italy's matches in the competition, each goal followed by his explosive and liberating outpouring of joy. For Italy it was Schillaci, wild eyes and all, that made those nights magical.

It all capped a meteoric rise for the Palermo-born striker who had been playing in Serie B with Messina just 12 months earlier. Then came a move to Juventus, who have always been better at spotting talent than most others. Expectations weren't high but coach Dino Zoff put his faith in him from the start and was rewarded by goals that helped them win the Coppa Italia against AC Milan as well as an all-Italian UEFA Cup Final with Fiorentina.

His goals for Juve, and his ability to be in the right spot at the right time, convinced the usually conservative Vicini that, even though this striker had only played once for Italy before the start of the competition, he was worth a place in his World Cup squad. Schillaci was what the Italians call a 'jolly': a possible trump card to be used if things become desperate.

And so he proved to be. It was the remarkable nature of his success, as well as his theatrics (and goals, of course), that made the whole nation fall in love with him.

\* \* \*

That Schillaci, a Sicilian, had managed to unite the nation was in itself something of an oddity. Among scholars, there's a long-standing debate as to whether the country was always split economically between north and south. Whereas some argue that this was always the case, others claim that upon unification in the mid-19th century they were on similar footings, and that it was the policies adopted in later years that led to a growing gap between the two.

Whatever the reason, it's undeniable that there was a distinct difference in the standard of living by the time Schillaci was growing up. Much of Italy's industrial wealth was concentrated in the north and, stuck in a cycle of unemployment, thousands of families from his native Sicily and the rest of the south were forced to emigrate in search of a better life. Many of them made their way to the north, where they filled factories and took up other menial jobs. Often, they had to live with the snobbery and ridicule of the locals, who reserved the denigrative label of *terroni* for these southern immigrants.

The north–south divide has also been reflected in Italian football, where the most successful clubs have always been from the rich heartlands of the north. Indeed, although at the time of the 1990 World Cup, Napoli had just won their second league title, which, as it would eventually transpire, came at a huge and ultimately unbearable financial cost, it's the rich clubs from Milan and Turin that have historically dominated.

Schillaci, however, seemed to transcend whatever animosity there was between the two poles. Born in the San Giovanni Apostolo area of Palermo, a housing district full of the usual social problems, he was someone that the common man – particularly those from the south – could identify with. Even the exaggerated mannerisms that accompanied his play, how he pleaded with referees when decisions went against him, looked distinctively southern.

Yet his passion for his country was something that anyone could appreciate. So too was his oversized desire to win, no matter what it took. Indeed, whereas in England his willingness to fall at the slightest touch was frowned upon, in Italy it was admired; it was considered less an example of cheating and more one of resourcefulness. In many ways, this is seen as part of the Italian character.

All this made Schillaci someone that any Italian could get behind; he was one of them, regardless of where he came from.

Yet the inclusion of Schillaci in the national team was in itself an anomaly. Apart from a brief period in the early 2000s when there were three Sicilian clubs in Serie A – Palermo, Messina and Cagliari – teams from the island have struggled to make it to the top tier of Italian football. Indeed, often there aren't any Sicilian clubs even in Serie B. While most Sicilians follow the game passionately, the majority support the big northern clubs of Juventus, Milan and Inter. It's a strange state of affairs that means local clubs often lack the financial resources to compete. That all of those three clubs faced bankruptcy in the years following their heyday and all had to restart from the very bottom of the Italian league structure tells its own story.

The absence of Sicilian clubs has a knock-on effect on Sicilian players, who struggle to find a route to the top of the game. It makes it harder for them to be noticed, which means that fewer make it to Serie A or get the opportunity to show what they can do. Indeed, since the 1980s only four of the 400-plus players called up to play for Italy have come from Sicily. And even that number is somewhat falsely boosted by the inclusion of Mario Balotelli, who was born on the island but who moved to Lombardy in early childhood.

Those are abysmal figures that place Sicily third from bottom of the 20 regions that make up Italy when it comes to players that have worn the national jersey over the past four decades. Considering that its five million inhabitants make up almost 10 per cent of Italy's population, that's a truly appalling statistic.

And yet there could – perhaps should – have been another Sicilian playing alongside Schillaci, making those nights magical. There was another who had the potential to shine even when asked to find a way past the dour defences of 1980s Serie A, a player celebrated by many who worked with him as one of the greatest talents ever to emerge from the island. It was also someone Toto knew very well. In fact, he came from the same family.

\* \* \*

As with his cousin, Maurizio Schillaci was born in Palermo and spent his early childhood kicking a ball wherever an empty space could be found to set up a pitch. His talent for the game was evident from an early age and soon Palermo Calcio were receiving reports of this wiry kid who could run with the ball as if it were glued to his feet. These became so frequent that Palermo eventually took notice and signed him up for their youth team.

It was there that he first came across a man who would figure prominently in his career. In the mid-1940s, Palermo had signed a Czech winger by the name of Čestmír Vycpálek, who became a legend at the club. In his first season he led them to promotion to Serie A and eventually became their captain, the first foreigner to do so in Serie A. Once his playing career wound down, he was named Palermo coach and, once again, led them to promotion to Serie A.

It was the start of a long career that saw Vycpálek coach across Sicily before, surprisingly, landing a job with Juventus' youth team and then eventually with the senior team. In Turin he enjoyed his biggest successes, winning back-to-back Serie A titles and leading Juve to a first European Cup Final, yet home for him remained Palermo. That was where he'd relocated his family after the Prague Spring, where he'd move once he retired and where he died in 2002.

Among those who joined Vycpálek's family was his sports-mad nephew, who opted to become a physical education teacher. Vycpálek, however, felt that he could do more and convinced him to take his first steps in coaching. Indeed, he did more than that, convincing Palermo to give him a job in the youth setup. So it was that when Maurizio Schillaci joined Palermo he was welcomed by an inexperienced Czech coach for whom this was a first major job – a certain Zdeněk Zeman.

Although young, Zeman already had clear ideas of how his teams should play, and Schillaci was the sort of forward he loved. Willing to work hard, creative on the ball and extremely fast, he had all the characteristics that the coach required of a striker for his ideas to work. And those ideas also worked for Schillaci, making him the star of the youth team and getting him noticed by the first-team coach, Antonio Renna.

On the final day of the 1981/82 season, Palermo had nothing to play for and neither did their opponents, Lazio, so Renna probably felt a bit more emboldened than usual. The 5,000 who had made it to the Stadio Barbera saw Lazio take an early lead before Palermo drew level. At that point, Renna threw on Schillaci, and his risk paid off. After just 20 minutes on the pitch, a loose ball gave Schillaci a sight of goal and he finished clinically, hitting the ball low and hard beyond the reach of the keeper.

With that kind of impact, it might have been expected that more opportunities would come to Schillaci. Unfortunately, it didn't pan out that way. Palermo endured a difficult follow-up season, avoiding relegation with a draw on the final day of the campaign. Renna lost his job midway through the season before being recalled to see the term out. However, there was little appetite to take risks, even on someone who was as promising as Schillaci, who, as a result, ended up playing just a couple more times for the first team.

Both Schillaci and the club realised that this wasn't going to work for him and, as has long been the tradition in Italian football, he went on a season-long loan to gain experience. The chosen destination was Rimini, a small club a division below Palermo, who had just appointed Giuseppe Materazzi, a young coach who would go on to enjoy a long career that included plenty of experience in Serie A.

Everything seemed set up for Schillaci to take flight but instead he was stuck on the sidelines once more. As with Palermo the previous term, Rimini's season didn't pan out as expected, and with the threat of relegation looming there was no desire to take risks on the young striker.

Such early setbacks can be fatal to a player's career, not only preventing any momentum from building but also silencing any praise that he'd earned in the past, which became just a forgotten memory. For Schillaci, that spell at Rimini could have done just that. It certainly put paid to any lingering desire at Palermo to take a chance on him. But, luckily, not everyone was as dismissive of his potential.

As Schillaci's dismal season was playing out, Zeman had finally outgrown the Palermo youth team and been given the opportunity to coach Licata, a minor Sicilian club that had just enjoyed their first season outside Italy's amateur leagues, in Serie C2, as the fourth division was called at the time. Zeman leant heavily on his Palermo connections, building a team that was a mixture of individuals born in the Sicilian capital and young local players. Among the players he identified, there was the former star of his youth team, Maurizio Schillaci.

Finally trusted by his coach, Schillaci excelled. Licata played the aggressive attacking football that their coach would come to be known for, and Schillaci, who had the benefit of knowing the tactics, fitted right in. At last he could show just what he was capable of, and that was scoring goals, ten in that first season, in which he finished as the top scorer in Italy's top-scoring team. No other professional club managed to score more than the 58 goals that Licata did. More importantly, Licata won their division and went deep in the cup, where Schillaci even enjoyed the satisfaction of beating Palermo.

Unsurprisingly, the following season was much harder and, despite a great start, Licata only confirmed their place in C1 on the final day of the season. This was no disappointment, however. Indeed, for a club that had been playing among the amateurs a couple of years earlier it was a fantastic achievement.

Schillaci also had reason to be satisfied on a personal level. Any doubts over his ability and whether he was good enough only for the bottom tier were dispelled as he proved capable of upsetting defenders at this level just as well as he'd done the previous season and once again ended the season as Licata's top scorer with nine goals, just one fewer than the previous year.

It's perhaps difficult to appreciate the extent of this achievement. Licata is a small club that had spent most of its existence outside league football. There was no rich benefactor pumping in money to fund success, in the way football clubs have tended to achieve such a rapid climb as Licata's. All they had was Zeman, his innovative tactics and ability to spot as well as nurture talent.

Yet, despite all this, he managed to mould a team capable of unexpected success. To this day, that team is affectionately referred to as the 'Grande Licata' (Great Licata) and that period remains the highlight of their history. The players who played regularly for Licata during those years remain heroes, although few are thought of as affectionately as the star of that team, Maurizio Schillaci, the man who either created the goals or scored them. Zeman's attacking tactics wouldn't have led to much if Schillaci hadn't been there to put the ball in the back of the net or lay it off to the others running in to fill the gaps. It's only slightly exaggerating matters to claim that he had the same impact on Licata that Maradona had on Napoli, such was the brilliance he added to their game.

For all his success – or perhaps because of it – it was at Licata that Schillaci's descent into darkness began. He'd begun to smoke weed before matches, initially with the excuse of taking the edge off his anxiety. In time, however, this became bad enough that he occasionally took to the pitch not knowing which way he was supposed to be kicking.

It was only his immense talent that carried him through. That immense talent also brought him to the attention of much bigger clubs, and while the possibility of Licata making it to Serie B seemed remote, it was never going to be the same for their striker.

Schillaci started 1986/87 in fine form, scoring three goals in four matches. Financially, however, Licata were struggling, so when Lazio came in with a club-record bid that in today's money equates to €1m, there was never any doubt that he was leaving.

This wasn't a vintage Lazio team, which in part explains why they were looking at the lower leagues. They'd been relegated to Serie B two seasons earlier and were struggling to stay afloat. Despite all that, however, they remained a big club, and for someone like Schillaci it presented the opportunity of a lifetime, the chance for him to move closer to the highest level. Instead it would prove to be the beginning of the end.

It all started in a friendly fixture. Eager to impress, Schillaci tried his utmost but something seemed off, rendering him incapable of showing any flashes of the talent that Lazio had signed him for. For the player, the reason for the poor showing was an injury, but the Lazio medical staff seemed unable to identify the problem, much less fix it.

Not only did this seemingly phantom injury keep him out and prevent him from gaining any consistency, but it also turned everyone against him. Schillaci had represented a rather big investment for Lazio but one that he couldn't begin to repay. Inevitably, this resulted in ill feeling towards him, transforming him into an outcast with an injury that seemingly existed only in his head.

That injury – which, it eventually turned out, wasn't a phantom one but a very real ruptured Achilles tendon – also left him with a lot of free time. Coupled with the frustration of not being able to show his worth, this could only cause problems. Vices started chasing Schillaci and, unlike opposition defenders, he couldn't shake them off. Parties, late nights and fast cars began to dominate his life. He amassed cars at the same rate that others buy, well, more than others buy anything, really. During that first year in the capital he bought 38. Given more money than he'd ever imagined, he simply didn't know what to do with it, so spent it frivolously.

Not only was it a recipe for disaster but it also attracted the wrong people around him. Unsurprisingly, then, it was in Rome that he had his first taste of hard drugs. Soon, he was unable to think of anything else but the next hit. Schillaci's career unravelled in Rome and pretty soon he was a forgotten man.

Not by everyone, however. After Licata, Zeman moved to Foggia then Parma, with both spells cut short. A return to Sicily with Messina was for him something of a last chance too, so he asked for Maurizio, a player he knew well and who was comfortable in his system. His plan was to partner him with a young talent who had come through the club's youth system, a talent who happened to be related to Maurizio: Toto Schillaci.

Given the liberty with which Zeman always let his teams play, together the two were sensational, with Maurizio creating chances and Toto finishing them off. It was an inspired decision that enthralled those watching and left a trail of broken defences behind them.

At Messina the fans witnessed some of the best football that Maurizio played in his career, as he himself admitted. Perhaps inspired by playing at a higher level, or by the desire to prove his critics at Lazio wrong, he excelled and once more started showing his worth. Even the injuries that kept him out more than once weren't enough to hold him back.

But the star of that team was undoubtedly the other Schillaci. Toto was already worshipped by the fans for having led the team from Serie C2 – where he made his debut as an 18-year-old – to Serie B but that season was the culmination. He scored 23 goals and it was clear to everyone that he was destined for bigger things.

There were no such beliefs about Maurizio. For all the value that he brought to the team he was seen as just another supporting actor.

Often, success in a player's career depends on the momentum they manage to generate. They move to a club, do well enough to be noticed by a bigger club and proceed to do well there. The more this cycle can be repeated, the higher level that player gets to play at. If the cycle is broken, however, it can be fatal. In most cases that break makes it extremely difficult to restart the positive momentum and get it going at the same pace as before. Not only has the player's confidence taken a knock but so too has the belief of the wider game. This lack of enthusiasm means fewer opportunities and a lower desire to overlook any flaws.

So it was for Schillaci. He played well enough for Messina – who had managed to identify the source of and clear his injury – but it was never going to get him back to where he was before the move to Lazio. Instead, he was seen as just another player who had failed to fulfil his potential and, whether he realised it or not at the time, his peak had come and gone.

A move to Juve Stabia – and a drop of three divisions – was all that was in store for him. The descent proved to be ruinous for reasons other than football. He'd dabbled with various drugs at different stages in his career but there, at the tail end of his career and away from the spotlight, the habit really kicked in. Cocaine first, then heroin, which started consuming his life until it became the only thing he cared about. He divorced his wife, lost all his money and ultimately practically all he owned, spending years either living in his car or trying to find refuge in parked trains at Palermo station. Football had led him to riches but it also set him on a path to the deepest of ruins.

Years after he'd last had him as a player, when the depths to which Schillaci had fallen made the news, Zeman wrote an open letter to talk about the former striker:

> I saw Maurizio grow in those years when football was still poetry, particularly in the south. Maurizio was the fans' idol and a leader for his team-mates. As such, I'll leave the man to one side and talk about the player.
>
> He was a great talent. Technically he was phenomenal. Going by his ability, skills and footballing intelligence, he could easily have played in Serie A at the highest level. In my 4-3-3 he played as a winger and he had everything you need for that role: speed, penetration, technique, an eye for goal and the willingness to sacrifice himself for others.

Maurizio was always kind with the others and for that reason everyone loved him. He helped everyone. It hurts to know that today he is all alone. Was he better than Toto? In the past I said that but, in truth, there's no need to make that comparison.

Moralising is often an easy by-product of such hard-luck stories and so too here. Indeed, how Maurizio could have been allowed to fall so low, especially by his famous cousin, seemed to be a recurring question of those who read Zeman's letter. And, indeed, it's a question worth asking.

For Toto, the 1990 World Cup proved to be the highlight of his career. Recurring injury problems curtailed his time with Juventus but his reputation still earned him a move to Inter. There too, however, he had little luck, playing just 30 times in two seasons (scoring 11 goals), with injury again playing a key, negative role.

That experience showed that his career at the highest level was over, so he made a move with an eye to securing his future – he joined Japanese club Jubilo Iwata. There he rediscovered his touch and, even though injuries remained an issue, he still scored prolifically and led them to the domestic title in 1997.

When he returned home, he found that the public sympathy gained during those magical nights in 1990 had lasted. He obtained roles, albeit minor ones, on television shows and even came third in the Italian version of *Celebrity Survivor*. But perhaps his most successful venture was a football school that he opened in his home city of Palermo.

It was there that the paths of the two cousins briefly crossed once more. Maurizio was given a coaching job but left soon afterwards. In one interview he admitted that the stigma of hearing parents object to having their kids coached by a drug addict had partly led to his decision to leave. Sadly, subsequent interviews, when his story had achieved a bit more prominence, omitted that aspect and instead turned into a criticism of his cousin, whom he accused of paying him a pittance that was barely enough to cover the cost of getting to work.

Ultimately, regardless of where the truth of that part of the story lies, it's just a sad epilogue to an even sadder life, one that was perfectly framed by the ever-eloquent Zeman. 'Certain careers don't always reward the individuals as much as they deserve,' he said. 'Unfortunately, this also applies to life.'

# Italia 90's Gift to Genoa Resonates Across Time and Generations

LIFE HAS rarely been easy for Genoa fans. Statistically, they're among the most successful teams in Italian football; with their nine league titles they're behind only the trio of Juventus, Inter and Milan when it comes to scudetti won. On this occasion, those who never trust statistics at face value would be justified. The harsh reality is that no living Genoa fan has been around long enough to have witnessed any of those title successes.

Set up by English businessmen living in Italy – as evidenced by the club's full name of Genoa Cricket and Football Club – they were among the pioneers of the game. Their links to England, where the game was much more advanced, made them one of the stronger teams when football in Italy began being played in an organised manner. The result was six title wins by 1904.

This dominance was curtailed after pressure from various clubs led to a limit on the number of foreign players each club could use. Unsurprisingly given their roots, Genoa had always fielded plenty of English players, so once that advantage was removed, their ability to dominate diminished. However, they still remained among the league's top teams and won three further titles over the next two decades, but after their triumph of 1923/24 they gradually gave way to others with greater financial might.

Genoa's downward slide was brutal. By the start of the 1950s they'd suffered their first relegation to Serie B and, in time, became more familiar with that division than the elite one. They even dropped to Serie C in the 1970s, a new level of misery for the fans to endure.

In the meantime, they'd witnessed two smaller clubs merge to give birth to a new challenger – Sampdoria – as the city's biggest club, not that Genoa really put up much of a fight for that label. Over the years their new neighbours came to symbolise the city of Genoa just as much as the more history-laden club.

The gap between the two clubs started to grow into a chasm after businessman Paolo Mantovani took over Sampdoria in the late 70s. Although he wasn't as rich as his counterparts financing the traditional giants of Juventus, Inter and Milan, Mantovani was a shrewd operator who could spot talent. Under his guidance, Sampdoria became a stable fixture in Serie A and had success both domestically and on the continent.

Genoa went in the opposite direction, not only falling from the heights that their founders had achieved but effectively becoming the second club in the city whose name they bore. Even worse, there seemed no hope for a better future. Not even the talent coming through could help push them higher because, as soon as anyone began to prove their worth, they were whisked away by others with better finances. The Genoa faithful only enjoyed a fleeting view of future internationals Bruno Conti and Roberto Pruzzo, for instance, before circumstances dictated they be sold to help prop up the club.

Those same fans didn't even dare dream of a side good enough to trouble the top end of Italian football; their desperation was absolute, which made what was to come all the sweeter. Because even though no one believed it, the good days were just around the corner.

\* \* \*

Genoa's modern golden era began when Aldo Spinelli, a businessman who had made his money in the transport and shipping industry, decided to buy the club. That was in 1985, the year that their neighbours won the Coppa Italia for the first time, arguably the most miserable moment in Genoa's modern history.

Spinelli breezed into the club with big ambitions and an even bigger ego. His determination was to build a team capable of honouring their history, while also, perhaps, earning him some of the hero worship that Mantovani was gaining at Sampdoria. His arrival shook things up at Genoa but their turn of fortunes hinged on two other arrivals, both of which came in the summer of 1990. The first was that of manager Osvaldo Bagnoli, the man who in 1986 had caused one of the greatest shocks in the history of football across Europe when he led unfancied Hellas Verona to the Italian league title.

Bagnoli was an experienced coach who valued players more than any tactical system, an exception in Italian football of that era. He also excelled at making his team greater than the sum of individual talents, improving the players but, more importantly, getting them to play better as a team.

Frankly, someone of his abilities shouldn't have been within Genoa's reach. Yet Bagnoli had stayed at Verona long after their title win, resisting the bigger offers that had come his way, opting instead to remain in a city where he felt at home. It was only when the club fell on hard times, financially speaking, that he accepted that the time had come for him to move on. And when that happened, there weren't many takers.

That was Genoa's – and Spinelli's – good fortune. For all his ambitions, Spinelli wasn't rich enough to finance a team of stars and, indeed, had only managed to gain promotion to Serie A at the fourth attempt, so a coach who could get the most out of the raw materials at his disposal was precisely what they needed.

Spinelli promised his new coach that he'd do his utmost to provide him with a squad that could compete, and to keep his end of the bargain he used Italia 90 to scout the man whose eventual signing would prove to be the second pivotal act in Genoa's change of fortune: a giant Czech striker by the name of Tomáš Skuhravý.

\* \* \*

Born in Přerov nad Labem, a small village on the outskirts of Prague, Skuhravý had taken to football from an early age and, as with all other kids in the village, started playing at local club TJ Sokol Přerov nad Labem. Skuhravý wasn't like the other kids, however, and by the time he turned 15 Sparta Prague convinced him that his future lay in the capital city with them. For Sparta it was a rather fortuitous discovery for which they could thank a youth team coach who opted to spend some time watching the local kids play as he holidayed in Skuhravý's village. He was the one who approached Skuhravý's father, offering a trial that opened a pathway for the young striker to move to the city club at such an early age.

Nothing was lucky in the manner that Skuhravý took up the opportunity, however. Initially the plan was to allow his talent to develop within Sparta's youth system. That was until their experienced manager Václav Ježek laid eyes on the precocious talent. The man who had led Czechoslovakia to the European Championship in 1976 instantly realised that this young striker was too good to be playing with kids over whom he towered. Instead, he played him with the adults, giving him his senior debut at the age of 16. By the end of that season, Skuhravý had made eight appearances, during which he scored one goal. More importantly, he'd proven that his coach's decision wasn't an impetuous one; he deserved to be there.

For all the faith that he'd been shown, Skuhravý wasn't a regular by the time Real Madrid visited Prague the following season for the first round of the 1983 UEFA Cup. He wasn't even amongst the substitutes, the club opting to use him in a youth team fixture instead. Not that he was missed as Sparta twice let a goal lead slip before scoring a third to record a famous win in front of an ecstatic home crowd.

Still stuck on the sidelines, Skuhravý scored a hat-trick for the reserves that probably preyed heavily on the coach's mind, when considering the possibility of taking this kid with him to Madrid for the second leg. He did so, and with Sparta trailing 1-0 with 20 minutes to go, decided that the situation was desperate enough to warrant another gamble on this 18-year-old.

It's hard to gauge what calculations had gone through Ježek's mind when he made his decision but it's unlikely that even he thought it would prove to be the right one so quickly. Just a couple of minutes after the substitution, a cross from the right-hand side seemed set to fly harmlessly over everyone's head. Until it didn't. Skuhravý, used to towering above all others even at that young age, leapt above everyone to nod the ball past the Real Madrid goalkeeper. It was his first European goal, scored in Sparta's colours with practically his first touch, and it was enough to silence the 70,000 fans at the Bernabéu and to seal the draw that his team needed to knock out the Spanish giants. It also took the Spanish cameramen by surprise; they didn't capture the goal and there are no recordings of it.

For Skuhravý, however, there was no forgetting that moment. When he rose above the opposition defenders he was also making the leap from junior football to the senior game. Never would he have to drop down to the reserves after scoring such a memorable goal. In fact, his place in the first team was solidified by further goals, the most memorable of which was a thunderous shot from the left-hand edge of the penalty area as Sparta dumped Watford out of the UEFA Cup with a 4-0 win. And while there wasn't much that the young striker could do in the quarter-finals as Sparta lost narrowly to Hajduk Split, he did end the season with his first major honours after Sparta registered a domestic league and cup double.

Despite his precocious ability, there was another insurmountable obstacle in Skuhravý's path: compulsory national service. At the time, men were forced to join the military for 18 months when they turned 19 and, having reached that age, Skuhravý had to comply, despite being a famous sportsman.

It wasn't necessarily a bad thing for him. Ježek had decided to leave the club that summer for a stint with FC Zürich, which meant that Skuhravý lost one of his biggest supporters. But even if nothing else had changed, the reality was that Skuhravý was still a very young player who needed to grow and mature. He needed to be playing regularly to gain experience, something that was unlikely to happen at a club like Sparta Prague, which was constantly expected to challenge for the country's top honours. A spell away from the spotlight would help him achieve that.

Another plus was that he wasn't the first to be faced with such a potentially career-defining dilemma. Indeed, there was a well-tested solution that allowed him to fulfil his military obligation and build his career: Skuhravý was sent to the Karlovy Vary region and allowed to join RH Cheb, a mid-table top-flight club from a small town of Cheb. There he played at a decent level alongside some of the country's top young talent. Over the two years Skuhravý spent with Cheb he counted future Czech internationals Michal Bílek and Pavel Nedvěd among his team-mates.

Skuhravý's first season as a regular was tough as he struggled to make any kind of impact, but it was precisely what he needed. And Skuhravý was a quick learner. By the end of his second year at Cheb he was confirming all the promise that he'd earlier shown, scoring 13 times to finish third in the scorers' chart. This was no insignificant feat given that Cheb were a mid-table team.

Physically, Skuhravý had long been capable of handling top-level football but those two years in the Czech countryside helped polish the rough edges. Now he was ready to lead the charge at the country's top club, which was just as well as Sparta Prague needed someone like him. As Skuhravý finished his military training, Sparta had just endured a poor season, at least by their standards, finishing second in the league and bowing out of the cup early. Drastic action was needed, so the call went out for the return of Václav Ježek to coach the team. Fortunately for the incoming coach, there was the new-look Skuhravý waiting and eager to show that he was ready to lead the team after his education at Cheb.

As reshuffles go, the one at Sparta quickly bore fruit. Another league title was added to their honours list, with Skuhravý hitting 18 goals to finish second in the goalscorers' table. There was more to their success than Skuhravý, however. The team that Ježek helped mould featured a core of players who were in their early 20s, such as Július Bielik, Ivan Hašek, Michal Bílek and Václav Němeček. Like Skuhravý, they had talent to burn and would allow Sparta to build a new dynasty.

Which is precisely what they did. With that group at its core Sparta became a dreadnought of Czech football, pulverising all opposition. They won four consecutive league titles and two Czech cups, improving each season irrespective of who the coach was, especially as they could also add the best talent from the rest of the league along the way, such as when Stanislav Griga re-joined the club in 1987/88.

Griga's return changed the dynamic up front. He was a penalty-box striker typical of the era who specialised at escaping his marker's attention and dispatching the ball past the keeper – nothing else. In football goalscoring can be difficult but players like Griga made it look easy. Of course, that was because others were doing a lot of the heavy lifting.

At Sparta Prague, that meant Skuhravý shifted from being the focus of the attack to the one who facilitated matters for others. His height and physical presence made him the ideal target man, capable of winning headers, knocking the ball into the path of his team-mates and forcing a way through defences. A striker of his size tends to occupy defenders' thoughts even before the match kicks off, which makes them a valuable commodity for that alone, because teams set up to stop the big man getting hold of the ball, so others tend to be overlooked, providing them with the space they need to slip in and score goals.

That's what Griga and others did with regularity for Sparta. Skuhravý's goal tally dried up after his first season back but as an attacking team Sparta were even more clinical than before. At least domestically, but in Europe it was a different matter. Despite the talent they had in the squad, they just couldn't get past the early rounds of the European Cup.

Nationally, Czechoslovakia had a mixed relationship with the World Cup. Twice finalists, in 1934 and 1962, they'd been almost permanent fixtures in the competition until 1970. They then failed to reach the final stages of three of the next four tournaments. Even their Spanish experience in 1982 had been a massive disappointment, with draws against Kuwait and France preceding a 2-0 defeat by England. However, they'd excelled on the European front, winning the 1976 European Championship and twice coming third in the same tournament (1960 and 1980) – yet they'd failed to maintain that rhythm.

So when they were drawn in a tough qualifying group that also featured Belgium, Portugal and Switzerland, hopes of making it to Italy for the 1990 World Cup finals weren't particularly high. That didn't bother Dr Jozef Venglo, who had returned as coach of the national team at the start of the qualification stage. Venglo was a man of science who pushed his players to eat the right food and was one of the earliest to embrace sports psychology. He was also a pragmatic man who appreciated that teams had to be built around individuals. As far as the Czech national team went, he understood that physicality was a big asset, particularly defensively, especially when it was combined with the technical skills his players clearly possessed. It was on that basis that he built a team that went through the qualification period by conceding just three goals, two of which came in a defeat against group winners Belgium.

Vengloš also appreciated what Skuhravý could bring to his team, replicating the little-and-large partnership up front that worked so well in club football. Again, Skuhravý wasn't always among the goalscorers, yet he was often the one who opened up the path through which the likes of Griga and Bílek could make their way to score. So fundamental had Skuhravý become that two of the matches they failed to win – a draw and defeat against Belgium – occurred when he wasn't in the team.

Ultimately those two negative results didn't matter too much as the Czechs qualified in second place in the group. It was, in many ways, the ideal way for them to make it to the World Cup. They were in the finals, which was all that mattered. At the same time, no one expected anything from them. Whatever they did in Italy or however they performed, it would come as a welcome boost.

Pressure on the Czechs was kept to a minimum, which helped them get off to a wonderful start when they attacked relentlessly against a somewhat naive USA. They should have scored much earlier than they actually did as they completely dominated the opening exchanges, but it took until the 26th minute for Skuhravý to flip roles and run into space that others' movement had created. He slotted the ball past the goalkeeper to give his nation the breakthrough.

From then on it became very easy for the Czechs, who scored a further four goals in the 5-1 victory. Skuhravý played a key role in most of the Czech goals, not to mention that he scored their third, a typical (for him) header from a corner that evaded all attempts to block it. Two goals on his World Cup debut was a good start.

The quality of opposition edged up a notch in their following two fixtures. In a dour match, they managed to sneak a winner against Austria that showed their maturity as a team, and, perhaps as importantly, effectively secured their qualification to the next round. Their final group match against Italy was a formality, even though the possibility of surprising the home nation was an enticing one. It wasn't to be, however, as Italy were just too strong and had the passion of the home crowd to carry them on. The hosts scored twice through their two revelations of the tournament, Toto Schillaci and Roberto Baggio, and that was that.

Not that it mattered much for the Czechs as they'd achieved the minimum target of getting through the first round. The good mood was certainly enhanced by the news that their opponents in the next round would be Costa Rica. For all the need to keep their feet on the ground, there was excitement at the prospect of overcoming one of the undeniably weaker teams left in the competition.

Scepticism or not, their expectations were justified when the Czechs ran out easy 4-1 winners. It was the Tomáš Skuhravý show, as the inspired striker scored three times in one of the finest attacking displays of the tournament. The Costa Rican defence simply had no way of countering him, which in reality means that they didn't have players who could stand up to him physically. Three times Skuhravý rose to head the ball and three times the Costa Rican goalkeeper was beaten. By the end of the match Skuhravý was the leading scorer, albeit temporarily.

Yet the presence and runs of Ivo Knoflíček, who repeatedly took defenders' attention and created space for the big striker to exploit, played a key if unheralded part in Skuhravý's success, although not one that everyone overlooked, as would become evident in later weeks.

The Costa Rica victory set up a quarter-final tie against West Germany. Franz Beckenbauer's team had gone into the tournament as one of the favourites, a reputation that they'd enhanced over the previous two weeks. Having already been beaten by another of the favourites – Italy – Czechoslovakia were aware of the gap in quality with the top nations but weren't about to let that overwhelm them.

Once the match started, however, it was clear that the Germans' favourites tag had been well earned. A Lothar Matthäus penalty on 25 minutes gave them a lead that they never looked like relinquishing. When the final whistle blew, Czechoslovakia were out of the competition and deservedly so.

Despite their elimination it was still a fantastic experience. Reaching the quarter-finals had been Venglos's personal target before the tournament started so it was mission accomplished. They'd also played some good football along the way to re-establish their reputation as one of the finest footballing nations. It was a platform on which they could build, improving as the years went on with a mixture of Italia 90 veterans and new talent that would eventually see the Czech Republic (Czechoslovakia was dissolved in 1992) reach the final of the European Championship in 1996.

For Skuhravý it had, arguably, gone far better than he'd have expected. His reputation was already good before the start of the competition, as he'd ended qualification as his country's top scorer, but his five goals in the finals marked him out as one of the World Cup's better finishers, ending one goal behind golden boot winner Schillaci. There had never been any doubt that his height was his best attribute, which had been confirmed by four of his goals coming through headers. His all-round play was also good – better than many gave him credit for – but in the air he was practically unbeatable.

The World Cup had provided him with a platform to show what he could do and he'd made the most of it. Skuhravý's name hadn't been known to many outside his home country before the competition but now many had come to appreciate his abilities.

\* \* \*

Some, however, had already been keeping an eye on Skuhravý. Genoa's wily owner Aldo Spinelli, on the lookout for players who could bring to life his coach's vision, was among them, and he decided to act immediately after Skuhravý's brace against the USA, putting in an offer for the striker. There was one problem, however: getting it approved.

As with most other countries from the Eastern bloc, players from Czechoslovakia couldn't simply opt to move to a foreign country. For anyone to be allowed to leave they first had to play more than a half-century of times for the national team, which, at a time when nations played significantly less football than they do today, often meant that a player had to wait until later in their career.

However, times were changing and the wind of freedom was sweeping Czechoslovakia. Skuhravý had no intention of returning home, especially when he'd experienced the thrill of putting himself up against some of the world's best. Winning yet another league with Sparta Prague, as would probably happen, might have been a nice ego boost but the routineness of it all meant it now lacked considerably in allure. It certainly couldn't compare to the challenge on offer elsewhere, which Skuhravý now craved.

When he informed the national federation of his decision, it was met with the usual rebuttals. The player knew, however, that he held the cards in the negotiations, at least while the World Cup was still ongoing. There were no threats or ultimatums, just his determined stance that he wasn't leaving Italy.

Eventually, the federation relented. Skuhravý stayed up late into the night, waiting for the outcome of the discussions that were being held before finally receiving the call that he'd been waiting for and that confirmed that the move to Genoa could now go ahead. The following day he rewarded the decision with that hat-trick against Costa Rica.

If the result was a significant victory for Skuhravý, it was also quite a coup for Genoa, whose plan revolved around getting the big centre-forward. Bagnoli was a pragmatic coach who preferred to allow players to focus on their roles; a right-back had to be a right-back, not an additional winger, for instance. In that vein, he expected Skuhravý to do what he did best, which was dominate in the air and in defenders' minds.

Exalted by his goals at the World Cup and eager for a hero to lead their team back to the higher echelons, the Genoa fans went mad for the giant Czech. It was a big moment for them, a sign that the years of mediocre players not deserving of wearing the shirt of such a noble club were nearing their end.

Yet Skuhravý's start wasn't particularly positive. His debut came in a 1-0 defeat to Arrigo Sacchi's Milan, and by matchday eight he was still waiting to score his first goal. As often happens, the initial joy was soon replaced by criticism of the striker's perceived inabilities. The disillusionment was great because the expectations had been so high. Perhaps, the Genoa fans thought, the World Cup wasn't as good an indicator of his abilities as they'd been led to believe. Probably, the most pessimistic among them thought, he's just another dud who had done well against no-mark teams.

Reprieve came in Florence. With Genoa 2-1 down to Fiorentina, Skuhravý took possession of the ball in the middle of the penalty area, dribbled past a defender and let go a fierce shot that couldn't be stopped. He was as relieved as anyone to finally score his first goal and his joy was reflected in his celebration, a somersault that was rendered all the more impressive because of his size. It would eventually become his trademark.

For all the relief that goal brought, it didn't immediately boost his form. While Skuhravý was used to playing at a reasonably high level, there was still a gap between that and the best league in the world, where he had to face the best defences in the game. He needed time to adjust, to shape his game in a manner that could be effective in his new surroundings.

There was also something of a crisis of confidence on his part as he himself later admitted: 'The initial impact was rather traumatic: when I read through the list of foreign players in Italy after the World Cup – Maradona, Völler, Gullit, Van Basten – I asked myself, "Where am I going? To play with all these champions?"'

The Genoa team that Skuhravý joined didn't have many stellar names but rather a good number of solid, experienced professionals who not only made him welcome but ensured that his head didn't drop when things weren't going his way. It also mattered that he was showing enough in matches and training for everyone at the club to retain their confidence in him. That faith would pay off handsomely, as Genoa fans began to witness.

The match that truly put Skuhravý on the map was the away fixture at Juventus. Early on, he'd been picked out by an exquisite lob in the penalty area but, perhaps surprised at the space he had, the striker fluffed his shot. Another's head might have dropped after such an embarrassing miss but not him and not with the confidence that he was receiving from his team-mates. When a few minutes later another cross made its way into the Juventus penalty area, he rose to challenge their two central defenders, both of whom panicked. Skuhravý was quickest to the resulting loose ball but Tacconi parried his header. Yet Skuhravý wasn't to be denied as he moved faster to the loose ball than anyone around him and this time there was no stopping his shot.

Having finally found his groove, Skuhravý simply couldn't stop scoring. In the second round of fixtures he scored 11 goals and dominated in the air, regularly anticipating defenders and bullying them into submission with his imposing physical strength. Against Lecce he scored twice, including an acrobatic scissor kick that remains one of the finest goals in the history of Serie A. He hit another two at Fiorentina and Lazio, while his goals were critical in securing home wins against Inter and Juventus.

The latter – the last match of the season – proved to be one of fundamental importance. While Juventus had started the season with their usual lofty ambitions – particularly as they boasted the two main domestic heroes of Italia 90 in Toto Schillaci and Roberto Baggio – their form had been abysmal to the extent that they went into the final day on the same points as Genoa. The Turin giants had never missed out on qualification for European competition but that proud record was at stake; Genoa, on the other hand, had never qualified. Yet here they were fighting it out for fourth place and the final Italian slot in Europe.

Ultimately, it didn't prove to be much of a fight. Already 1-0 up by half-time, Skuhravý latched on to a pass from midfield and, with the Juventus defence disintegrating around him, slotted the ball past the goalkeeper to seal Genoa's passage to Europe. A couple of weeks earlier, neighbours Sampdoria had celebrated their historic title win but the scenes of jubilation witnessed at the Marassi at the final whistle against Juventus matched those title celebrations.

Much of the merit for Skuhravý's upturn in form went to his coach. 'We trained at shooting on goal or beating our man, football at its simplest,' Skuhravý recounted in an interview with *La Gazzetta dello Sport*. 'At the end of every half Bagnoli would always tell me, "What the f**k are you doing? Why don't you shoot on goal ten or fifteen times?" And he was right. Even in our tactics: we had to move together, keeping tight and the whole team within thirty metres of each other.'

By then the whole team was working in wonderful synchronicity but the fans' favourite was undoubtedly the giant forward. '*Si chiama Tomáš Skuhravý con le sue reti si vola, fai un'altra capriola, fai un'altra capriola!*' sang the Genoa fans ('His name is Tomáš Skuhravý and with his goals we're flying, do another somersault, do another somersault!')

Yet, despite being seen as the team's leading man, Skuhravý's partner up front wasn't far behind. Carlos 'El Pato' Aguilera was his alter ego, the smaller partner in the little-and-large duo. If Skuhravý's job was to worry the central defenders by his mere presence, Uruguayan internatioanal Aguilera was tasked with making the rest of the defence dizzy with his running and technique. As Skuhravý always insisted:

For me, Pato was the best player in the world. Playing with him was like having eyes at the back of your head. If you had Pato, you go towards goal and score. That's it. That was my home, I left the building to others: my battlefield was in front of goal.

The dirty work, that of keeping defenders busy, was my responsibility. He always used to tell me 'all that matters is that you get in front of goal, I'll put it there for you'. We could find each other with our eyes closed; we also spent a lot of time together even off the pitch. When he touched the ball with his toes, I knew already where he was going to place it.

The devastating partnership was even more effective the following season when they scored 37 goals between them. A decent start to the league campaign was encouraging enough but the real focus was on Genoa's debut UEFA Cup adventure, something that became all the more evident as the season wore on.

In truth, that experience could have ended before it really took off. They'd hoped for an easier first-round draw than the one that pitted them against Real Oviedo and, although the Spaniards were just as inexperienced in Europe, they proved to be a challenging opponent, so much so that Genoa lost their European debut, going down 1-0 in Spain. However, when Skuhravý stooped to head home in the opening minutes of the second leg, it seemed as if the floodgates were about to open. As one of the few Genoa players with experience of European football, Skuhravý held an advantage over his team-mates, yet even they realised that the defensive mix-up that allowed Oviedo an easy equaliser late in the first half could have been the killer blow.

But Bagnoli's team were made of sterner stuff. They kept on going, equalising through Caricola midway through the second half, before finding the third, crucial, goal in the 89th minute. The scorer was once again their Czech giant, who rose above everyone to head past the keeper and send the stadium into delirium. For many of a Genoa persuasion, it remains one of their favourite moments.

The next two rounds were much less dramatic, with two Romanian teams – Dinamo Bucharest and Steaua Bucharest – dispatched with relative ease. There was another Skuhravý goal (the winner in the first leg against Steaua) yet the gap in class was evident in both instances, which meant that the European novices had made it as far as the last eight in one of the toughest continental competitions.

As a reward for their progress, they were drawn against an aristocrat of the European game. With four European Cups and two UEFA Cups, Liverpool were on the other end of the spectrum insofar as experience was concerned. At least theoretically. For this was their first season back in Europe after the Heysel-induced ban that had lasted seven years. In many ways their players were even greener about the demands of European football than their rivals.

Indeed, the Genoa players weren't really bothered by reputation and tore into the English team from the kick-off. The first half saw them create a host of chances, with the clearest falling to Skuhravý, who headed against the bar before seeing his rebound blocked by a desperate last-ditch tackle. Although they were used to facing little-and-large striking combinations – back then a staple of English football – the threat posed by Skuhravý and Aguilera was causing chaos among the Liverpool defenders. The Czech could bully his way past any opponent, while the Uruguayan's running drove the Liverpool players dizzy; yet both were technically gifted enough to be multi-dimensional.

They also knew each other to perfection, so when Skuhravý headed on a punt into the box, Aguilera was already moving in anticipation to where the ball was going to fall, flicking it into the path of Valeriano Fiorin to open the scoring. When the Brazilian full-back Branco hit one of his trademark thunderous free kicks late on to double Genoa's lead, he also made the score more reflective of the home team's dominance.

Despite the solid lead, there was still apprehension when Genoa travelled to England two weeks later. Anfield was a foreboding place to visit, one where no Italian team had ever emerged victorious. Once more Skuhravý was the most experienced of the Genoa players, having already played in a similar environment at the Bernabéu. However, his team's lack of experience barely showed when the match kicked off, despite Liverpool pushing forward in determined fashion, eager to score. And they would have, had it not been for the Genoa goalkeeper Braglia being in inspired form.

Having soaked up the pressure, the Italians then went ahead with a clinical and typical counter-attack that saw them breaking free on the right. The Liverpool defenders rightly assumed that the ball was going to be crossed into the box and crowded around Skuhravý to deny him an opportunity. In doing so, however, they completely overlooked Aguilera, who gleefully used the space that his strike partner had opened for him to score.

Whatever doubt there had been before was no more; Genoa were going to the semi-final. Liverpool did manage to score an equaliser in the second half but Aguilera scored again late on to give them a famous first Italian win at Anfield. They were rewarded with a standing ovation from the home crowd.

Having got so far, Skuhravý wanted to go all the way. Yet it wasn't to be. A young Ajax team coached by Luis van Gaal that would soon go on to win the European Cup were too strong for them. The memories of that glorious night at Anfield would be all that Genoa would end up with.

Those memories, along with the others gathered over the previous 18 months, would prove very precious for the Genoa fans as their club slid back to its previous mediocrity. Their European form wasn't matched domestically, and they ended the season in the lower half of the table. Worse, Bagnoli opted to accept an offer to manage Inter, and Aguilera moved to Torino. The brief golden period was over.

Skuhravý stayed on, however. Not that there weren't plenty of eager observers. Both Bernard Tapie's Olympique Marseille and Silvio Berlusconi's AC Milan made big offers for the Czech striker, yet Spinelli simply couldn't let him go.

Despite a constant rotation of coaches – Genoa made eight changes over the following three seasons – Skuhravý found no reason to push for a move from the city that had won his heart. He kept on scoring too, never hitting fewer than ten goals, despite the quality around him not matching up to his talent.

In the end, heartbreak awaited. Having narrowly avoided relegation twice, Genoa finally succumbed at the end of 1994/95. Skuhravý kept fighting to the very end, scoring a dramatic winner against Torino on the final day of the season and forcing a play-off against Padova. He marked that match with another goal but, unable of going beyond a draw, their fate was decided by a penalty shoot-out that they lost.

Skuhravý briefly stayed on in Serie B but then moved to Sporting Lisbon in November 1995. Yet the years of being the focus of Genoa's attack – and the tackles of opposing defenders looking to take him down – had taken their toll. He played just four times in Portugal before moving back to the Czech Republic to wind down his career with Viktoria Žižkov.

Despite being just 31 years old, by the time his national team took on Germany in the final of the European Championship in 1996, Skuhravý had already retired. The Czechs had found another giant to lead the attack in Jan Koller but also played with greater freedom and conviction than they had in 1990. Yet that European final would have been unlikely if Skuhravý hadn't led the attack so admirably in Italy and forced a move away from his home country that opened that path for others. That run to the quarter-finals at Italia 90 reignited Czech confidence in themselves and their ability, providing the foundation for a decade of success.

Skuhravý's own time in Italy extended well beyond those three weeks of the World Cup, even though they were fundamental for his career: 'In 1990, I was 25 years old, and the World Cup in Italy was an extraordinary opportunity for me to showcase myself. At that time, Italian football was at its peak. Each team could have a maximum of three foreign players, and the best players from every nation played here.'

He came to love his adoptive home and remained there even after his career came to an end. He occasionally puts on the Genoa shirt for charity matches and remains a beloved figure among their support. With good reason. His joining their club was Italia 90's greatest gift to Genoa, having a far greater impact than the four matches in the tournament that took place at their Luigi Ferraris Stadium.

For a generation of Genoa fans, Tomáš Skuhravý came to represent the golden sky at the end of the storm. The victories against Juventus, Real Oviedo and – above all – Liverpool provided memories that have kept them going in the decades since.

# Acting Goalkeeper

OF THE many movies built around the game of football, only one has had any lasting impact: *Escape to Victory* (or *Victory*, as it was marketed in the US). There are many reasons for this but arguably the main one is the credibility with which the actual game is portrayed. Little wonder, given that the cast included a whole host of football stars from the time, such as Osvaldo Ardiles, Bobby Moore and, of course, Pelé.

But while those players gave the movie credibility, pulling power came in the form of Sylvester Stallone. Fresh from the big successes of the *Rocky* franchise, he knew what it took to make a sport-driven movie. The problem was that, contrary to boxing, Stallone had no idea about playing football. He had even less interest in it, telling the movie critic Roger Ebert that he thought it was 'a sissy sport ... until they kicked the ball into my stomach and I crossed the border into Austria with haematomas on both hips'.

With so much attention having gone into making the football of the movie believable, it would have been counterproductive to try to shoehorn Stallone into an outfield position. The solution to this conundrum was to put him in goal with a nice back-story, that of Hatch, a former American football player who desperately wanted to get into the team because it offered a better chance of escaping. He wasn't any good with his feet but he could use his hands and that's all that there is to being a goalkeeper.

Far-fetched it might be but frankly it was much more believable than the idea of an American player forcing his way into a Rest of the World XI during the 1940s. Apart from a brief flirtation with the sport in the 1970s, Americans had shown very little interest in the game of football, so when the movie came out in 1981 that idea would have been as alien as the era it was supposed to be set in.

While *Escape to Victory* was profitable and became a cult classic across Europe, it didn't have a significant or lasting impact in the US. There certainly wasn't an uptick in interest in the sport. Hardly surprising given that legendary director John Huston, who had been hired to shoot it, wasn't particularly proud of it himself. He later admitted that he accepted the job purely for the money and it didn't even get a mention in his autobiography.

So football in the US remained largely a sport for immigrants and expats. Certain concepts at the core of the game, such as the notions of draws or low-scoring matches, were considered alien to American culture. Only those who had brought the game with them from the old continent could have a connection to it. For the rest, there was no looking beyond the traditional American sports of baseball, basketball, gridiron and ice hockey.

American failure at the highest level contributed to this lack of interest. The national team had been missing from the World Cup since a team made up of amateurs had beaten England 1-0 in the 1950 edition. Most of the time they were crowded out by Mexico, the dominant team of the CONCACAF (Confederation of North, Central America and Caribbean Association Football) region, but even on those occasions when the Mexicans weren't an obstacle – such as 1986, when they received an automatic slot as hosts – the USA contrived to lose at home to Costa Rica to miss out on qualification.

It was almost the same in 1990. Once again, the Mexican obstacle was missing – they'd been suspended after being caught using over-age players during the Olympic qualification tournament – but this didn't necessarily mean an easy qualification for the USA. Most of their players were either semi-professional or playing for lower-league clubs across Europe. And those were the lucky ones. Home-based players didn't have a national league to play in so they weren't guaranteed regular football of decent quality.

The state of US football at the time is best exemplified by the story of their coaches. At the start of their qualification campaign the team was led by Lothar Osiander, a German who had been living in the US for three decades and with a well-regarded coaching reputation. It was Osiander who got them on the right path, earning entry to the group stage of qualification. Yet once there, he decided to step down. The reason wasn't the usual story of a difference in views with the federation or an issue over playing style, it was just that this was a part-time gig for him and he simply couldn't quit his job as a maître d' at Graziano's, a San Francisco restaurant.

Osiander's replacement, Bob Gansler, also took on the job on a part-time basis but at least in his case he was juggling this with a similar role at the University of Wisconsin-Milwaukee. Under Gansler's charge the team kicked off qualification struggling for consistency and after three matches their record stood at a win, a draw and a defeat. It was at that stage that the coach opted for a rather radical change, deciding to call up and install as the team's goalkeeper a 20-year-old who was a second-year student at the University of Virginia: Tony Meola.

In keeping with the way football was viewed in the US at the time, the game was in Meola's blood. His father, Vincenzo, had played for Avellino in Serie C when he was in his early 20s. Yet the Campania region wasn't a happy one in those post-war years. While Italy enjoyed a post-war economic miracle as a result of the Marshall Plan and the demand for manufactured goods created by the Korean War, the bulk of the investment was concentrated in the north, where industry boomed. By the early 60s, average wages in the four main northern regions was more than double those in the south. In part this was the result of political decisions that, rather than encouraging an equitable spread of investment, allowed a natural redistribution of population. By every possible measure, southern regions were worse off than the rest of the country, from the number of hospital beds to railway infrastructure, going through to the rate of illiteracy.

Unable to find work at home and faced with stifling poverty, many southerners were left with few options other than leaving their homes in search of a better future. Almost five million Italians moved away from their regions of birth in the years between 1951 and 1965 but two-thirds of these came from the south of Italy. Calabria, Campania, Sicily and Puglia witnessed a heart-breaking exodus of more than two million sons and daughters.

So when in the late 50s the older Meola married his beloved Maria, he was, like many other young men, aware that raising a family was going to be difficult if he stayed at home. His love for *calcio* and Avellino had to take a back seat to his new responsibilities, so in 1961 he joined the exodus, emigrating to the US, where he eventually settled in New York.

It was there that he raised his family, which, like many other immigrants, grew to love the culture of their adoptive nation without ever forgetting the one from which they'd come. In the Meola household that meant the kids were encouraged to adopt not only the traditional American sports but also football.

The instinctively athletic young Meola didn't really need too much encouragement. As he grew, his physique kept up with the increased demands of his favoured sports. Even in his late teens it was hard not to notice the kid with the massive shoulders and solid build that hinted at a past similar to Hatch's, one spent playing American sports that largely relied on hand-eye coordination. When it came to soccer, that skillset meant he was ideally suited for one role above all – that of a goalkeeper.

'I liked all sport,' Meola said. 'At college I played both basketball and baseball. But he [his father] insisted. He told me that I shouldn't wander too far from my origins. Between the end of the 70s and the start of the 80s he used to follow his former club on the radio after they got to Serie A. I couldn't disappoint him. So I became a goalkeeper.'

Not that he had the choice over which position to play. 'He just stuck me in goal because he thought I was fat and couldn't run,' Meola later recounted of his early experiences with the game and the reaction of his first coach. 'None of the kids ever wanted to go in goal because they wouldn't get to run around. But I liked being the team's last defence.' Still, Meola liked it, so much so that he even rejected the New York Yankees, who tried to draft him out of high school.

Opting for goalkeepers' gloves still turned out to be a good move, especially as he grew to be an imposing athlete, one who was 6ft-plus tall but who looked even more commanding thanks to his broad shoulders. He was good enough to earn a scholarship – albeit not just for football but also baseball – and managed to excel, winning All-American honours in each of the two years he played the sport at university level. Throughout a period of almost 3,000 minutes of playing time, he conceded just 11 goals.

It was that consistency that caught Gansler's attention and earned him a spot in the national team. With Meola in goal, they went on a three-match run without conceding a goal. Unfortunately, two of those ended as draws, which meant they had to win their final match away to Trinidad and Tobago to snatch the final qualification spot.

A couple of months earlier, the US had been awarded the hosting of the 1994 World Cup but that was still too far off in the future. The team needed more immediate validation. To do so they needed to do something no other American team had done in two decades – win an away match. It was a tough call, especially as Trinidad and Tobago, their hosts, were also in line to qualify and needed just one point to do so.

Indeed, when the USA players arrived on the island, they were met by a jubilant nation that perhaps on some level thought that qualification was already theirs. The mood at the stadium was equally euphoric but the festivities stopped in the 30th minute when a Paul Caligiuri shot looped into the back of the net to give the USA the lead they were looking for.

From that point on, it was wave after wave of Trinidadian attacks but the USA defence stood firm. On the rare occasions that a shot did manage to get past them, there was Meola, always well positioned to save. When the final whistle blew, most of the USA players stood rooted where they were, managing only to raise their hands in celebration, such had been the energy they'd expended during the match. Only later did they really begin to appreciate what they'd achieved. For the first time in four decades, they were going to the World Cup.

Meola had been at the heart of that achievement, a pivotal figure in the success story. His reward was a contract with the USA national team, with the federation stepping in to fill the void that the absence of a structured league had left. It was the only way to ensure that their players could focus on their training, rather than having to juggle it with their other commitments. In Meola's case, it meant that he dropped out of university and parked his studies. Italy was to be his only focus.

While playing at the World Cup has to rank highly in any player's dreams and was something the Americans had worked so hard to achieve, their efforts didn't always get the appreciation they deserved. There was plenty of dissatisfaction at the low-ball contract the players had been offered, while the facilities weren't always the greatest. Not just at home but even in Italy itself. Originally given the option to train in the same complex as the Italian national team, plans had to be redrafted quickly when the two were drawn in the same group. As a result, the USA were placed in an Olympic training centre in the Tuscan town of Tirrenia that offered rather basic facilities. Being cut off from their families and the rest of the world hardly helped. Already facing a mighty challenge, the young and inexperienced squad would certainly have hoped for a less strenuous lead-up to the competition.

The real trial was still to come and if anyone needed a reminder of the gap that existed with the more established football nations, that came in their opening match of the tournament against Czechoslovakia. The USA players where physically dominated by the Czechs, who were not only better technically but had the necessary experience to handle the defensive approach that the Americans adopted. When the final whistle was blown, Czechoslovakia had come away with a resounding 5-1 win.

It was a huge reality check for all the USA players as the excitement about playing in the World Cup suddenly turned into anxiety. Matters weren't helped by the knowledge that the host nation was to be their next opponent. Certainly not with some journalists asking the Italian coach whether his team would score more than ten goals. More than a few of those journalists had their eyes on the record books.

Not that it was simply those in the media who shared that confidence. On the road to the stadium, the coach carrying the USA squad passed several Italian fans with arms raised and hands open. Some players waved back in reply to the salutation that they were receiving, for that's what they thought those fans were doing. The truth was, as an interpreter informed them, that those lining the streets were telling them they'd get beaten by ten goals.

Such a disrespectful attitude obviously stung but there wasn't much that the American players could do, other than hope that the lessons served by the Czechs had been learned. Yet the nightmare scenario seemed to unfold when a free-flowing move in the 12th minute saw Giuseppe Giannini break into the USA penalty box and fire past Meola. Then 20 minutes later it could have become worse when the Italians were given a (rather soft) penalty, but Gianluca Vialli's shot hit the post and rebounded to safety.

Slowly, however, the American defence started to get a hold of things and Italian forays forward abated. When they did manage to get through, they found Meola perfectly placed to smother any danger. Instead of the expected thrashing, the Italians ended up worriedly playing sideways, looking to kill time. As for the fans who had gone to the stadium expecting a flurry of goals, they ended up jeering their own players in frustration. While the match ended in another defeat, the manner of it was a moral victory for the Americans.

Confidence adequately boosted, they went into their final match against Austria eager for some kind of result. Hopes were further heightened when the Austrians had a man sent off midway through the first half. Once more, however, the Americans' lack of experience showed and, as they pressed forward in search for a breakthrough, the Austrians hit back on the counter to score twice. The USA's first foray in the World Cup for 40 years thus came to a close with the record of played three, lost three.

Beyond those results, it hadn't been all bad. Interest in the game back home was still minimal – a positive result might have made the news, but no one was going to get excited about defeats – but the players had shown the wider football world that they were worthy of respect, that there was talent there.

At 21 years of age, Meola certainly had plenty to be pleased about. He'd gone from playing college football just a year earlier to facing the world's best. His ascent had been meteoric, with little to suggest that the momentum wouldn't be maintained.

Before the World Cup there had been talk of European clubs expressing an interest in Meola. Benfica, runners-up in the previous season's European Cup, were said to be looking at him, as were numerous Italian clubs. Despite letting in eight goals in three matches during Italia 90, none were his fault or ones where he could have done better. If anything, he'd been a calming influence on the rest of the team when they needed it most. Meola's reputation had, arguably, been significantly enhanced by the World Cup.

When it came to it, however, reality wasn't that bright. None of his rumoured suitors stepped up and the only club willing to take a bet on him were Brighton & Hove Albion, then in England's Second Division. Perhaps unsurprisingly – he was still 21 years old at the time – Brighton saw him as a challenger to their number-one goalkeeper Perry Digweed, at least in the short term. Despite just having played in the World Cup, he was simply too inexperienced.

Fate, however, seemed to have different ideas. Two matches into the new season, Digweed suffered an injury that opened up the way to his deputy. Meola stepped up and played fantastically well – he was voted man of the match against a Wolves team that featured Steve Bull, a deadly striker at that level who, like Meola, had been in Italy that summer, as part of the England squad.

Doing so well encouraged Meola, who also got to play another match thanks to Digweed's absence. In football, however, there's no discussing the position of the regular keeper. So when Digweed recovered he immediately won back his place, with Meola dropped to make way. Having impressed when he'd played, it must have been frustrating for Meola to find himself once again on the outside looking in.

Perhaps more opportunities could have come his way had he persisted at Brighton but, instead, Watford came in for him. Legend has it that Elton John had been impressed enough by the goalkeeper to sign him for his club. In truth, that's probably just a nice myth, given that the musician had sold the club a year earlier. Whatever the motivation, Meola was happy enough with the move. 'It feels great that this saga is finally over,' he said. 'It is very exciting for me to sign with my first full-time professional team. I feel it is a great step forward, not only for me but hopefully for all future American goalkeepers.'

Sadly, he'd spoken far too early. Within a couple of weeks his work permit had been refused, and after just one match with Watford it was all over. A three-month spell training with French outfit Toulouse followed but that too came to nothing due to complicated work permit rules. Meola found himself back where he started. Arguably, he was in a worse place. With the dream of a move to Europe seemingly dead, and lacking an established professional league in the US, there weren't that many options open to him.

He had a brief spell at the Fort Lauderdale Strikers as football in the US looked for a comeback through the setting up of the American Soccer League in 1988. Yet by the time Meola joined, both club and league were going through difficult times and folded after just a handful of years of struggle. Meola didn't endure much of that because his stay was short-lived. The brief experience was enough to highlight once more the disinterest of the American public in football, that there wasn't enough of a following to allow for the survival of a professional league.

The only way the game was going to gain a foothold in the US, it seemed, was if the World Cup due to be held there was successful. If the presence of the world's biggest teams and stars wasn't going to excite the public enough for them to turn up and then keep the interest alive afterwards, nothing was going to be able to save football in the US.

That was the big bet that FIFA had taken when they awarded the World Cup to the US, so much so that one of the conditions set when the tournament was awarded insisted that a nationwide professional league must be set up. The aim was obvious: football was already the most popular sport in the world but, financially, it needed to grow in the world's most advanced economy as well.

For that to happen the USA national team needed to do well. With just a handful of players in Europe and minimal opportunities back home, the US federation once more stepped in to give professional contracts to all the players on the American roster. Effectively, for those players the national team would also be their club. It wasn't the ideal situation but it was one that worked. Under the guidance of the much travelled and inspirational coach Bora Milutinović the USA evolved from a team that clearly felt like intruders on the biggest stage to one confident in its ability.

That confidence found its release one year before the start of the World Cup as the national team faced England in a lucrative friendly held at the Foxboro arena in Boston as part of a competition held in preparation for the main event. Over 37,000 American fans packed into the stadium to see their team register an impressive 2-0 win against the English, arguably American football's best result since beating the same opposition in the World Cup in 1950.

A narrow defeat to the reigning world champions, Germany, a few days later seemed to confirm that the Americans were on the right track. In truth, the only confirmation that came out of that match was over Meola's importance to the team. Beyond the final score (3-4) the Germans had outclassed the Americans and by the end of the match had registered a massive 28 shots at goal. Almost certainly they'd have won by an embarrassing margin had it not been for the American goalkeeper making 11 saves to keep the scoreline respectable.

Still, there was more to be encouraged by rather than disappointed. Football wisdom has it that no team can do well without a solid spine, starting from the goalkeeper. If any confirmation were needed that the Americans at least had that basic ingredient of a solid shot-stopper, then that 1993 tournament proved it.

Meola proved just as vital in the World Cup a year later. In the first match, against Switzerland, a 1-1 draw, he pulled off several fine saves to earn a valuable point for the USA. He was just as solid in the second match, an unexpected 2-1 win over Colombia that, sadly, is mostly remembered for Andrés Escobar's own goal that ultimately cost him his life.

Not many of Meola's saves were of a spectacular nature. Often it was simply down to his positioning and being where he needed to be when he needed to be there. He was a little less confident in the final group match – a 1-0 defeat to Romania where he was caught out by Dan Petrescu's shot at the near post – but in the larger scheme of things it mattered very little; the USA had made it to the next round as one of the best third-placed teams in the groups.

Four years earlier, they'd gone into the match against the Italians with the locals predicting a ten-goal win. A measure of the progress that the Americans had made during the intervening period came in the respect that Brazil showed them before their match in the last 16. No one was under any illusion that the Brazilians weren't the favourites, not when their attack featured the deadly duo of Romário and Bebeto, but also no one was predicting an easy rout of the hosts.

It was the biggest match in the history of football in the US and the Americans played in a manner that befitted the occasion. The Brazilians were visibly the better team but a combination of bad misses and dogged defending kept them at bay for 74 minutes before the two strikers combined to gain Bebeto that slice of space he needed to slot the ball past

Meola. The traditional footballing hierarchies had imposed themselves once more but the massive crowd of 84,000 who watched at Stanford Stadium and the millions more who followed on TV realised that they'd seen a momentous match. Football in the US wasn't going to be the same ever again.

Ironically, given what was on the horizon, it was at this stage that Meola's career went in the opposite direction of the fictional Hatch. Many of his team-mates were making moves to Europe to try their luck there and it could have been the same for Meola. More clubs than four years earlier were now interested in him but he veered his career on a whole new trajectory when he received a radically different kind of opportunity: the National Football League's (NFL) New York Jets had been as impressed as anyone else out there and wanted him to join their setup as a kicker.

Placekickers are specialised roles within American football. As the name suggests, they are responsible for the kicking duties of field goals and extra points, as well as being the team's kick-off specialists or punters. Such duties mean that they also tend to be the ones who score most of a team's points – the top-scoring players in NFL history have all tended to be placekickers – and often entire games hinge on their ability to convert kicks, winning vital points for their team.

Just as for the writers of *Escape to Victory* it made sense that an American used to playing their version of football might make for a natural goalkeeper, it seems that someone at the Jets felt that a goalkeeper might also make for a good kicker. It's easy to see why they felt that way. While placekickers are normally protected from physical contact on field goal attempts, it's not the same in kick-off instances, where the kicker can end up being involved in the action once the kick is returned.

Nevertheless, the risk is minimised for these players. It's why many kickers tend to be slighter players, certainly when compared to their team-mates. It's also why they tend to end up playing in the league for longer than most other players. They simply don't suffer the same level of attrition as the rest of the team. Yet, while minimal, the risk is still there, which was probably what made the idea of recruiting Meola all the more attractive. He had the experience of kicking a ball with his feet but with the bonus that he was used to players charging into him – although there's a big difference between a striker jumping into a goalkeeper to win the ball and an American footballer charging at him with the same idea in mind – and had the build to handle it.

That same summer the Jets also signed Nick Lowery, who at the time was seen as one of the finest kickers ever in the NFL. Still, Lowery was 38 at that stage, so there were doubts over how long he could continue playing and how effective his kicking could remain, especially for the duration of a whole game. A rule change had added five yards to the kick-off lines, making it vital that whoever was tasked with kicks had to have the strength needed to deliver.

Perhaps the Jets' thinking was that Meola would be able to learn from Lowery, blending the skills that he'd already developed with those needed to be a successful kicker. He wouldn't have been the first to tread that path. Among the many former football players who eventually became kickers, the Dane Morten Andersen stands tallest. He'd played football in his native Denmark and narrowly missed out on a call-up to the national team of his age category. During a trip to the US, however, he tried NFL-style kicking and eventually became one of the game's finest, even making it to the Pro Football Hall of Fame.

Unfortunately, Meola wasn't set to follow a similar path. From early on during practice, he earned the nickname of 'Captain Hook' for his tendency to send the ball to the left-hand side of the field. This showed underlying issues with his technique, which transpired in other ways, such as an inability to keep the ball in the air long enough, making his kicks less effective. After three pre-season games, the coaching staff at the Jets had seen enough and decided to cut him from the squad. The idea of a player moving seamlessly from one sport to another might work in fiction but reality tends to be harsher.

Despite the disappointment that rejection undoubtedly caused, the fact that the opportunity had come about revealed plenty about Meola, of his confidence and capacity to back himself in different kinds of challenges and the ability to make the most out of every opportunity that came his way.

That strength of character explains why he was so fundamental to the USA team during those early days of the rebirth of football in the US. Others might have balked at the idea of facing the world's best at the 1990 World Cup when the only football they'd played was at university. Not Meola, who instead revelled in the challenge, inspiring those around him in the process. And when things didn't go his way he simply dusted himself off, got up and kept going, regardless of whether the setback was a heavy loss on your World Cup debut or having the dream of a career in Europe knocked back because of a piece of paper.

Any other attitude would have made it impossible to survive those early years when football received just cursory attention, and media reports on the USA's matches at the biggest stage barely garnered a few paragraphs in most broadsheets' sports pages. For it ensured that they kept on going in the hope of finally making it.

Which they ultimately did. Yet there were plenty of further setbacks waiting along the road. Once the American football route was exhausted, Meola looked around for new opportunities but not many were forthcoming. The best one came from the Buffalo Blizzard, one of the top teams in indoor football.

The reduced version of the game was, for a time, more popular in the US than the real one because it was faster and focused on skill rather than an emphasis on tactical aspects. It was also easier to find venues where matches could take place. Its popularity was such that most of the top American players of that era at one point or another played indoor football during their career.

Meola doing so, then, was nothing unusual, even if a player who had starred at two World Cups might have expected something better. What was extraordinary, however, was the reason why he ultimately left the Blizzard: Broadway. In one of those moves that makes real life more unbelievable than the world of fiction – even *Escape to Victory* didn't go this far – Meola received the opportunity to play the role of the titular character Anthony Angelo Nunzio in the off-Broadway production of *Tony n' Tina's Wedding*.

It was described by the show's website as 'an immersive comedy show staged as an evening of nuptials for two Italian-American families. It invites the audience to actively participate in all festivities … everyone is a welcome guest at the ceremony and reception, there's real food, real dance, and real mingling with the cast of loveable characters.' It might not be one of the most famous of productions, but it was still quite a successful one. It had a run in the smaller theatres around New York that lasted over 20 years and has been staged in over 100 locations across the world 'including cities in Canada, Japan, Germany, the United Kingdom, and Australia'.

Meola had apparently been taking acting lessons for some time and harboured ambitions to make it in the movie business. He spoke of how he was going to 'be the ninth Tony in the play and seven of the Tonys have gone on to major motion pictures'. Clearly, he had big ambitions.

Tellingly, however, Meola wasn't even the most famous sportsperson in the cast. That honour fell to Vito Antuofermo, a former world middleweight boxing champion who went on to appear (very briefly) in *The Sopranos*. In fact, one of the ways that such a production has to gain publicity is to offer guest roles to well-known people, safe in the knowledge that in itself this will attract an audience curious to see how it turns out. A few years before Meola, it had featured the baseball star Lee Mazzilli, a 1986 World Series winner with the New York Mets, who had just retired from the sport and was also looking for a way into the movie business.

Regardless of the motive, Meola did well enough for his contract with the production to be extended for three months after his initial four-week deal. Unfortunately, there were no further extensions and his acting dreams had to be shelved next to his American football ones.

Fortunately, football's time in the wilderness in the US was nearing its end. The World Cup had done better than anyone could have predicted. The number of people attending matches exceeded the previous best by one million and average attendances almost hit 70,000. Financially, the tournament also did spectacularly well and the US federation walked away with a surplus in excess of $50 million, which allowed it to not only honour its commitment to FIFA to set up a professional league but also have real clout to ensure that it survived infancy.

Having been announced in 1993, Major League Soccer kicked off in 1996 and at last offered professional football for local players. Meola had spent some weeks training with Parma but when nothing concrete came out of that he was assigned to the NY/NJ MetroStars – a sensible move to provide a home-town hero to the team.

He wasn't the only high-profile, with fellow USA national team star Tab Ramos being drafted alongside him as well as the veteran Italian midfielder Roberto Donadoni, a player that Meola had faced way back at the 1990 World Cup. The experienced Eddie Firmani – who had tasted success in the North American Soccer League – was installed as coach amid expectations that the team would be among the leading lights of the fledgling league.

Those expectations were dashed after the team failed to recover from a debut loss to an own goal. Firmani was sacked after eight matches, with replacement Carlos Queiroz failing to significantly improve results. They finished third in their conference but were quickly dispatched from the play-offs.

For all their struggles, Meola still enjoyed an excellent season in which he led the league in the number of clean sheets kept, with nine. This was recognised the following season when, after the club's first captain, Peter Vermes, was traded to the Colorado Rapids, Meola was elevated to the role of club captain.

Despite all attempts, the team not only failed to improve the following season but actually did worse. They did manage to get back to the play-offs in the league's third edition but again that was short-lived. Part of the problem was the flailing around for an immediate solution, rather than the presence of a long-term plan to help the team grow into a success. It was this search for a quick fix that led to Meola leaving. Typical of the rather chaotic nature with which the MetroStars (the New York/New Jersey moniker had been dropped from the club's name a year earlier) were run, they first told him that he was definitely staying before opting to send him and fellow national team icon Alexi Lalas to the Kansas City Wizards just weeks before the start of the new league season.

Meola was angered by the broken promises and didn't really want to be at Kansas City. An injury suffered during training early in the season that kept him on the sidelines for almost five months didn't help. What drove him on was a conversation with Bob Gansler, the man who had given him his debut with the USA national team and who had taken over as the Wizards' manager. He'd agreed to trade him back to New York at the end of the season.

By this time Meola was no longer a regular part of the USA team – he'd asked not to be included after the 1994 World Cup, citing personal reasons – but he was still one of the finest goalkeepers in the country, despite a series of injuries setting him back. Gansler realised how good he was and worked on the player to convince him against leaving as he built his team around him.

It was a successful strategy. Gansler brought in several experienced players that other teams weren't too keen on and, perhaps stung by that rejection, the Wizards quickly gelled together. They developed one of the meanest defences in the league and Meola set a new MLS record of 681 minutes without conceding a goal as he registered 16 clean sheets as they first won their conference title before fighting their way to the play-offs final.

By the time that final came, Meola had already been voted as the league's Most Valuable Player – thus confirming Gansler's judgement – yet the Wizards were seen as the underdogs against the Chicago Fire due to their opponents' strong attack that was led by Bulgarian legend Hristo Stoichkov. Yet it was Kansas City who struck early on in the 11th minute and then relied on the solidity of their defence to see the match out. Meola played a starring role, making several saves but, in reality, it was a team effort as they frustrated their opposition. At the end of the 90 minutes the score was still 1-0 in their favour.

For Meola, the boy drafted into a man's game out of college, who had grown to be one of his country's finest-ever players and one of those who had ushered the national team in from the wilderness, it was his career's crowning achievement. He played in Kansas for a further four seasons before returning to New York to wind down his career back home. In 2002 he made it to another World Cup, although, by this stage, he was third choice behind Kasey Keller and Brad Friedel. Still, he kept on playing and on 11 April 2006 earned his 100th cap for his country in a friendly against Jamaica.

At the end of the 2006 season, he called time on his career, although, somewhat ironically for a man who had considered other options away from the sport years earlier, he did play for another season with the New Jersey Ironmen indoor football team.

Over the years, there have been dozens of American goalkeepers who have played at the highest levels in Europe. Meola never managed to achieve that, partly because of circumstances but also because of a personal desire to remain close to his family. Yet he was the one who led the way for American goalkeepers; the example he established in getting the USA to the 1990 World Cup has been followed. And it's partly thanks to him that latecomers to *Escape to Victory* might not be too surprised to see an American keeping goal for the combined World XI.

# In Thy Name

WHAT CAN you do when your father decides that he's going to name you after one of the greatest and most famous footballers ever? And we're not talking about something that could potentially be waved off as a funny coincidence, like a Cristiano or Leo. We're talking about something obvious that no one can hide from. Something like Pelé.

In that case, there are only two possible options: you either decide to completely ignore the game of football so that you cultivate a group of friends for whom the name is largely irrelevant; or, if you go in the other direction and choose to embrace it, then you work as hard as you possibly can at being so good at football that no one can make fun of your name.

The latter was the path chosen by Gavril Pele Balint. His father – also named Gavril – had come across the middle name five years before the younger Balint's birth in 1963. It was difficult to catch a glimpse of the 1958 World Cup in Romania. Only a few of the elite had access to television in one of the most repressive countries behind the Iron Curtain and, in any case, just a handful of matches were transmitted by local channels. Access was easier through the radio, so the football-mad former amateur player listened to as many commentaries as he could. Despite the lack of visuals, he too was captivated by the 17-year-old Brazilian sensation who took his nation to their historic first World Cup success. And even though he'd never actually seen Pelé play, Gavril liked the way the commentators described him and the fluidity of his movement.

A former player and later coach of the local team from Sângeorz-Băi, Balint snr's greatest wish was to have a son who would go on to do great things with a ball at his feet. In that moment, as the matches from Sweden and Pelé's exploits filled the airwaves, a thought first formed in his head, one that later consolidated into the decision that if he ever had a son, he'd name him after this young phenom in the hope that, like the young Brazilian, he too would one day win something important in the game of football.

Fortunately for both Balints, the young boy not only inherited his father's passion for the game but, crucially, had talent to match the burning ambition that had been kindled since an early age. He'd begun to show it on the pitches of Bistriţa, where he first started kicking a ball, eventually joining local side Gloria, where he'd continued to shine. It was inevitable that someone with his talent would garner attention, and eventually national recruiters came knocking with an invitation to join a centralised football boarding school that filtered the brightest prospects. This was where students went through rigorous training regimes from an early age to improve their chances of excelling at international level, thus securing glory for the country and, by association, for the ruling regime.

It was a harsh, brutal system that robbed the boys of their childhood and forced them to grow up quickly. Yet it was also one that bore results. The country's famed programme that helped develop a host of the world's top gymnasts and that stunned the world when Nadia Comăneci became the first gymnast to register a perfect score in the 1976 Montreal Olympics had been built on the same model. Talent was scouted from across the country and, from an early age, put under the guidance of the best coaches, with attention focused exclusively on the sport.

Stories of the horrific abuse that went on in the gymnastics programme emerged decades later but at the time it was seen as an honour to be invited. That's certainly how young Balint saw it when he was asked to be on the first intake at Luceafărul Bucureşti in 1978, although there's nothing to suggest that those in the football school were subjected to similar abuse. For all his desire to succeed, the decision to leave his family behind still wasn't an easy one. Few have the stomach to leave behind a crying mother, heartbroken at the departure of her child, let alone a boy barely into his teenage years. Yet he realised that the best place for him was at the school where the main aim was to prepare the boys in the best possible manner to achieve youth tournament success.

Within three years they had their first success. Despite being 18 years of age, Balint was called up for the Romanian Under-20 team that had qualified for the 1981 World Youth Championships held in Australia. Many of his team-mates had already celebrated their 20th birthday, so it's a sign of how well thought of Balint was that he was a regular in the team. It was also a mark of the work done at raising the level of Romanian football that they finished in third place, beaten only in extra time by eventual winners Germany. It was their only defeat of the tournament, which included a 1-0 win over England in the third-place play-off.

For Romanian football, this was a colossal result that validated their approach to nurturing talent, proving that it worked not only for individual sports and armed them with the conviction needed to remain on this path. The prize in focus was one that every authoritarian regime craved: doing well on an international stage. By the early 1980s Romania's relationship with the World Cup was a peculiar one. They'd been one of the few European nations to take part in the inaugural edition held in Uruguay way back in 1930 and had then gone on to compete at the next two tournaments as well. Yet all they had to show from those fairly miserable experiences was one win, a 3-1 success over Peru on their debut.

After 1938, it was as if Romania had fallen off the map of world football as they struggled to get back in to the elite competition. Only once did they make it to the World Cup finals (Mexico 1970) over a period of more than five decades, and even then results were poor. Getting past the qualification rounds was proving to be a step too far for them time and time again. It had been much the same in the European Championship, where they'd only managed one qualification in the tournament's existence.

Those failures were seen as a reputational stain for the Romanian elite, one that had to be erased as quickly as possible. The success in the World Junior Championships had raised hopes and signalled that something special was brewing for Romanian football. Further encouragement came from Romanian participation in European club competitions, specifically in the results of one team: Steaua Bucharest.

The biggest club in the country and also the one backed by the powerful Ministry of Defence, talent had been funnelled to Steaua for years. Even so, they'd been on a domestic drought of honours for six years from the tail end of the 70s to the mid-80s. Frustrated by that run, the club turned to Emerich Jenei, a former player and a mercurial coach who had led them to the league title in the past – this was his third stint as head coach – in the hope that he'd yield the desired results. In an attempt to hedge their bets or prepare for the future – depending on your level of charity – they also brought in as assistant another of the club's most legendary players, the recently retired Anghel Iordănescu.

The new setup clicked from the start. Jenei was a shrewd man-manager and a visionary coach who demanded quick, precise passing from his players. 'In training, we did one-touch football,' he used to say, succinctly summarising how he prepared his team. 'Only when the boys lost their focus, because it's very difficult to keep that up, did I accept two-touch football.' His philosophy, coupled with a group of talented players and Iordănescu's coaching, immediately brought success. The domestic drought was ended when they won the league in 1984/85, which, in turn, opened up a route to the biggest continental prize.

Up to 1985/86, whenever they'd qualified for the European Cup, Steaua had never managed to get past one round. They could take some comfort in the knowledge they'd pushed a strong AS Roma all the way in the previous year's Cup Winners' Cup before losing 1-0 in Rome. Yet not even the most fanatical of fans would have dreamed of what was in store.

A rather fortuitous draw set them up with Vejle Boldklub, Honvéd, Kuusysi and Anderlecht, all of whom were overcome to set up a final against Barcelona in Seville. What's most remembered of that match – apart from how stultifyingly boring it was – was Steaua goalkeeper Helmuth Duckadam managing to save all four Barcelona penalty kicks in the shoot-out after the goalless draw. Those overshadowed Andoni Zubizarreta's saves that stopped the first two Romanian penalties, and the final two Steaua penalties that actually went in. Marius Lăcătuş scored the first. The second – the one that sealed victory for Steaua – was calmly rolled into the bottom left-hand corner by the Romanian Pelé, Gavril Balint.

\* \* \*

Balint had joined Steaua's youth teams in 1980 – his was a typical example of how talent was channelled to the biggest clubs – and made his top-flight debut in 1981. By the time that Jenei had taken over he was a first-team regular, but under the new coach he became a fundamental part of the team, playing on the right side of a three-man forward line.

While Steaua's European successes surprised many, it was no fluke. Talent was funnelled to the top clubs, the ones backed by the most powerful ministries. Apart from Balint and Lăcătuş, the 1986 team included the elegant defender Miodrag Belodedici, and Victor Piţurcă up front, a willing striker always capable of finishing off any opportunities that came his way.

A year after that success, Gheorghe Hagi joined from FC Sportul Studenţesc, and the midfielder, arguably the greatest player in Romanian history, took them to a new level. They reached another European Cup Final in 1989, although on that occasion they were outplayed by Arrigo Sacchi's AC Milan, plus another semi-final in 1988. Domestically, they had no peers. Between 1984 and 1989 they won five consecutive league titles and the domestic cup on four occasions. In the middle of that period there was a 107-match unbeaten run. It was as comprehensive a dominance as any in the history of the game and Balint was at the heart of it all the way.

Not that he had much choice. Under Nicolae Ceauşescu's dictatorial rule and his failed economic policies, Romania was one of the most impoverished countries in Europe. It was also one of the most repressive that, while not under the influence of the USSR and at least in appearance harbouring good relationships with the West, tried to control every aspect of its people's lives. Arguably top of the list of prohibited activities was the freedom to travel to the West, irrespective of whether for fun or work.

Football and footballers were no exception. There were minimal opportunities for any clubs not backed by the more powerful state agencies to succeed as their better players were always receiving suggestions of who to join. Those same players only had the illusion of choice because their freedom to move was restricted by what others thought best for the regime.

In the 1970s, Real Madrid were desperate to sign attacking midfielder Nicolae Dobrin, a three-time Romanian Player of the Year who had caught their eye after a scintillating display when he faced them with Arges Pitești in the 1972/73 European Cup. His dribbling skills so enamoured Real's president Santiago Bernabéu that he travelled to Romania for a personal meeting with Ceaușescu, offering a then huge $2m transfer fee, plus the promise to cover the costs of floodlights at Pitești's stadium. It wasn't enough. Dobrin was seen as a national treasure and allowing him to leave would have sent the wrong signal to the rest of the Romanian population, especially with Spain being a fascist dictatorship at the time.

Juventus received a similar reply when they tried to sign Rapid Bucharest striker Florea Dumitrache. Their offer of $1.5m plus the promise to open a car manufacturing plant in Romania weren't enough to convince the regime that Dumitrache could leave. As a 24-year-old at the peak of his abilities, he was simply too important a symbol to risk losing.

Only those willing to take the most drastic of actions made it out. In 1981, Ballon d'Or nominee Marcel Răducanu defected to West Germany to secure a move to Borussia Dortmund. He was following in the footsteps of Viorel Năstase, who had rejected his country to make a move to Young Boys Bern, and Alexandru Sătmăreanu, who remained in Germany illegally after a European Cup match before joining VfB Stuttgart.

Those running Romanian football, however, were clever enough to introduce carrots to keep players happy. Not only did they benefit from better living conditions than the rest of the population but they were also allowed to move to foreign clubs. There was a catch, though: they could only do this when they received official approval, which often came when players turned 32 and, effectively, were no longer useful to Romanian football.

It was when they reached that age that both Jenei and Iordănescu were allowed to leave, at which point they moved to minor clubs in Turkey and Cyprus, respectively. And that's how it was for generations of Romanian players. That's also how it would have been for Balint and the rest of Steaua's great team. They'd have grown old and then been allowed a token move to make a little bit of extra money before winding down their careers.

All that changed in 1989 when, inspired by what had happened elsewhere in countries within the Warsaw Pact and fed up with the conditions in which they were being forced to live, the people of Romania rose up against the regime. After more than two decades of dictatorship, Ceaușescu was brutally deposed in December, with free elections following five months later.

\* \* \*

By the time the World Cup rolled up in the summer of 1990, a hopeful mood was sweeping through Romanian cities. And surfing on top of that mood were football players, perhaps the finest generation ever to come out of the country, who were suddenly alive with the possibility of a move overseas and the riches this could deliver.

The first to leave was inevitably Hagi. Real Madrid didn't wait for the World Cup to see what he could do at the highest level. In May, their club president, Ramon Mendoza, travelled to Bucharest to wrap up the deal for $4m. A few weeks later, fellow Steaua and national team midfielder Iosif Rotariu followed suit when he moved to Turkey's Galatasaray.

The rest of the national team were willing to wait for the World Cup to see what offers would come their way. This proved to be the right decision. Like children finally being allowed into a toy shop that had previously been off limits, Western clubs simply couldn't get enough of the buffet that the liberalisation of Eastern bloc economies was offering them.

The Romanians had identified the Telese Terme city in Campania to hold their training camp ahead of the World Cup. It was supposed to be a quiet, idyllic escape from the pressures of the competition but was instead transformed into a madhouse of activity as clubs piled in to get their pick of the cheap Romanian talent. One newspaper captured the mood perfectly, claiming that 'in the hustle and bustle of the airport in Rome, you had more privacy in the 90s than in the national team training camp'.

When the dust settled, eight players had new clubs. The chaos of those days was capped by a crazy transfer saga that verged on the unbelievable. Gica Popescu signed for PSV Eindhoven, having been specifically identified by their new coach, Bobby Robson. All seemed fine until it emerged that he'd also signed for Serie A club Lecce, a deal that Popescu claimed he'd forgotten about. And while that might seem like a ludicrous excuse, it's merely a reflection of the naivety of the Romanian players, who simply weren't used to having a choice.

The conditions were ideal for what became the great exodus from Romanian football, and even players from lower-league clubs were looking abroad in search of the kind of life denied to them at home. That they were receiving offers reflects the level of talent that the country was developing during those years.

\* \* \*

For all that talent available to the national selectors, Romania could have easily missed out on the World Cup. They went into the final match of the qualification campaign trailing Denmark and with the odds against them. On the plus side, they were hosting the leaders. Even though the Danes knew that a draw would be enough to qualify for the finals, they started in attacking mood and within six minutes were ahead. Qualification seemed theirs. Balint, however, had other thoughts. In the 26th minute he did what he always seemed to do: find himself in the right spot at the right time. A misplaced header reached him and he did the rest. It was a feat that he repeated in the 61st minute when he latched on to a loose ball to hammer home Romania's third goal and put the result beyond doubt.

A show of character and skill against highly rated Denmark signalled that the Romanians were coming of age. Further evidence of the quality within the Romanian camp assembled for Italia 90 came in their opening match. Despite all the distractions their players had faced during preparation, they still had enough composure to control their opening match against the USSR – losing finalists in the European Championship two years earlier – before scoring twice in the second half through Marius Lăcătuş to earn an impressive 2-0 victory.

Although he'd scored the crucial goal that earned Romania qualification, Balint had been dropped from the starting XI. Jenei had opted for Lăcătuş, along with 20-year-old sensation Florin Răducioiu, with Balint left to make do with the final minutes of the two opening group-stage matches. That was still enough. Brought on against Cameroon in the second match with Romania two goals behind, he managed to latch on to a hopeful punt into the box and score their consolation.

It was a pivotal moment for him. Jenei wasn't dogmatic in his choices and, for all Răducioiu's talent, he appreciated that perhaps something different was needed. Balint was not only quick and technically gifted, but he was also an opportunistic finisher with an uncanny ability to position himself in the right spot. Over the course of his career he'd scored his fair share of spectacular goals but the typical Balint goals were scrappy, stolen goals. And in a World Cup as defensive and tight as Italia 90, that was an incredibly precious commodity.

That's what Jenei recognised after the Cameroon match, which is why he went with Balint in the key group finale against Argentina, a match they knew they needed to get something from. Both teams did. With the USSR comfortably beating the already-qualified Cameroon in the other match, the two teams played a nervy game. Then, all of a sudden, Argentina found a way through. Defeat would have been disastrous for the Romanians. Given such pressure they might easily have panicked but instead their mix of character and talent shone through. They regrouped and redoubled their efforts in search of a way past the aggressively defensive Argentina. For a time it didn't seem as if it was going to be their day but then Jenei's pre-match choice paid off. Balint did what he did best, appearing just where he was needed, latching on to a mix-up in the penalty area to head home from close range. Romania, in their first World Cup for two decades, were through to the next round.

What happened next is a moment that's widely remembered and celebrated across Ireland, while garnering the opposite reaction in Romania. Both teams were wary of each other. The Irish knew that, technically, the Romanians were their superiors but, equally, the tactic of sending long balls into attacking areas adopted by Jack Charlton had Jenei's team worried. Typically given such wariness, the two played out a dour 0-0 draw that couldn't be decided in extra time. Penalties followed, and while the Irish scored all their kicks, Daniel Timofte couldn't get his past Packie Bonner. Romania's World Cup adventure was over.

For Balint it had been a bittersweet experience. He'd managed to walk in the footsteps of his father's hero and his namesake by playing in the World Cup. He'd also been the only Romanian player to score goals in two matches, managing to edge out Răducioiu, who had gone into the tournament as their bright young hope, in the process. Yet he too shared in the Romanian dissatisfaction at their elimination at the hands of a team they felt was beatable.

For him there was also the personal disappointment at being one of the minority of players in the Romania squad who hadn't been lured elsewhere. He was still 27 years old, had just scored on the biggest stage and had a European Cup to his name. At Steaua he was a vital, ever-present player in a team that had dominated domestically and excelled internationally. He had five league titles and three cups to his name. Apart from that European Cup success he'd also been in the Steaua team that reached a semi-final and a final of that competition on two other occasions. They'd even added a European Super Cup to their honours roll after beating Dynamo Kiev.

So Balint wasn't just some flash in the pan or a lucky bystander along for the ride in a great team. He'd been a core player in one of the finest teams in European football in the second half of the 80s. How was it that clubs weren't lining up to sign him?

Whatever the reason, when the new Romanian league season kicked off he was there once again, although he was surrounded by a lot of new faces. Of the team that usually played during 1989/90 only three others remained when Steaua lined up for their opening fixture of 1990/91 against Universitatea Craiova. And this wasn't some ideological decision by the club's administration, determined to keep a player around whom they could build a new team. There simply wasn't anyone interested enough in Balint.

Then, just as a degree of resignation about his future was setting in, came the offer that he'd been waiting for. It all happened quickly after their first match as Real moved to sign him and within days he was off to Spain. Only this wasn't the same Real that his long-time team-mate Hagi had joined earlier in the year. Nor was it one of two other historic Reals, those from Sociedad and Betis. It wasn't even the less glamorous and only occasionally in the top-flight Valladolid, Zaragoza or Oviedo.

No, the club that made the move for Balint was the pretty much unknown one of Real Burgos. From a team that was used to winning the domestic league title, he was moving to one that – technically – had never even played in the top flight.

\* \* \*

The history of the city of Burgos is a rich one. Established in AD884 as a way to push the frontiers of Christendom, over the centuries it has housed kings of Leon and Castille, been the scene of many wars and served as a base for Franco's fascist government during the Spanish Civil War. It was in a nearby village that the famous Spanish national icon El Cid was born and it's in Burgos Cathedral – a world heritage site – that he's buried.

Football hasn't contributed to that richness of history. The most popular sport in the region is arguably basketball. Club Baloncesto San Pablo Burgos, the professional team that represents the region, routinely fills the 10,000-capacity Coliseum Burgos, as one would expect of a team that won back-to-back Basketball Champions Leagues in 2020 and 2021.

That's not to say that football has never had a foothold here. The first football teams appeared in 1912 and within a decade more than 20 had mushroomed across the city. In a way, the ease with which clubs rose worked against the establishment of one team that could really make a mark. Over the decades, the trend for clubs to be formed and then disappear a couple of years later continued, until in 1946 football enthusiasts in Burgos finally settled on Burgos Club de Futbol.

Even though the city's fans had now united behind one team, it wasn't a rich club, so the first three decades of its life were spent alternating between the second and third divisions of Spanish football. Stability only came in the mid-60s when they enjoyed an extended period in the second division that allowed for a slow progression that finally resulted in top-flight football in 1971. It was the start of their golden era of the 70s, which was spent largely in the Primera Liga.

While this was quite a ride, it was also one that the club couldn't afford. In 1983, Burgos went into financial meltdown. With creditors pressing for money and having none available to hand out, the club folded.

That was the end of one story but also the start of another. As with many other Spanish clubs, Burgos also had a second team – the equivalent of their reserves – playing in the Tercera Division (which, despite the name, is the fourth tier). The registration of that team – at the time known as Burgos Promesas – was unaffected by the main club's dissolution, so when the fallout settled, it changed name to take on the Real moniker, while also suddenly becoming the city's main team in the process.

Despite depending largely on youth players from the club's previous iteration, Real Burgos were too big for the division. A record 111 goals were scored in that first season, but promotion eluded them after a play-off defeat to Barcelona's B team. It was merely the postponement of an inevitable result achieved a year later as the club once more embarked upon an upward trajectory of constant progression that by the end of 1989/90 saw them dominate in the Segunda Liga to deliver Burgos once again to Spain's top flight.

The team that delivered promotion was one that played good football and had a core of decent players, with the star being the Yugoslav striker Predrag Jurić, signed a year earlier from Velež Mostar. Several experienced (if unspectacular) players were brought in over the summer, players who added depth but hardly the touch of quality a team looking to stave off relegation needed. Those running the club knew this, so numerous potential targets were sounded out. Closing the deal with their limited financial means was, however, proving to be difficult. So, weeks after the rest of the squad had gathered for pre-season training, the star addition was still missing.

It was at this point that they embarked on an odyssey. Having identified Balint as the man who could provide the spark they needed, two of the club's top administrators were sent to Brussels, where Balint was in pre-season training with the rest of the Steaua squad. When they got there, however, they found that they'd just missed the Romanian team's training camp, so once more they got on to a plane, this time destined for Bucharest. There they were faced by Steaua's president who, having already lost so many players, wasn't willing to let another star name leave. At least not cheaply. The Spanish representatives were told that only an offer in excess of $4m could make the deal happen.

Balint himself was eager to follow his team-mates abroad and he'd already agreed to Real Burgos's contract terms. He tried to force the move through but such strong-arm tactics weren't going to work with a military man who had decided that he was going to dig his heels in and a federation that felt no more players could be lost to foreign leagues.

So Balint stayed put and the Spaniards returned home frustrated. No one could accuse them of not persevering, however, and when fate opened another window they climbed through. That summer Steaua were due to play a friendly away to Logroñés, so the Burgos hierarchy used this opportunity to make one final attempt to sign the player they wanted. To their surprise, they found that the stance had shifted significantly and the prospect of Balint moving wasn't as unfeasible as it had been earlier in the summer.

This news wasn't without its downside, as now other clubs were sniffing around their man. Fortunately for Burgos, they had the pre-agreement contract they'd earlier signed with Balint and they used this to convince everyone that no one else could push them out of the deal. The player wanted them and they had the paperwork to prove it.

The tactic worked. Aware that times had changed, that the control he had on the players was no longer absolute and also that his bargaining position had been eroded by the signing of the contract, the colonel heading the club relented and Gavril Balint moved to Real Burgos from Steaua Bucharest for $1million. Finally, they had their man.

\* \* \*

The news was celebrated like no other. 'Balint, the star of Real Burgos, is home' screamed the headline of the local daily *Diario de Burgos*. Fans took to the streets to celebrate the news.

Such excitement was understandable. When, upon promotion, fans had been promised a top-quality addition to the squad, deep down they felt that this was just cheap talk. Few expected that something would actually happen. And yet here was the man they'd been promised. This was a man who had scored the winning penalty in the European Cup Final. Just a few weeks earlier they'd seen him on TV scoring against Diego Maradona's Argentina. No previous Burgos team had ever managed to attract a player like him.

Of course, before 1990, no Burgos team would have had the opportunity to dream of signing someone of that calibre. It was only the opening of the Eastern bloc football market and with it the possibility to gain access to superstars who were massively underpaid by Western standards that allowed it. The whole system was ripe for plundering. Ill-prepared and ill-equipped to deal with the new realities of a market system, Eastern European clubs failed to capitalise on their assets and were drained of talent. The many intermediaries who introduced themselves into most of those deals also led to a large percentage of any money made failing to reach the clubs' bank accounts. Having given his all to Steaua Bucharest's cause over the course of a decade, that mattered little to Balint, who could finally make the most of his talent, from a financial perspective. It mattered even less to Burgos, who had made a serious jump in quality.

But while Balint's arrival led to celebrations in Burgos, the rest of Spain was less impressed. The Romanian was a star but there wasn't much to acclaim in the rest of the team. Most of his new team-mates were either journeymen or other teams' rejects. There simply wasn't enough to foster any belief that Real Burgos could avoid a quick return to the league from which they came. But what many hadn't taken into account was those players' character. Perhaps inspired by the rejections they'd suffered and certainly because of the tactical discipline of a coach, José Manuel Díaz Novoa, who prized defensive solidity above all else, their return to the top flight wasn't the calamity many had predicted.

The first team to have their noses bloodied by the Real Burgos fighting spirit were Real Madrid. When the Spanish champions visited El Plantío in early October they were expected to win easily. Their team was stocked with world-class players everywhere you looked, particularly in attack where they boasted the fearsome duo of Emilio Butragueño and Hugo Sánchez. And while Burgos put in a shift to deny them, a goal by Real Madrid's Mexican early in the second half seemingly confirmed the inevitable. But Burgos weren't giving up. Midway into the half, Balint peeled off his defender, latched on to a pass and then wrong-footed the whole defence with a low cross that Jurić simply had to tap in. From then on the impetus passed to Burgos, who managed to find a last-minute winner. It was a stunning result and one that was repeated in the return fixture.

Real Madrid weren't the only ones to be stung by the newly promoted team. Barcelona and Atlético Madrid were both held to draws, while Valencia were beaten at home, all results that earned Burgos the nickname of *matigigantes* (giant-killers). There was also a nickname waiting for Balint. His ten goals saw him top the team's scoring charts, which, combined with his birthplace of Transylvania, led to the rather predictable 'vampire of the goal'.

The nickname also showed how well loved Balint was. Unsurprisingly, he was crucial to the team. Tactically built on a good defensive base and a solid midfield, his intelligence, movement and eye for goal were perfect for a team that mainly looked to hit on the counter. Their football was rarely spectacular but it was effective and that was often down to Balint's ability to make the most of any situation.

A goal against Osasuna underlined this. While defenders were trying to judge the trajectory of a punt upfield by the Burgos goalkeeper, Balint was already on the move. He looked over his shoulder to confirm that his judgement was correct, then as soon as the ball landed in front of him he hammered it past the goalkeeper – a clinical combination of technique, speed and an eye for goal. It was a key reason why staying in the top league, the main target before the start of the season, was achieved with a relative degree of ease.

For small clubs like Real Burgos, however, the second season after promotion brings with it new challenges. Most find that it's the one where they really struggle. The momentum gained with promotion starts to slow down and the novelty wears off. Other teams start to get a feel of how to play them, and players' hunger begins to fade.

Not for Burgos, though. They built on their first campaign and attacked the season with more confidence. There were more giant-killings but with them there was an added consistency in results overall. It was a season that saw Balint score 12 goals, confirming that even in a league filled with some of the world's best talent and despite not playing for the leading club as he'd done with Steaua, he was a top player who made the difference. Even though Burgos just missed out on European qualification with a ninth-place finish, it was a fantastic achievement for both club and player.

Sadly, that would prove to be as good as it got for both. Burgos's relative success made it difficult to keep the squad together, with some players – including key men such as Jurić – being lured elsewhere and, perhaps more devastatingly, coach José Manuel Díaz Novoa opting to move to a bigger club in Espanyol. With the soul of the team ripped out, it was impossible to maintain the fighting spirit that had made them the *matagigantes* in the first place.

What followed was predictable. The 1992/93 version of Real Burgos were a pale imitation of the team that had been pushing for European qualification months earlier. Over the course of a disastrous season, they won just four times and finished bottom with a mere 22 points. Their stay at the top was over.

For Balint, relegation wasn't even the worst of it. A serious meniscus injury suffered midway through the season stopped him from helping his team in their struggles. But as the weeks went on and a host of professors examined his knee, the prognosis became worse instead of better. Eventually he was told the most devastating news for a player still at the peak of his powers, that there was no way back for him. At just 30 years of age, Balint's career was over.

This proved to be a killer for Real Burgos. A fit Balint could have been sold to make some money. Not so an injured one. Debts had been mounting for years and without any assets at hand to help pay them off they were back in sadly familiar territory. Another relegation followed after a season in the second division, not because of what the team had done on the pitch but due to failure to pay players. They played for one more season before dropping out of league football altogether, then re-emerging in 2011, albeit as a team that only plays in the Burgos regional league.

It wasn't easy for Balint either. He had to watch his former national team-mates from home as they went on to achieve the best result in the history of Romanian football when they made it to the quarter-finals of the 1994 World Cup.

With time came acceptance. Balint still visits Burgos regularly to catch up with former team-mates as well as to reminisce with the fans, who can only dream of having a team in La Liga. The years he spent in Spain weren't the best of his career – nothing could compare to winning titles with Steaua Bucharest or playing at the World Cup – but they weren't bereft of satisfaction either. The move to Burgos had been born at least partially out of fear of being left behind when all around him were fleeing from the Romanian league, and that perhaps explains why he joined such an unheralded club. But while back home he was never the main man, at Burgos he became the undoubted star and revelled in that position.

Actually he did much more than that – he dragged the team to a higher level than it could otherwise aspire to, in a manner that only the best talents can. He proved that he was one of the best players in La Liga, a star in the truest sense of the word. And while he might not have hit the heights of the man he was named after, Gavril Pele Balint turned out not to have been misnamed after all.

# The World Cup that Changed it All

IT'S FAR too easy to allow nostalgia to colour views of Italia 90. That it was a pivotal tournament that kick-started the modern era of football – for better or worse – is beyond doubt. For a whole generation it was the first World Cup they truly remember, so it's only natural that they look back at it with a certain feeling of wistfulness. Of course, the football itself wasn't always great but the drama and spectacle of the event more than made up for that. And, after years of underperformance, England for a change exceeded expectations to get to a semi-final.

All of which is true. Yet that shouldn't overshadow the treatment of fans, particularly English ones, which was often horrendous. The Italians authorities looked at English fans with suspicion. Actually, dislike better describes their views. If everyone is innocent until proven guilty in the eyes of the law, as far as the Italian police were concerned, English fans were seen as criminals until proven otherwise.

There were historical reasons for that.

\* \* \*

Back in 1980, the last time Italy had hosted a major football tournament, the European Championship, English fans had made their mark. Fighting broke out when locals, attending England's opening match against Belgium, began celebrating a Belgian goal. The Italian police responded by firing tear gas into the crowd, which wasn't really the smartest of moves as the wind blew it on to the pitch, badly affecting the players.

Play had to be halted for a few minutes to allow the players to recover, which in the hosts' eyes meant a further loss of face. It also fuelled fear in the mayor of Turin over England's upcoming matches, as the city was due to host the crucial match between Italy and England. The mayor threatened to have the match cancelled. None of that came to be and all matches went ahead, albeit with a higher police presence than usual. And, even though there was only minimal trouble over the remainder of the tournament, the already-tarnished reputation of English fans was forever cemented.

It influenced the manner in which all fans were treated every time an English team played in Italy for years to come. When Liverpool fans travelled to Rome for a European Cup Final in 1984, they were subjected to attacks from locals and contempt from police. That was in itself the prelude to the Heysel tragedy a year later, where 39 Italian fans sadly lost their lives after a wall collapsed under pressure as fans were running away from clashes on the terraces. It was a horrible and needless loss of life that confirmed the beliefs among Italians that all English people at a football match were hooligans.

That barely a year before the World Cup English fans were involved in another tragedy hardly helped quell those beliefs. A string of subsequent investigations all decisively proved that Liverpool fans played no part in the Hillsborough tragedy and the blame lay with the inadequate policing decisions that funnelled fans into pens that couldn't contain them. Yet that wasn't the message the British establishment pushed in the hours and days after the tragedy. Instead, they peddled the idea that Hillsborough was caused by drunken fans who had arrived late. That's what parts of the English media reported in the aftermath of the tragedy and that's the belief that the rest of Europe swallowed in the days afterwards.

So when the Italian authorities looked at Hillsborough, all they saw was another reminder that English fans had to be treated for what they were: drunken louts who used football as an excuse to cause trouble and mayhem. Had they had their way they'd have kept pushing for a ban on English supporters making it to Italia 90 and, most probably, they'd have had the support of the English establishment, which had historically not viewed either football or its supporters with any kind of favour. In fact, despite knowing that the Taylor Report commissioned in the aftermath of Hillsborough was going to exonerate the fans, a government committee discussed the option that they should block England's participation in the World Cup because that would be a focal point for hooligans.

It was a suggestion that played to Prime Minister Margaret Thatcher's instinctive dislike of football fans. She'd already successfully put pressure on the English Football Association (FA) to cancel a friendly against Italy and would do so once more to prevent a friendly against the Netherlands after her trusted press secretary Bernard Ingham told her that the FA was 'behaving extraordinarily stupidly' in organising such a fixture.

Not that this was just the view of the government. Denis Howell, the Labour Party sports spokesperson at the time, piped up with views that 'the thugs of Holland and the thugs of this country are arranging their own fixture already', before demanding that everything should be done to 'stop the thugs leaving these shores for the World Cup'. Indeed, Howell had criticised the government for not being tough enough on English football hooligans.

Ultimately, however, the conclusion was against stopping England from taking part. 'Withdrawal from the World Cup is an altogether larger issue. If England withdrew, the likelihood is that the determined hooligans will make their way to Italy anyway and find a different cause to champion,' Thatcher's deputy Geoffrey Howe wrote in a letter summarising the discussion.

Not that it was ever really an option, given that FIFA viewed the World Cup as a celebration of the sport. It would have been difficult for them to argue their case while at the same time stopping people from attending their celebration. So the Italians had to come up with a different solution for the problem of English fans. And eventually they did just that. If they couldn't stop English fans from going to the World Cup, they'd keep them as far away from the rest of the competition as possible.

To do so they went for Cagliari, the capital city of Sardinia, as host for the English squad. While the setting was as beautiful as any other that the rest of the competition had to offer, its infrastructure wasn't as advanced as other cities. In particular, it wasn't easy for England fans to get to Cagliari. There were no cheap flights there – in fact there were few direct air links – while it was impossible to drive there. This made it hard for the fans to follow their team.

What that also meant was total control over who made it in. From the organisers' point of view, hosting England on an island made it impossible to get there unobserved, contrary to what would have happened had England been allowed on the mainland. That would likely have attracted the worst elements of the English support, who could have flooded through overland. But not in Sardinia. Everyone had to go through some form of passport control, which meant that every individual could be screened.

Theoretically, at least, that made sense. The Italians had been provided with a long list of fans who had been banned from football in England. Anyone coming in would be checked against it, a plan that would have worked if everyone used their own passport. But, obviously, those who wanted to cause trouble knew that as much as the police. They were also the ones who typically knew what they had to do to get around such tactics.

The list that the Italians had obtained was headed by renowned Nottingham Forest hooligan Paul Scarrott, who had over 40 convictions for bodily harm, most of them around football. His passport had been revoked, which meant it should have been impossible for him to make it to Italy. Yet a few days before the opening match he sent a photo of himself in front of the coliseum to the *Daily Star* with a letter announcing that he was there to fight the Dutch fans. He'd made it into Italy thanks to a false passport and would probably have made it to Sardinia if he hadn't got too drunk, allowing the Rome police to fortuitously come across him among vagrants.

A show was made of his expulsion from Italy with everything aimed at sending the message that all was under control. That Scarrott had made it to Italy was in itself proof of exactly the opposite, that such problems would never be solved by adopting such a harsh standpoint, which only punished those who genuinely were there for the football.

Naturally none of this seemed to bother the hosts. In fact, they were self-satisfied because, beyond the control measures that the island offered, Sardinia would in itself act as a deterrent. This in many ways illustrates how little those organising the World Cup knew of fan culture. Perhaps to them the idea that the fans would do anything to follow their team seemed an alien notion; that the inaccessibility would be enough to stop those same fans from making the trip. Instead, all it did was increase the cost and the discomfort for those eager to see England play. Those who couldn't afford the tickets for the chartered flights simply got creative and first went to Rome before catching a ferry across to the island.

Many Irish fans, who were drawn in England's group and thus ended up in Cagliari as well, followed their team in their final pre-tournament friendly in Malta before catching a boat from there to Sardinia.

Leonardo Coen, one of the founders of the *La Repubblica* newspaper but also someone who dedicated much of his career to reporting on sporting events, chose to join those travelling to the island, reporting on what he found. His is one of the finest descriptions of the chaos caused by hosting a group on Sardinia that had three teams with huge followings, and of the inhumane treatment that fans had to withstand:

> A visit to the small, insufficient airport of Cagliari Elmas. It has never seen so many charters in one day, 24 of them, meaning 5,000 fans. At the end of this World Cup, there will be 40,000 passengers for Elmas. The director Mario Del Curatolo has sounded the alarm: this airport can't handle it. The airport can accommodate a maximum of 600 people on arrival. Besides, there are no computers for coordination, only paper and pen are used. Where did the boasted efficiency of Italia 90 go?

As a result, Pinochet's systems are being imitated. Fans are welcomed in a kind of grey cement camp. Some benches. Don't protest. Fortunately, the Irish are quiet, even submissive people. They waited six hours last night, like animals in a cage. They endured it all for the love of football, and they will return to Malta tonight immediately, where they are being treated more civilly.

Some wanted to make the segregation absolute. 'It would be to everyone's advantage if the Irish, the Dutch and the Egyptians stayed in Palermo and flew in for their games,' Paolo Casarin, an Italian on FIFA's security committee opined. 'For security reasons, it is not possible for the Irish to stay in a hotel 3km from England's residence, and all of the other hotels are unsuitable.'

'If people come to Italy for violence, then the police will be very tough,' Luca Cordero di Montezemolo, who headed the Italia 90 organising committee, warned.

Coen continued in his piece, subtly chiding the authorities – and everyone else – for buying into the idea that all English fans were looking for trouble:

There is rough sea offshore, and the unfortunate passengers of the two Tirrenia ferries from Civitavecchia know something about it. Before departing, the Italians threatened and insulted the British, shouting 'go back home' as the British supporters complained.

They were expecting 600 passengers, but only half of them arrived. But where did the real hooligans hide? Police truncheons are visible, but the fair play of the World Cup seems like a lie as soon as one passes the port gate. As soon as these British arrive, it only takes them five minutes to understand what's going on in Cagliari. For them, it's the Beirut of football. Even last night, punches and bottles (empty) were thrown among drunken fans, intolerant locals, and inflexible police officers.

Drunkenness was seen as a big cause of issues so, to stem it, the selling of alcohol was prohibited for the 24 hours that preceded a match as well as the same period after it. What this did, however, was push the sale of alcoholic drinks underground and a healthy black market arose to make sure that those who wanted a drink – and were willing to pay over the odds for it – wouldn't be denied.

Things came to a head at what came to be known as the Battle of Sardinia. While on the pitch England and the Netherlands played out a tedious 0-0 draw, Italian police embarked on a much more vigorous exercise against English fans. Coached by the British police on how to deal with these issues – the same people who had failed fans so badly just a year earlier – the Italians acted hard and without hesitation at the merest hint of any trouble. About 500 English fans were detained and their identities were checked against a list of known hooligans.

The desire to stamp out any problem as early as possible sometimes led the police to make wrong assumptions. An Italian prostitute, who had chosen to wear a kilt in a misplaced belief that this would help her attract more customers, was mistaken for an English fan and chased all the way to the seaside promenade. It's a funny story, but also one that illustrates the ignorance of those who were there supposedly to protect.

Even so, some were itching for their own form of justice. 'Some people are revelling in the tension. Some would like to seek justice against all these English hooligans. The Cagliari ultras are said to be on the verge of war. They are not joking when it comes to using their fists: just ask how they behaved in Turin after a match or the night the team got promoted to Serie A,' Coen wrote, once more bursting the sanctimonious notion among many in the organising committee that it was just the English who used football as an excuse for violence.

Of course, it wasn't just the locals who saw English fans as troublemakers who had to be dealt with harshly. Even the *Los Angeles Times*, which barely acknowledged football at the time, reported on what had happened, cheeringly starting the report with the phrase: 'Italian police 1, English hooligans 0'. Then again it was hard to justify any other reaction when even Colin Moynihan, then the British Minister for Sport, applauded the treatment: 'I'm grateful to the police for their swift, tough and decisive action, which defused this situation and prevented other incidents – avoiding serious confrontation between English and Dutch supporters.'

Such comments contrasted dramatically to how others viewed their own. Lex Mellink, a spokesman for the Dutch police at the World Cup, said of the Oranje fans, 'They have a bad reputation, but they have behaved well as a group in the last few years.' Similarly, there was no public rebuke when police in Genoa were forced to fire over the heads of 200 drunken German fans to quell them.

The English were simply a menace who had to be repelled and beaten back. Recalling the incidents, the Sardinian web portal Vistanet reported as recently as 2021 that 'many of them, as several correspondents from the most important international newspapers reported, were literally thrown into the sea. Not by law enforcement but by numerous Sardinian volunteers who came from all over the island and decided to assert themselves in this way. The British government appreciated it.'

All of which sounds and was terribly bleak. But amid that harshness there was a bud of hope, one that Coen captured:

> A leaflet circulates with instructions on how to behave, prepared by the FSA, the Federation of Anglo-Saxon Supporters: avoid wandering around shirtless, don't show tattoos, and be careful around the police. Italian police officers are quick to arrest. If you are stopped, don't be overly concerned. It's normal for many people to be arrested on such occasions. If you haven't done anything wrong, stay calm. You will be released.

The mere fact that those there for football, rather than to create trouble, even had such support was a seismic shift. The real FSA (Football Supporters' Association) had been formed five years earlier, in 1985, in the aftermath of the Heysel disaster, by Liverpool fans Rogan Taylor and Peter Garrett. They'd written to *The Guardian* sharing their hopes of a 'critical mass of fans to organise and defend the game', inviting 'traditional supporters from every club in Britain to join this entirely independent body', hopeful that this 'could trigger the birth of similar groups in all the footballing countries of Europe'.

It was an ambitious and audacious vision, especially at such a dark moment in English football's history. But it also gave birth to a movement that would start to flourish by the time of the Italy World Cup. Indeed, that letter had sparked a conversation that ended in a whole society beginning to emerge across England that brought together numerous smaller initiatives that had the same goal.

Eager to start actively shaping how fans were treated, they set up an FSA World Cup sub-committee that was headed by Steve Beauchampe, editor of the fanzine *Off the Ball*, and made plans to set up their 'own form of tourist information which will also be able to give out the latest on matches and ticket allocation'. Beauchampe's deputy, John Tummon, further explained their vision in an interview with the *Manchester Evening News* that flew in the face of much of the rhetoric about football fans at the time:

> England has gained a bad reputation through the years. But some of the criticism being handed out is unfair and unfounded. This is a crucial time for our national game and we want to ensure that the World Cup goes well. There are thugs, but they are vastly outnumbered by the ordinary and decent supporter.
>
> We will have Italian-speaking people with us and we intend to create the best possible kind of image we can.
>
> In the past some of us have felt that bad reporting by the press has actually inflamed incidents and sparked off soccer violence. We do not want to see that happening at the World Cup.

This was a somewhat revolutionary idea but one that worked. In time the message began to filter through. After the tension of the early days, when fans were seemingly willed on to try anything so they could be quelled, the view began to change. As England progressed in the tournament – meaning they could no longer be confined to Sardinia – one would have expected problems to increase considerably. Yet that didn't happen. In fact, it was just the opposite as most of those who followed the English national team truly did so because of the football.

By working hard to make sure that fans knew how to react if they were placed in a difficult position, the FSA effectively gave them an alternative to rebelling at the overly hostile attitude that they were often greeted with. Not everyone took their advice but enough did for the change to be noticeable.

Gradually, the media began to wake up to this reality and started reporting it. Instead of looking for stories about fights and confrontations, they began to speak about the conditions that those fans were facing, criticising the heavy-handed policing to which they were subjected.

As the former hooligans turned writers Doug and Eddy Brimson noted, 'The fallout from Italia 90 was considerable. Despite hysterical ranting from Moynihan, it was clear, and becoming clearer even to the British media, that the vast majority of English fans at the tournament behaved themselves.'

By the time England and Italy faced off against each other in the play-off for third and fourth place, there was a party atmosphere in the stands, with both sets of fans sharing in a feeling of mutual bonhomie.

The change in football culture had been emerging for years before the 1990 World Cup, even if those on the outside were reluctant to admit that violence was on the decrease. At the same time, the game itself wasn't in a healthy place. Even though it was becoming safer to go to matches, average attendances for the First Division at the end of the decade stood at around the 20,000 figure, just as they had for years. This was hardly surprising; after all, who would want to consume their entertainment in dilapidated stadia that desperately needed investment and where, to top it all off, they were treated as criminals who had to be caged in so they wouldn't cause any issues? Especially when the Bradford fire and Hillsborough had confirmed that fan safety was barely a consideration.

England's success at the World Cup, coupled with the fans' largely positive behaviour in Italy, began the shift. While members of government had been advocating keeping the national team out of Italia 90 before the start of the tournament, attitudes had changed enough by the time England reached the semi-final that a parliamentary session was interrupted to allow MPs to follow the match. They didn't get to see the victory they were hoping for but for the three hours of the event, England was united. It's estimated that half the nation's population watched the game. Indeed, in the minutes that followed England's elimination, the country experienced a huge energy surge, such was the demand for electricity from people putting their kettles on!

It could even be argued that the semi-final defeat served England better than a World Cup triumph would have. For, despite the sense of disappointment, there was also the justifiable pride at how the players had done and how everyone – those on the pitch and the ones off it – had shown a capacity for dignity in defeat. It reconnected the masses to the game, reigniting an interest and passion that had waned over the years. All this was brilliantly summed up by Jeff Powell, who, writing in the *Daily Mail*, said that the World Cup was 'rekindling the English love affair with the great game invented on our island'.

When the England team returned home following a lost play-off for third place, it was to a heroes' welcome. More than 200,000 fans gathered to cheer Bobby Robson's men and, in return, were rewarded with the iconic image of Paul Gascoigne wearing a pair of plastic breasts. Gazza's antics would have been labelled as those of a typical beer-fuelled football yob a few weeks earlier, but now the darling of the English media who had cried upon realising that a booking in the semi-final would mean suspension for the final, was celebrated for his spirit. In fact, it's impossible to reconcile all that enthusiasm with the knowledge that a few months earlier there were those who were working to stop the English team making it to the World Cup.

The positivity continued flowing when six days after the tournament, UEFA announced that the ban on English clubs' participation in Europe that had lasted since Heysel was being lifted (with the exception of Liverpool, who would return a year later). A dark era had come to an end with a far brighter one emerging on the horizon, and all this thanks largely to a few magical weeks in Italy that had rehabilitated the English reputation.

All that positivity melted away when fans returned to league football a couple of months later to be welcomed back by the crumbling stadia that they called home. As the Taylor Report, the final version of which had been published in January of 1990, eloquently described:

> Football spectators are invited by the clubs for entertainment and enjoyment. Often, however, the facilities provided for them have been lamentable.
>
> Apart from the discomfort of standing on a terrace exposed to the elements, the ordinary provisions to be expected at a place of

entertainment are sometimes not merely basic but squalid. At some grounds the lavatories are primitive in design, poorly maintained and inadequate in number.

It's arguable that the Taylor Report was the second-most important event of 1990 for English football, just behind the World Cup run itself. It was breathtakingly visionary in its outlook and championing of better conditions for football fans.

A somewhat similar report had been written in 1985 after Bradford's Valley Parade tragedy but most of the recommendations that came out of that were draconian. Indeed, that report also covered a now largely forgotten tragedy in Birmingham in which the 15-year-old Ian Hambridge lost his life after a wall crumbled on top of him at St Andrew's amid some of the most violent fighting between the home support and that of visiting Leeds.

Influenced by the scenes witnessed in Birmingham, the Valley Parade inquiry came out with recommendations such as membership cards to screen football fans attending matches, and the widespread installation of CCTV technology to better monitor what was happening in the stands. There were no major recommendations when it came to the stadia themselves – despite the fact that the wall at St Andrew's had crumbled because the ground was so run down – apart from suggestions such as 'improving evacuation procedures, the training of stewards, the provision of fire-fighting equipment and increasing the scope of safety certificates'.

The Taylor Report also picked up the argument in favour of membership schemes. Beyond that, however, it went into much greater detail over what should be done, also because its remit specifically asked it to do so, identifying the failings of English stadia but also a whole structure to help improve the situation. Yet this was the ninth report produced in Britain over how to improve safety at football. That the Hillsborough tragedy still happened despite the various recommendations and the meticulous examination of previous tragedies, implies that the authorities in charge, including the government, football associations and clubs, simply didn't give sufficient consideration to the importance of ensuring the safety of the fans.

It's quite plausible that the bulk of the Taylor Report recommendations would have also been ignored had the English national team not done so well and shone a spotlight back on the national game. What it was arguing for weren't some mere alterations to stadia but wholesale changes, including the rebuilding of those grounds that were no longer fit for purpose or that couldn't be properly renovated. This meant that owners, who had previously happily allowed the condition of those stadia to deteriorate, would suddenly be asked to spend heavily so that they could give the fans the kind of facilities they deserved.

At the time this seemed inconceivable, but it's precisely what happened. The fencing that penned football fans in – to deadly effect at Hillsborough but also with countless other near misses before that tragedy took place – came down as well. Just as significant was the move to all-seater stadia, something that the British government made obligatory soon after the Taylor Report was published.

While the Taylor Report never made it mandatory for grounds to be all-seater (the strongest suggestion was for a reversal of the situation of the time, where one-third of stadia was seated and the rest standing) it did argue that seating made attending matches safer. The arguments used weren't exactly scientific: 'When a spectator is seated he has his own small piece of territory in which he can feel reasonably secure. He will not be in close physical contact with those around him.' But they were forceful enough in their logic.

What Lord Taylor did do, ironically, was refer to a study among the registered members of the FSA – that same association that had been a lone voice in helping English fans during the World Cup in Italy – that touched upon the argument of seating: '53.6 per cent claimed they would actually support the drive for more seating if they were reasonably priced and covered.' The addition of these last two points – concessions on price and cover – also seemed to have dramatic effects in reducing levels of opposition to the prospects of all-seated facilities.

Flimsy though the arguments were, they were also appealing. Supported by government grants and the Football Trust, clubs started to renovate whole sections and move towards all-seater. Again, the Taylor Report had been rather forward-looking and argued against fans having to bear the cost of these renovations through increasing ticket prices. That, however, became one of the recommendations that was ignored.

In hindsight, there was a level of naivety by Lord Taylor in even suggesting that, as if he saw football club owners as being local benefactors looking to share their money with the masses. There might have been a level of truth in that, as back in 1990 practically every club was owned by wealthy local families and individuals. Yet those same individuals had been more than happy to let fans visit stadia that were, in Lord Taylor's own words, squalid. There was no way they were going to bear the costs of the changes that they were being asked to implement.

Soon, a solution emerged that meant even the ticket price hikes would seem immaterial. It was a solution that Lord Taylor also touched upon in his report: 'The television companies know that football on the screen has a vast following,' he said. 'They should be expected to pay a substantial price for the rights to relay popular matches.'

That might not necessarily have been the case when Lord Taylor wrote his report, given the disenchantment that had settled over the game. There were the big cup finals that traditionally had a huge following but, other than that, a weekly highlights show seemed more than enough to satisfy the interest of the general public.

It's a belief that Italia 90 blew away. As Gary Lineker commented, 'It was a seminal moment almost, in terms of football in this country. Lots of different kinds of people got interested in football, all different classes of people. I think it had a significant effect on the growth of football.'

The huge numbers who watched England's matches on television proved that there was a latent interest in the game. It showed that it wasn't just the working classes that followed the sport but rather people from every background. Perhaps the traditional television channels that had always had access to football didn't appreciate that enough or took it for granted but it was something that a new player in the market was determined to access.

At the time, ITV held the rights for top-flight football, having agreed a deal worth £44 million over a four-year period. Today, that seems like a pitiful sum, but as Greg Dyke – then chairman of ITV – told *The Guardian* in a 2017 interview, he was heavily criticised within the broadcaster for paying that much.

The big-five clubs had already hinted at a breakaway league. They were led by the Arsenal chairman, David

Dein, who, like Lord Taylor, was impressed by American sport's ability to transform their events into a spectacle, with entertainment before and during the games. He felt that football should have a similar vision, which would make it much more valuable. Whatever his thoughts and regardless of the changes that he had in mind, none of that would have mattered had it just been the traditional players of the BBC and ITV fighting it out. Neither was willing to spend over the odds for football.

While the initial bid for a new league was staved off, it was only temporary. The resurgent interest in football post-Italia 90, along with a more family-friendly environment at matches, made the clubs realise just how precious an asset they had. Again, spurred by the leading clubs, another attempt was made to set up a new league, with this new plan being centred around a departure from the Football League and setting up a new competition under the umbrella of the FA.

The involvement of the latter wasn't incidental; it provided crucial, if flimsy, justification for the move beyond pure greed. It was argued at the time that England couldn't succeed in international tournaments if top clubs remained under the control of the Football League, which had no direct interest in the success of the national team. Having a league governed by the FA was the only way to ensure that the needs of the national team were met.

This was largely untrue and the clubs did very little differently to accommodate the England team, regardless of which league they were in. Yet having the FA in their corner gave the clubs the necessary legitimacy. Crucially, this also meant that any TV revenues that the league negotiated didn't need to be split with all the clubs in the Football League. Which was fortuitous because, aided by numerous individuals within club ownership who wanted it to succeed, BSkyB managed to win the rights to the competition by agreeing to pay £304 million. It was a huge deal, especially compared to what the clubs had been receiving beforehand, but is dwarfed by the figures paid today, which run into the billions.

Yet that deal was enough to establish two behemoths. Sky had been haemorrhaging money before winning those rights but the new capacity to transmit live football reinvigorated it. From that point on it went from strength to strength, becoming one of the leaders in its industry. So too did the Premier League, which confidently leapt on the wave of enthusiasm that Italia 90 had raised and has never really got off. Today it's the richest and most-watched football league in the world. Other countries are envious of English stadia and the atmosphere that's created during matches, with people from all over the world flying to England to attend. They crave the experience of watching a match in England and are willing to pay handsomely for it. English football has become a destination.

All this would have been impossible to imagine back in 1990, before Bobby Robson's men went on a run that almost brought the World Cup to England and, in the process, helped create the right conditions that would transform English football forever more. Italia 90 was truly the World Cup that changed English football forever.

# Front-Row Seat to Irish History

WHEN KEVIN Moran scored late on to seal a 2-0 win for the Republic of Ireland over Bulgaria, the 32,000 who had packed into Lansdowne Road went wild. The tension that had been building for the previous days could finally be released into celebration as the Irish knew that they'd done all that they could possibly do. Everything else was out of their hands.

This was October 1987 and the match was their last in Group 7 of the qualifying stage for Euro 1988. The win put them top of the group – at a time when the winners qualified for the finals – but nothing was confirmed at that stage. Their main rivals, Belgium, still had two matches to play, which, if won, would see them overtake the Irish. Even the defeated Bulgarians were still in the running as a home win against Scotland in their final match would put them on 12 points, one more than the Irish.

What happened next was the stuff of fables. Scotland, who had only managed one previous win in the group, against bottom-placed Luxembourg, first beat Belgium 2-0 at home and then shocked Bulgaria, winning 1-0 away. The Irish were going to their first major continental tournament thanks to their neighbours' helping hand. The Republic of Ireland would go on to make the most of that qualification, beating England in one of the most memorable matches in their history and opening what would become a golden era for the national team.

It was also the making of Jack Charlton. When the Football Association of Ireland (FAI) was looking for a new national team coach in late 1985, Charlton hadn't been among the favourites; most expected either Leeds legend Johnny Giles or the Under-19s coach, Liam Tuohy, to be chosen. That an Englishman was appointed to lead Ireland didn't go down well and this sentiment boiled over in the press conference during which Charlton was presented to the media. 'The circumstances of my selection are unimportant, they had nothing to do with me,' Charlton told the journalists. 'I'll be perfectly happy to be judged on what I do in the job.'

Time would prove him right and eventually he'd stop being seen as an Englishman but, rather, 'one of our own' by the Irish, as you'd expect of a man who led the Republic of Ireland to results that no one else had ever achieved before. His tenure was the perfect example of how success can shape a person's image and how people view them.

A counter to how Jack Charlton eventually became a quasi-revered figure is that of his predecessor, Eoin Hand. Appointed as the coach in 1981 after achieving domestic success with Limerick United, Hand suddenly found himself in charge of a supremely talented group that included Liam Brady, Frank Stapleton, Steve Heighway, Michael Robinson, David O'Leary and Mark Lawrenson. Such was the quality available that there are those who argue that it was their greatest-ever national squad.

That there's even a debate about that is mainly down to what that group managed to achieve, or rather didn't. Drawn alongside France, Belgium and the Netherlands in a 'group of death' in the qualification phase for the 1982 World Cup, the Irish still did fantastically well. Both the Netherlands and France were beaten at home, while the matches against Belgium were evenly matched. In fact, the Irish should have at least claimed a draw in Brussels. That they didn't was down to an inept display of refereeing by the Portuguese Raul Nazare, one that ruled out a perfectly legitimate Ireland goal before giving a soft free kick two minutes from the end from which the Belgians scored their winner. It robbed Ireland of a crucial point and infuriated the coaching staff so much that some confronted the referee afterwards. Not that it mattered, although some felt that the absence of a reaction on his part was indicative. Years later it emerged that in 1984 Belgian club Anderlecht had bribed Spanish referee Emilio Carlos Guruceta to ensure they qualified for the UEFA Cup Final. There's nothing to suggest that the same had happened with Nazare, although nothing will dissuade Irish fans of a particular vintage about what occurred.

To add insult to injury, FIFA replied to a request by the FAI to make the referee assessor's official report public by sending snippets of what was noted, including how the assessor had rated the display 'good to excellent', while also pointing out that the assessor had 'especially mentioned the decision to disallow the goal by your team. This decision was correct.'

The Irish bounced back well from the setback, drawing in the Netherlands and beating France at home. Yet, having played all their matches, they were dependent on others dropping points. Specifically, they needed the Netherlands to hold France to a draw.

Contrary to what would happen six years later, results didn't go their way. France beat the Dutch 2-0 at home before securing a routine 4-0 win against Cyprus. The

Belgians topped the group with 11 points – thanks to their controversial win against Ireland – while France and the Republic both ended on ten points. The French had managed to hit seven in their away fixture against Cyprus, a crucial factor given their parity with the Irish, as it gave them the healthier goal difference that they needed to clinch the decisive second spot.

Coach Hand had been among those who confronted Nazare after the Belgium match, recalling years later, 'To me it was blatant, and I accused him of it after the game. "You have taken money, it's a disgrace ..." And really, I should have been reported for that ... but nothing happened.'

Yet there was nothing to be done except regroup and work in the hope that the team would make up for the missed opportunity by qualifying for the European Championship. Sadly for him, and for Ireland, they never really got going in that competition, which meant that, after five years, Hand's time in charge was up.

In football it's rarely useful to dwell on what-ifs but it's hard not to think about how things might have turned out had Nazare made the right calls in that Belgium match. Ireland would probably have qualified for the World Cup and, given the talent they had, it's a safe assumption that they'd have done well.

It would certainly have made a huge difference for Eoin Hand. Although he remained a respected figure within national team circles and would return to work for the FAI in later years, he received nothing like the adulation bestowed on Charlton when he finally managed to qualify for a major tournament. The legendary status that was reserved for Charlton could have been Hand's.

Perhaps a more consoling way of looking at his fate is that he'd managed to soak up so much bad fortune that when Charlton's team needed a bit of help, the universe felt that a bit of good luck – which Scotland's results provided – was more than justified. As the media would later note, Charlton had enjoyed the fabled luck of the Irish; Hand had simply been the one who made it possible for fortune to smile so kindly on the Englishman.

In reality, Hand had done much more that would eventually help Charlton. For instance, he'd already started recruiting players born in England to Irish parents, well before Charlton famously started digging into people's ancestry to identify potential additions to his squad. One of those players Hand identified actually played a key role in Ireland's win over Bulgaria that helped ensure qualification for Euro 88.

John Byrne had come on in the 77th minute with the Irish looking to keep the pressure up despite being a goal ahead. And that's precisely what he helped them do. In the 84th minute he received the ball on the left-hand side of the Bulgarian penalty area. With his back to the goal and a defender tightly marking him, it seemed that there was nowhere for him to go. A beautiful bit of skill allowed him to escape his marker, enough to volley the ball into the penalty area. The defenders managed to clear but once again Byrne moved faster than everyone else to get to the loose ball, which he once more lofted towards goal. This time Kevin Moran managed to get his head to it to score the all-important second.

Yet Byrne might not have been there if it hadn't been for Hand. Born in Manchester in 1961 he'd come through at York City, making his debut at 18 before going on to play almost 200 times for them over the course of five years. In his final full season at York, 1983/84, he was the team's undoubted star, adored by the fans for his natural footballing ability and dribbling skills that made life in the Fourth Division substantially more enjoyable. Over the years he'd managed to iron out the inconsistencies that are common among most young players to become one of the division's finest strikers.

There was more to that York team than Byrne, however. Managed by Denis Smith, they were one of the best teams ever to play in the division, something they showed throughout a majestic season in which they hit 101 points to win the title with ease. Byrne was one of three players who was ever-present that season, scoring 28 goals. With such a record, one might have expected a club much higher up the league ladder to swoop in for Byrne. That, however, didn't happen. In fact, he'd have probably spent the following season playing Third Division football were it not for a chance encounter with QPR.

The two teams were drawn to play each other in the second round of the League Cup, with the First Division team easily winning both legs, 4-2 and 4-1. Later that season, York would knock out Arsenal and take Liverpool to a replay in the FA Cup, yet on this occasion they were largely outplayed by QPR. Even so, John Byrne did enough to impress the QPR manager, Alan Mullery, who realised that the young striker had the potential to play at a much higher level than the Third Division. Just days after the second leg, QPR put in an offer of £100,000 and Byrne was off.

A couple of weeks later he made his debut appearance in the First Division, as a substitute in a 2-0 defeat at Norwich. By the turn of the year he'd become a regular starter for the Hoops.

It was at that point that the Mancunian, who had taken a roundabout journey to the top, came into the Ireland reckoning. The Irish had failed to qualify for the 1984

European Championship and Hand knew that he was living on borrowed time. Even so – or perhaps because of it – he decided to experiment a bit with his team selection. He opted to give a debut to Paul McGrath, a defender who over the coming years would become a cult hero for his home nation (not to mention score Ireland's first against Bulgaria in that key match). Yet McGrath's introduction was rather low-key; he was an early substitute replacing the injured Mark Lawrenson.

By contrast, John Byrne's entry came through the main door. Although born and raised in England, the Irish selectors had found out that his father came from the old Irish capital of Carlow before moving across the Irish Sea. So Byrne was named in the team to face Italy and played most of the match. Ireland lost the match – which was at risk of not taking place because so many fans turned up that there were even people climbing on top of the stands to catch a glimpse of the Italians – but for Byrne it was still a magical night. A year earlier he'd been playing in the lowest level of English football; now here he was facing the reigning world champions.

Changes in management didn't seem to have a negative effect on him. At QPR, Alan Mullery was sacked just weeks after signing Byrne, but his replacement, Frank Sibley, kept faith in him and was the one who made him a first-team regular. The same happened when Sibley gave way to Jim Smith at the end of that same season.

At national level, Jack Charlton came in and, as with any new coach, tried changing things and experimenting with some new call-ups. Yet Byrne was always there, a valued member of the squad and a regular substitute, even if not as often a starter as he might have hoped for. That he was playing top-flight football regularly helped. QPR had barely avoided relegation in his first season but were much more comfortable the second time round. At the heart of their improvement was Byrne's continued development as he established a fruitful partnership up front with Gary Bannister.

On occasions the two were unplayable. Chelsea found that out when they visited Loftus Road on Easter Monday of 1986. The visitors were in fourth place and favourites to win as they looked to keep up the pressure at the top. A week earlier they'd travelled to Wembley, where they beat Manchester City 5-4 to win the first edition of the now forgotten Full Members' Cup. Yet their form and reputation mattered little on the day as Bannister and Byrne put on a show, with the former scoring three and latter getting two in a resounding 6-0 victory.

'It was an unbelievable game to play in. We just played so, so well and everything we did came off. They couldn't handle us that day,' Byrne recalled years later.

The pick of the bunch, however, was QPR's third. Byrne, who had already played a key role in the opening two goals, received the ball on the halfway line and promptly lost his marker with a deft drop of the shoulder. He then sped towards the penalty box, waltzing his way past four defenders before calmly chipping the ball over the oncoming keeper. That goal perfectly captured what Byrne was all about. He had the skill and flair to pull off moves that most other players couldn't dream of. At QPR, a club with a rich tradition of creative No. 10s, he fitted in perfectly.

On the flip side, he lacked the consistency to really make a mark at the highest level. There were instances where he seemed unplayable – as against Chelsea – but on other occasions he seemed quite lacklustre. One of those occasions came a few weeks after the thrashing of their London rivals.

QPR had made it to the final of the League Cup and were clear favourites for a win against First Division strugglers Oxford United. Disappointingly, however, they massively under-performed. Perhaps the big stage got to them or the favourites tag placed them under too much pressure but they never really got going and ended up losing 3-0. For Byrne, it would be one of the closest opportunities he'd get to a major honour and the failure to play anything close to his best would haunt him for the rest of his career.

Byrne's trajectory plateaued a bit following that defeat. QPR struggled the following season and, even though he was regularly called up to the Ireland squad, he was often left on the bench. But that he was still being selected was in itself proof of his abilities, especially as Charlton wasn't really a big fan of flair players, preferring instead those with a more direct approach. Not that he could be criticised for the choices he made. Initially he could rely on Frank Stapleton and John Aldridge, while in later years there were also Niall Quinn and Tony Cascarino. Not only were these strikers a better fit for Charlton's system but they were all remarkably reliable.

This was one of the reasons why Byrne never got on the pitch at Euro 88, despite playing such a crucial role in them getting to those finals. And, while on a professional level he was disappointed not to have been given the opportunity, he understood his coach's motivation; Ireland had done exceptionally well in beating England and drawing against the Soviet Union. A slender 1-0 defeat to the Netherlands was hard to take as it meant elimination, yet as debut tournaments went, this was as good as anyone could have expected.

Perhaps it was that failure to get on the pitch in Germany that inspired Byrne's next decision. Or it could be that the increasing insularity of English football – the exclusion from European competition coincided with the rise of the long-ball game and a shunning of players with Byrne's skillset – got him pondering his future at home. That QPR's progress had plateaued by that point and his prospects weren't particularly bright if he stayed may also have played a role. Whatever it was, he was clearly itching for a new experience. A handful of players had made the move to European clubs, so someone like Byrne going in that direction wasn't particularly surprising.

What was undeniably strange was the choice of club. For Byrne didn't go to a QPR equivalent in Spain, Italy or Germany but opted instead for a French club trying to get out of the second division. Le Havre, his chosen destination, couldn't even lay claim to a rich history or being a fallen giant. They'd been a lower-tier club for most of their history. In fact, until a decade before Byrne's move they'd been an amateur club playing in the fourth division. It was only the arrival of an ambitious president in 1979 that saw them first return to professionalism and then gradually climb their way to Ligue 1 within the space of a few seasons.

That's where they played until 1988, when they suffered relegation back to the second tier. It was that setback that attracted them to Byrne's availability. The success of English clubs in Europe was still fresh in most people's memories, plus Byrne had just been at the European Championship. That he hadn't made it off the bench didn't really matter; he had the experience and was of the calibre that any ambitious club would value and would be willing to pay for.

Still, it was a strange move that many failed to understand. Not only was Byrne walking away from the English top flight but he was doing so to go to France. While the French league wasn't considered a backwater football-wise, it wasn't as highly regarded as those of Italy and Spain. No French club had ever won a European competition, so how good could they be?

Even beyond that, this was a different era; freedom of movement hadn't yet extended to football. Clubs were still limited in the number of foreign players they could register and many didn't fill their allocated allowance. Cross-border movement was still an alien thought. Particularly in England, the prevailing feeling was that any player moving to a different country was showing a lack of ambition of sorts.

Perhaps the attraction of Le Havre was that Byrne could be the team's star. Not only was he coming from English football but he was a full international. His combination of flair and grit provided the ideal mix, quickly becoming a mainstay in attack as well as a fans' favourite. He even convinced his Ireland team-mate Frank Stapleton, who had just been released by Ajax, to join him at Le Havre. The two struck up a good relationship on the pitch, even though it lasted only half a season and didn't result in the much-desired promotion. Stapleton decided to return to England with Blackburn Rovers but Byrne opted to stay, further cementing his reputation among the fans. Once more he failed to guide them to promotion but he'd still done very well for them, scoring 16 times in 49 appearances.

Even though he was playing in relative anonymity, Byrne was still well regarded by Charlton. The Irish had made a slow start to their World Cup qualification, failing to score in any of their opening three matches. Then a home win against Spain gave them the confidence boost they needed and from that point they won their remaining matches without conceding a goal. It was a momentous achievement, one that elevated Charlton as a quasi-deity for leading the Republic to another tournament that they'd never previously played in.

It was achieved on the back of a straightforward tactic Charlton stuck by: a strong defence that didn't concede too many chances and strikers who clinically took any that came their way. Byrne didn't really fit that mould and hadn't played during the qualification campaign, yet when the squad to go to Italy was named he was in there once more.

His selection was made all the more surprising by the tactics of Charlton, who retained a pragmatic approach. There was a lot of talent in that Irish squad; Charlton had famously pushed the limits when selecting his players, tapping into the Irish diaspora to add to the homegrown talent. Indeed, of the 22 players that he called up for Italy, 16 had been born in England to Irish parents or grandparents. Later it would emerge that one of them, Tony Cascarino, didn't qualify on those criteria as his mother had been adopted and the Irish grandmother that entitled him to put on an Irish shirt wasn't a blood relative.

Charlton had shaped the squad much as one would do with a club team, bringing in the right elements to play the kind of football he wanted to set out. Whatever their birthplace, the squad he assembled was as devoted to the green shirt as any that had come before. That had been proven by getting to the finals. A miserly defence had conceded just twice in eight qualification matches. The quality of opposition at the finals of the World Cup would be higher but, in a way, that made the safety-first approach a reasonable one. Amid all that, Byrne's selection provided Charlton with a decent insurance policy. Should the team be struggling for goals, he could put on his flair player to change that.

It didn't turn out that way.

\* \* \*

Having been surprised by Ireland on their debut at the European Championship, England were determined not to be caught out again in the opening group fixture at the finals. Gary Lineker gave them an early lead and they set about defending it. However, they failed, and Ireland equalised in the second half with a goal that typified Charlton's football philosophy – a long punt upfield from goalkeeper Packie Bonner and, after a bit of a scramble, Sheedy put it away. Quick, efficient and deadly.

It was a good point for the Irish, which couldn't be said about their goalless draw against Egypt – often cited as the worst match in what's considered to be a poor World Cup. The result put pressure on them to get something out of the final match against the Netherlands.

Once more, Ireland went a goal down early on when Gullit waltzed through their defence to score. It looked as if a long night and disappointment awaited. Yet Ireland kept calm and in the second half drew level. Again, it was a repeat of the England match. A long punt by Bonner should have been cleared by Berry van Aerle, who instead hit it awkwardly back to goalkeeper Hans van Breukelen. He, in turn, failed to get a hold of the ball and in the blink of an eye Niall Quinn was on it to power in the equaliser.

Both Van Aerle and Van Breukelen were incredibly experienced players who had won domestic leagues, European trophies and the European Championship. They should have dealt with the ball easily, yet they'd also been subjected to constant pressure from the Irish strikers. This was all part of Charlton's plan, so much so that when he noticed John Aldridge was tiring, he doubled down on the tactic, sending on another tall and physical striker in Tony Cascarino.

That draw meant that Ireland had completed their group matches unbeaten. Three points might not seem like a great outcome but it was good enough to secure second place in the group behind England. They'd found it hard to score goals but, by playing to their strengths, they'd also proven to be very hard to beat.

It was much the same against Romania in the next round. On paper, the Romanians had arguably the better players but they'd stumbled in their group against a defensively minded Cameroon and that perhaps played on their minds. They'd seen how Ireland liked to play, so their desire not to be caught out by the long balls that had the potential to take out their midfield in one go meant they ended up playing conservatively.

The result was a rather tedious 120 minutes that was almost completely devoid of any action of note. It meant a penalty shoot-out to decide who would go through, which, rather surprisingly, caught the Irish somewhat unprepared. Penalties hadn't been discussed beforehand, so there was no pre-set list of penalty takers.

That proved clear when David O'Leary stepped up to take Ireland's final penalty. Bonner had just pulled off a magnificent save from Daniel Timofte to give Ireland a golden opportunity to qualify. Yet O'Leary wasn't exactly the kind of prolific striker you'd want in such a moment. In fact, he'd barely even featured for Ireland at the World Cup and had only come on as a substitute for Steve Staunton, who, ironically, was good at penalties. O'Leary seemed unfazed, taking his time to place the ball on the penalty spot and then having to re-set it after the referee indicated that it wasn't positioned correctly. All the while the country waited, or, as the commentator on Irish television aptly put it, 'The nation holds its breath.'

O'Leary would soon have them all celebrating. He sent the goalkeeper the wrong way to score the vital penalty and send Ireland through to the quarter-finals. He later reminisced, 'I always thought I'd love to test myself in a situation like taking the last putt in a major. To see if you could do it on your own without your team-mates ... There was an explosion of green ... the biggest mistake was standing still, I nearly got killed by all my team-mates!'

Explosion was the right word because the whole nation burst out in celebration over the success. Novelist Colm Toibin, who was writing for an Irish newspaper, spoke of how the Irish partied until they dropped. Literally. 'And where to sleep? That night in Genoa many simply lay down and fell asleep where they were. There would be enough time for sleeping in beds, a whole lifetime. And in the morning they would set off for Rome, the Irish supporters.'

Such was the emotion that even Jack Charlton, someone who had actually won the World Cup with England, was moved to comment, 'If I live to be a hundred, I don't think I'll forget what I've just seen out there.'

Having reached the quarter-finals – well beyond what many felt they were capable of – the pressure was off the Irish, particularly as they were due to face home nation Italy at the Rome stadium that had been a bastion of invincibility for them during the competition.

Perhaps it was that absence of any expectation that allowed Ireland to have the best of the opening exchanges. Charlton hadn't changed his tactics but in that quarter-final players were more comfortable keeping the ball at their feet than they'd been in earlier matches. This, in turn, surprised the Italians, who found it hard to recalibrate from the kind of match they'd prepared for.

Based on those opening exchanges, another slog into extra time was a possibility. And it probably would have turned out that way had Italy not fielded Toto Schillaci, who enjoyed the finest two months of his career. He was in the right spot and had the right amount of fortune in the 39th minute. Roberto Donadoni fired a shot from outside the penalty area that Bonner parried to the side before stumbling to his knees. In another match, that ball may have bounced away to safety or Bonner would have stayed on his feet. Not this time. The ball fell to Schillaci, who fired into the empty goal before Bonner could get back to his feet.

Going behind made it much harder for the Irish, who had struggled for goals throughout the tournament. They still battled hard and had a couple of half-chances. The Italians, however, were the better team and could easily have scored another. The Irish adventure had come to an end.

Given how they'd started the match, and the perceived favouritism for the home team by referee Carlos Valente, some in the Irish camp were disappointed by their elimination. Disappointment was certainly what Byrne felt, although his reasons were different. Once more he'd travelled to an international tournament and ended up not playing a single minute.

'It was disappointing,' he said. 'During the competition I was training hard and I felt so sharp. Everything was going right. I was banging the goals in and I thought I would get my chance. I remember John Aldridge said to me he was amazed Jack hadn't given me a chance. I guess I didn't figure in his plans but because we weren't scoring, I wanted him to take a gamble on me.'

Still, Byrne's overall memories are positive. 'It was superb,' he said. 'We were away for six weeks and it was the best party I've ever been to. We had a tremendous squad of players and the support from the Irish fans was amazing. They never cause any trouble and know how to enjoy themselves. We went to the Vatican one day and saw the Sistine Chapel and met the Pope. Some of the Roman Catholic lads cried. We got to see and do things that you never could otherwise. And we ended up going all the way to the quarter-finals, which was fantastic. Expectations weren't that high in Ireland and that made it all the more special.'

After the World Cup, Byrne left Le Havre to return to England, signing for Brighton & Hove Albion, who were in the Second Division. It was a bittersweet season. Byrne scored 11 goals to finish as their second-top scorer as Brighton registered a remarkable run to the play-off final. Sadly for them, the ultimate success would evade them as they were soundly beaten 3-1 by Notts County. Brighton's only goal came in the final seconds, after Byrne had first tenaciously won the ball and then set off on a mazy dribble – a display of the mix of determination and skill that had allowed him to forge his career.

That summer Denis Smith, the man who had kick-started Byrne's career at York, gave him the opportunity to join Sunderland. Again, it was another bittersweet move. Sunderland did poorly in the league, barely avoiding relegation, and Smith was sacked by December. To compensate, there was a magnificent run in the FA Cup, where they managed to reach the final. Byrne played a key role in that, scoring in every round, including the winner in the semi-final against Norwich. Again, however, it wasn't to be. Sunderland started brightly – they were the better team in the first half – and Byrne had a glorious opportunity to score but fluffed the chance. In the second half, Liverpool took command, scoring two goals to kill the contest.

For Byrne, that was the beginning of the end. His family had failed to settle in the north, so he opted to move to Millwall, who were managed by his former Ireland team-mate Mick McCarthy. There followed two more spells at Brighton, which sandwiched two seasons at Oxford, where he'd been signed once more by Denis Smith.

His career came to an end with Shoreham in the Sussex County League, where he stayed until he was 38. The pull of the game was too much. Indeed, he even made a brief return when he turned 40 to play for Whitehawk in the same league. By then, however, he'd already embarked on a new career. His initial instinct was to stay within the game that had provided him with so many emotions, albeit, rather than going down the managerial route, his desire was to go into physiotherapy. A conversation with Norman Whiteside changed all that and convinced Byrne to opt instead for podiatry.

'It is probably the hardest thing I have ever done. My brain had been dormant for 20 years playing football, but I've been qualified now for nearly 10 years … I get a lot of job satisfaction improving patients' foot problems.'

The blonde mullet that was his trademark throughout his career was shaved off a few years back, making it harder for people to recognise him. Some still do, and it often ends with them just eager to 'talk about football instead of their current medical condition'. All of which helps to serve as a reminder of the lasting impact he's had on the game. The disappointment of not making it on to the pitch in Italy is now but a distant memory, one that's overshadowed by the echoes of fans' celebrations and Byrne having a front-row seat to a historic moment in Irish football history.

Above all, there's his small but vital contribution that kick-started Ireland's golden era and provided Jack Charlton with the goodwill needed to take his team to Italy and beyond.

# Breaking the Curse

'*DESGRAÇADO É o goleiro, até onde ele pisa não nasce grama.*' 'Disgraceful is the goalkeeper, no grass grows where he walks.'

During the 1950s, José Martins de Araújo Júnior – better known as Don Rossé Cavaca – was one of Brazil's most-beloved personalities, a journalist, comedian and broadcaster rolled into one. Humour and wit were his trademark, both in his private and professional life. Once, having been invited to follow Atlético Portuguesa on a European trip, he sent his young daughters a postcard depicting a gorilla wearing a football shirt. 'It is so cold here that I've had to grow fur,' he wrote. 'Do I look different?' The story goes that it took his wife quite a bit of time to calm the crying girls enough to explain that it wasn't really their father in the picture.

Even though he passed away in 1965, when he was just 42 years old, some of Don Rossé's aphorisms have remained popular to this day. Few, however, as much as his sarcastic description of the role of a goalkeeper. Perhaps because there's a visual element to it: before modern technology made most top-class pitches perfect all year round it was common to see penalty areas bereft of any grass in front of goal. Most probably, however, that sentence remained popular because it captured the traditional Brazilian mindset about goalkeepers, those men who took it upon themselves to do everything, including using their hands, to stop goals from being scored, as the antithesis of football.

\* \* \*

The root of Brazilian antipathy for goalkeepers lies in how the game has traditionally been viewed and played in a country where a history of slavery has had a deep impact. Mário Filho, another giant of Brazilian journalism, explains in his book *O Negro no Futebol Brasileiro* (*The Negro in Brazilian Football*) that referees in the 1920s and 1930s were so biased that they'd never blow for fouls by white players on black ones. They weren't as lenient when it was the other way round.

This meant that black players had to develop a new way of playing that avoided contact as much as possible. Skill and the ability to glide past opponents – pollinated in part from samba, another staple of the poor, largely black classes – was their way around the issue and, over time, it came to define how the game was viewed. Football was a spectacle and through their skills players had to entertain.

It also meant that, more than anywhere else, no one really wanted to be a goalkeeper. Glory was reserved for the strikers, maybe the midfielders, as long as they could find paths past those trying to stop them. Defenders were accepted as a sort of necessary evil but even they often brought a high dose of skill to their game.

But goalkeepers? They were just an unnatural aberration. Not only were they trying to stop the magicians from entertaining but they even used their hands to do it. Little wonder then that it was goalkeepers who tended to get the blame for any failings in the Brazilian game.

\* \* \*

Over the years, the story of Moacir Barbosa has become an infamous example of the cruel nature of the game but also of life and how those perceived as being at fault are treated.

In 1950, Brazil entered the World Cup that they were hosting expecting to win it. In the run-up to the final they crushed Sweden 7-1 and Spain 6-1. So stellar was the team and so thrilling their play that before the final kicked off, they were hailed by the local press as the new world champions.

When Brazil scored early in the second half of the final they were dominating, it seemingly justified those evening newspapers that had made such an arrogant declaration. But instead, Uruguay raised their game and clawed their way back, scoring two wonderful goals to stun the Maracanã and the Brazilian public. The second goal saw Alcides Ghiggia beat Brazilian left-back Bigode before shooting at goal. Thirteen minutes earlier, at the end of a similar move, Ghiggia had passed to Juan Alberto Schiaffino, who had scored the equaliser. With that memory still fresh, Barbosa had moved slightly out of goal, so when Ghiggia instead opted to shoot, he was caught out. A desperate dive wasn't enough, as the fiercely hit ball had too much power and it squirmed underneath Barbosa into the back of the net.

Barbosa was an excellent goalkeeper, indeed he was considered to be one of the world's best. He'd joined Vasco da Gama in 1945 and been the rock on which they built their successes, winning the state championship in 1945, 1947 and 1949, along with the Campeonato Sul-Americano de Campeões (a precursor to the Copa Libertadores) in 1948. He'd even tasted success with the national team, being their goalkeeper during the 1949 Copa America tournament, including the 7-0 thrashing of Paraguay that confirmed them as continental champions.

All this is important in light of what came next for him. Unable to comprehend why they'd lost, the Brazilian public wanted a scapegoat and their goalkeeper who had allowed the shot to trick him was the one who got most of the blame.

Barbosa's career continued and he even won another state championship, but he could never fully shake off the reputation that he'd cost Brazil the World Cup. In 1994, he was even banned from meeting national team players by the manager, Mario Zagallo, who feared that his curse would taint the team, bringing them bad luck.

Indeed, Barbosa always spoke of the hurt he felt 20 years after the final when, at a local market, a mother pointed him out to her son and said, 'Look at him, son. He is the man that made all of Brazil cry.' To a close friend, he repeatedly said, 'I'm not guilty. There were 11 of us.' In a documentary he once said, 'Under Brazilian law the maximum sentence is 30 years. But my imprisonment has been for 50 years.'

The treatment that Barbosa received helped shape the narrative around goalkeepers. As he pointed out, there were ten other players in that final but none were subjected to as much condemnation as he was. Star forwards Zizinho and Ademir de Menezes remained celebrated figures, even though they hadn't managed to turn Brazil's superiority into goals. Forgiveness came much easier for those who, like them, brought joy to the masses. And that highlighted the dilemma facing those who chose – or were pushed – to play as goalkeepers. They'd never enjoy the glory, only the condemnation.

That was what befell later goalkeepers such as Waldir Peres, the man between the sticks at the 1982 World Cup, when another generation of incredibly talented, offensive-minded players failed to deliver on their potential. He wasn't subjected to the same level of vilification as Barbosa but he was still seen as the main reason for the team's failure. The idea that the fault might also be because the team fielded too many attack-minded players who weren't as interested in tracking back as they needed to be never really received much attention.

\* \* \*

For many decades, Brazil was known worldwide for being the country of great strikers, but that it did not have great goalkeepers. This was not true. Brazilian football has had excellent goalkeepers who stood out in their performance since the beginning of the 20th century but ended up being overshadowed by the unparalleled brilliance of players such as Pelé, Garrincha, Rivellino, Didi, Zico, Socrates, Careca, Romário, Ronaldo, Kaká, Rivaldo, Adriano and Neymar.

Paulo Guilherme is one of Brazil's most respected sports journalists and also the author of the 2005 book *Goleiros – Heróis e Anti-heróis da Camisa 1 (Goalkeepers – Heroes and Anti-Heroes of the Number 1 Shirt)*. Perhaps because he's looked at the role more closely than many others, he rejects the theory that Brazil's goalkeepers, traditionally, were poor. Truth be told, he speaks like a man exasperated by the myth:

> In each of Brazil's five world titles, the performance of the goalkeepers was very important. The first goalkeeper to play for the Brazilian team, Marcos Carneiro de Mendonca, in 1914, was considered one of the greatest in South America at that time. Barbosa, the goalkeeper of the 1950 World Cup, is to this day the best in the position in the history of Vasco da Gama, the club for which he played.

Gylmar was the two-time world champion goalkeeper in 1958 and 1962 and considered a reference in the position. Felix, goalkeeper from 1970, made important saves in the games against England and Uruguay, which guaranteed the good campaign of that fantastic team. Taffarel, in 1994, was decisive, as was Marcos, in winning the 2002 World Cup.

Guilherme's is a valid argument. Yet his is perhaps a more enlightened view than that of the general public, whose attention is more selective. The reality is that historically the focus tended to turn to Brazilian goalkeepers only after disappointments. When the *Seleção* did well, it was the attacking play that got the glory. Strikers win you matches, goalkeepers lose them. In such a culture goalkeepers simply couldn't win.

This isn't simply a Brazilian tendency; goalkeepers face a tougher time than most wherever you go. Yet the antagonism seemed more so in Brazil. And this lack of faith in Brazilian goalkeepers was also reflected in how foreign clubs who went to Brazil looking for talent tended to act. Their attention was reserved for outfield players, mostly midfielders and strikers but, occasionally, defenders. No one ever went to Brazil looking for goalkeepers. For a country where football has often offered a way out of poverty, this meant that those asked to guard the net were effectively being condemned to a career with no prospects of landing a lucrative contract abroad.

This wasn't necessarily a negative. Guilherme feels that whereas 'players stayed for a short time with Brazilian clubs, being quickly traded to teams in Europe, the goalkeeper, on the other hand, ends up spending more time in the clubs, and becomes the reference of that team for the fans'. Yet this lack of career prospects makes it hard to look at the position and not feel that it was only those left with no other option.

* * *

For Brazil, Italia 90 was a humbling tournament. Their elimination in the round of 16 remains the earliest they've exited the finals and they did so without a whimper. Yet Italia 90 was also the decisive event that splits the narrative arc of Brazilian goalkeeping into a before and after.

The country's rich tradition of supremely talented attacking players had over the years fostered the expectation of a national team that played in one mode: open attacking play. This was enough during the decade where Pelé was leading the frontline – although those teams also featured exceptional defenders who often didn't receive the attention they deserved – but after 1970 it increasingly became a burden.

Still, despite worsening results at the World Cup, that anticipation persisted, and unsurprisingly so. In recent years much has been made about the need for any successful football team to have a philosophy, a way of viewing and playing the game that's clearly stamped on everything they do. This common idea of how to do things makes it easier to identify talent, coach players and use it as the lens through which external challenges are viewed. While the idea was popularised after the success of Spain's *tiki-taka* teams, the notion itself isn't a modern one. The Netherlands have been seen as the team of 'total football' since the 70s, while Italy have long been associated with the defensive *catenaccio*. Whatever they do now, those labels will remain.

Brazil's football identity was forged by attacking play. Everyone expected Brazil to play their way around defences with a carefree approach that aimed at outscoring the team facing them. That philosophy had served them well when their attack was good enough to overwhelm all opposition. Yet the tactical evolution that was unfolding elsewhere made this increasingly unlikely to succeed.

Results at World Cup level had been getting worse with the passing of every tournament, even though they were always among the favourites. It was the same in 1990. On the face of it the squad picked by Sebastião Lazaroni was brimming with attacking talent, including Careca – Maradona's attacking partner at Napoli – Bebeto and Romário. In truth, there was talent everywhere you looked: Aldair and Ricardo Gomes at centre-back, Branco's cannon shot from full-back, and the controlling presence of Dunga and Alemão in midfield. A year earlier practically the same squad had managed to win the Copa América. Lazaroni was a tactical pragmatist who realised that by not being better disciplined defensively Brazilian football was being left behind. This was reflected in the way he asked his teams to play, which included a *libero* at the back and traditional touchline-hugging wingers.

While Lazaroni was trying to imitate the European way of playing, the professionalism of the likes of West Germany and Italy meant that a hallmark was missing for Brazil. During the 1990 World Cup, for the first time ever, relatives were allowed to visit the club's training camp, while the often-critical Brazilian media weren't granted access. Players' focus was also frequently interrupted by agents eager to secure lucrative moves to Europe for their charges.

On the pitch, matters got off to a good start with three wins in the group stage. The first, against Sweden (2-1), was impressive; the other two – Costa Rica (1-0) and Scotland

(1-0) – less so. They'd done the bare minimum and got away with it.

This set up a match up against their eternal rivals Argentina. The reigning holders had barely scraped through to the last 16, finishing third in a group they'd been expected to top. All the odds favoured the Brazilians and they started the match playing the kind of football that confirmed this. Yet as the minutes ticked by they failed to get the breakthrough they deserved. As frustration grew, thinking became muddied, which made good football impossible. The stage was set for Diego Maradona to run at the Brazilian defence with ten minutes to go, laying the ball to Claudio Caniggia, who slotted home the winner.

\* \* \*

The reception that Brazil received on their return home was typically scathing. The media, who had been kept away from the squad, took their revenge as they latched on to every failing. Lazaroni left soon afterwards amid criticism for agreeing to join Fiorentina when he should have been focusing on the national team. Little did it matter. Had he not jumped then most certainly he'd have been pushed. It wasn't just the coach who got blamed, though; players' reputations and their rumoured lack of professionalism also came in for a severe beating.

Yet within that failure there were the embers of success. The core of the team remained and learned from their humiliation. It forced on them a realisation that, while tactics played a key role, it was their unity, willingness to work hard and blocking of external distractions that were the key ingredients to success.

In 1990, all that lay in the future. The immediate fallout was severe and the criticism of players who had let down their country was savage. And yet there had been a shift in the narrative. No longer were attacking players being excused from the national team's failings, with all blame shifted to those at the back. In hindsight, this was huge.

That was also down to the realisation that in goal there was a special talent. Cláudio Taffarel went into the World Cup still riding the wave of excitement about his immense promise. For the first time, a goalkeeper was excelling to the point where even Brazilians had to sit back and appreciate his talent. They were hardly given a choice when he saved three penalties in Brazil's semi-final win against West Germany at the 1988 Olympics and had an immaculate Copa América. In the latter, he conceded just once, in Brazil's opening match, before going a full nine matches without letting anyone or anything get past him.

'The 1990 World Cup was a failure, so much so that even we players admit it,' Taffarel said. 'We lost that World Cup because while it was a big group with great players they weren't united, and that led us to defeat. I'm very sorry, because looking at the other opponents we were fully capable of reaching the final and winning. But we lost to Argentina, which in my opinion, during the game, we were superior and we massacred them. They, in one opportunity, managed to eliminate us.'

Those words of dejection expressed in an interview years later reflect the attitude of a man whose mentality was focused only on winning. It mattered little to him that he emerged from 1990 as one of the few Brazilians with his reputation enhanced.

'I played well and had good performances [but] I don't want to make it sound that I should be excluded from any criticism, because I too am responsible for that failure.'

His hurt at what happened during Italia 90 is evident from the way he speaks about the experience, even though decades have passed. But that also provides a glimpse into his mindset, one that doesn't leave room for excuses or spare anyone from blame. And that mental strength is telling. Every goalkeeper knows that they can have the best of matches but still end up costing the team with one mistake. Taffarel probably knew it more than most, growing up in a country still obsessed by Barbosa. You need to be mentally tough to know all that and still decide to play in goal.

It paid off. He couldn't do enough to take Brazil to World Cup success in 1990, but it did earn him a ground-breaking move to what was then the best league in world football.

\* \* \*

In 1990 Parma had just been promoted to Serie A but they had a rich owner who had big ambitions for the club. They'd already signed Sweden's star striker Tomas Brolin and the Belgian defender Georges Grün before they made Taffarel their third foreign player (at the time, Italian teams were only allowed three).

It was a surprising move, partly because Italians prided themselves on having the world's best goalkeepers, but also because no one had ever thought of going to Brazil for a goalkeeper. Yet Taffarel proved to be an instant hit in a team that quickly began challenging Italy's elite. In 1992 they won the Coppa Italia and then the European Cup Winners' Cup a year later.

Taffarel's penalty saves in 1994 made him the hero as Brazil won the World Cup and he then enjoyed an extremely successful spell in Turkey with Galatasaray, where he not only won domestic honours but also the UEFA Cup. In

1998 he once more played a pivotal role in Brazil getting to the World Cup Final, saving three penalties as they overcame the Netherlands in a semi-final shoot-out. Sadly, there wouldn't be a repeat of their earlier success but his heroics further enhanced his legend. And each one of his successes chipped away at the previous doubts over Brazilian goalkeepers until all that was left was rubble.

Taffarel was a very pragmatic goalkeeper. He didn't have the imposing physique typically attributed to those in the role but he had the courage and determination that are vital. His drive to succeed was reflected in his training zeal and constant desire to do all that was necessary to improve. Even as a young man, he was a student of the game, particularly of goalkeepers, always looking to see what he could learn. Preparation was key and it paid off.

At 5ft 11in, Taffarel wasn't the tallest of goalkeepers but, while for many this would have been a disadvantage, he managed to turn the situation in his favour by improving other areas of his play. Indeed, what he lacked in inches he more than made up for in anticipation and explosiveness. The latter was down to a youth spent playing beach volleyball that strengthened his foot muscles, the former due to preparation, aware that he couldn't rely on size to stop shots, so he worked on improving his reading of the game.

This proved to be a vital skill at a time when the role of the goalkeeper was changing. After the 1990 World Cup, changes in the laws prevented goalkeepers from picking up back-passes, which, indirectly, meant that they had to be more dynamic. For that, Taffarel had the ideal skillset, with his awareness not only allowing him to fine-tune his positioning but also better judge when he needed to rush out of goal.

There might have been more to his move to Italy than just talent. Calisto Tanzi, Parma's owner and the man who had built up the Parmalat empire, once said that he'd signed Taffarel because it made good business sense: he was expanding his brand in South America, so having a Brazilian playing with the Parmalat logo on his shirt made it easier to gain customers.

But while there might have been some truth in that – a small club like Parma is always more likely to get exposure if they have a high-profile player from that country – they were also shrewd operators who spotted talent well before everyone else. And Taffarel was undoubtedly talented. Twice he was voted among the world's best three goalkeepers and while his performances at the 1990 World Cup had been eye-catching, Parma had been following him for much longer than that. This wasn't an opportunistic move.

That much was confirmed by what Taffarel managed to achieve in Parma and beyond. Perhaps more importantly in the wider scope of things, Taffarel changed how Brazilian goalkeepers were viewed by the rest of the world. He showed that it wasn't just midfielders or strikers who could get a move to Europe; in a world where borders were blurring, there was space for anyone as long as they were talented.

* * *

In chaos theory there's what's known as the butterfly effect, which, dumbed down, is the idea that the simple act of a butterfly flapping its wings can put in motion a series of events that eventually leads to a tornado. It's quite a visual manner of illustrating the way in which seemingly minor actions can have greater consequences. For Brazilian goalkeepers, Taffarel's success was the equivalent of a butterfly's wings flapping.

'Taffarel was instrumental in ending Brazil's reputation for not having great goalkeepers,' Paulo Guilherme states. 'His performance at the 1988 Seoul Olympic Games and the 1990 World Cup in Italy changed the eyes of the world in relation to Brazil's goalkeepers. In addition, Taffarel opened the doors of the international market to Brazilian goalkeepers when he went to play for Parma, in Italy. And soon others followed suit.'

His move ensured that others had a path that they could follow. And soon a tiny trickle became a flood. Since Italia 90, Brazil has produced some of the world's best goalkeepers: Dida, Júlio César, Ederson and Alisson Becker. All four are superb goalkeepers who have managed to provide a rock-solid foundation on which the rest of the team could be built. Would they have made it to Europe if Taffarel hadn't been the first? Probably, but, having dispelled ideas about the poor quality of their goalkeepers, it became only a matter of time before European clubs came looking to identify the next big No. 1.

And they found them because, for the first time, the quality of goalkeeping was on the rise. This latter aspect wasn't accidental.

\* \* \*

With focus so often being dominated by their attacking talent, something that's regularly overlooked about Brazilian football is that it has often been at the forefront of innovation. As early as the 1950s the national team had a dedicated physical trainer, years before others saw the wisdom in this. Pushed by the military dictatorship who ran the country from 1964, the attention placed on the physical training of players and the innovative practices adopted went beyond what others were willing to accept.

João Saldanha, who coached the team to a World Cup success in 1970, credited the NASA-inspired training that the team undertook prior to the competition for them doing so well. It allowed them to cope with the altitude, particularly in the group stage in Guadalajara. While others struggled to cope, they won all their matches and established the momentum needed to carry them to victory.

Even so, there are those who believe that this focus on physical fitness came at the cost of technical talent, which is why Brazil didn't then win a World Cup for 24 years. That seems a bit extreme when you look at the players who put on the yellow shirt during that period. What's certain, however, is that when combined with the Brazilian love for flair, that drive to develop stronger players led to the evolution of the perfect goalkeepers for the modern game.

Brazil have had great goalkeepers in the past. Yet never has it been so widely accepted that they're among the best in the world, which is the situation now with two of their goalkeepers. Often, the man chosen as the country's No. 1 is Alisson. John Achterberg, Liverpool's first-team goalkeeping coach, says about him:

> The consistency he has shown since he has been here is there for all to see. This allows him to cover spaces quickly and get to the corners of the goal quickly. And when the ball goes over the top, even if he's in a race with a forward who is quick, he can beat them to it ... he is very fast and that is maybe something people do not recognise in him.
>
> Goalkeeping has changed so much recently. What you have seen is goalkeepers try to get used

to playing out from the back. And when you have a keeper who is really good at it, like Alisson, it really does help.

David Seaman says of Ederson, the other contender for the Brazilian No.1 shirt:

> Some have done it really well … Ederson doesn't just play it out from the back, he can also set up an attack.
>
> He has that long, raking pass, and he is so accurate as well. But it's not just about that with him because his goalkeeping is really good as well. He's not a flash goalkeeper. He's no show-off, he makes the save and if he has to dive, he dives; if he doesn't have to dive, he doesn't dive.
>
> Some keepers do what we call 'camera saves': it's there and instead of touching it over they do three twists and a somersault! Ederson doesn't do that.

Both these goalkeepers have achieved success because of their talent and hard work. Their skills are the perfect fusion for the possession-based, intensive press of the modern game. And yet their talents might easily have been overlooked had Cláudio Taffarel's displays at the 1990 World Cup not been what was needed to breach the invisible barrier that had held all Brazilian keepers before him back. Once he'd broken through – and in doing so indirectly created a role model for young Brazilians to follow – it became inevitable that a country so invested in the game would begin producing others ready to tread the same path.

* * *

As Cláudio Taffarel flung himself to his left to block Daniele Massaro's penalty, he wasn't just exorcising 24 years of pain for Brazil by winning the 1994 World Cup – he was also turning the historical tide of opinion over Brazilian goalkeepers.

For him it was the culmination of a learning process that had begun four years earlier in another World Cup he still believes Brazil should have won. Italia 90 had been a failure. But it also laid the foundations for their future success and their emergence as a nation that produces as many world-class goalkeepers as it does strikers.

# Back-Pass Pain

WHEN FOOTBALL was first played it looked nothing like the game we're familiar with today. Originally contested between towns and villages, early matches tended to have few rules. This resulted in violent affairs that were little more than organised mass brawls.

Industrialisation forced many people away from their villages and reduced free time, so the free-for-alls that had prevailed were no longer possible. Rules were introduced, shaping football to the point where most of those who played adopted similar laws – those of association football – that came to be the widely accepted standards.

Even so, the initial set of rules still resulted in a game that would seem alien to modern followers. The FA's first laws didn't make any specific reference to goalkeepers, with every player allowed to catch or knock the ball onwards. It was almost a decade later that handling was prohibited for all players, although that was soon amended, finally introducing a goalkeeper who was allowed to handle the ball 'for the protection of his goal'.

Football in those days was administered similarly to a modern start-up, where changes were made quickly and, based on the feedback, amended just as rapidly to best serve the growing paying public. Thus it was that over a period of roughly 15 years, new rules came out to specify that goalkeepers couldn't carry the ball, then they could carry it but only for two steps, then they couldn't handle in the opposition half, and then they could handle for any purpose and not just the defence of a goal.

It's possible to visualise every rule change coming into force and enterprising goalkeepers looking at the text, trying to find any grey areas that they could exploit to give their team an advantage, which, in turn, would result in a new amendment.

Eventually the game settled down. In 1912 it was specified that goalkeepers could handle the ball exclusively in the penalty area, and then in 1931 this was tweaked slightly to ensure that keepers could take up to four steps while carrying the ball. And with that, the changes to the rules governing the art of goalkeeping – at least major ones – came to an end. Management styles came and went; tactics evolved to take in new roles but always with one basic premise of a goalkeeper being able to freely handle the ball as long as it was within the confines of the penalty area.

The rigidity of those beliefs meant that for decades very little was expected of goalkeepers apart from good reflexes and a certain level of fearlessness to throw themselves head-on where others went with their feet. It was a respected role and no team could imagine winning without a good shot-stopper. But to a large extent it was also seen as a unique role that was a bit apart from the team, so much so that when tactical shapes were discussed, goalkeepers weren't even included. The likes of 4-4-2 or WM tactics only took into consideration the outfield players because they were seen as the ones who played an active role.

Yet this attitude towards the role of the goalkeeper also reflected an underlying survival of the sporting ethos of the game of football. Once it had settled down and its main rules set, not much was done to abuse privileges afforded to goalkeepers. For decades, no one really looked at goalkeepers' ability to handle as a way to gain an advantage.

\* \* \*

As England once more took the lead against West Germany in the final of the 1966 World Cup, their players' celebrations were muted, even allowing for the rather conservative celebrations of the era. In truth, the heat and the size of the Wembley pitch had sapped energy out of their legs; they were physically struggling to get to the end of the match.

Yet they knew that the Germans would respond as they had before, by pushing forward in search of an equaliser. The easiest option for the English players in that moment was to look at a way to waste a few precious moments, helping the clock tick on towards the final whistle. Even so, they weren't tempted to pass the ball back to Gordon Banks, allowing him to hold on to it for a few seconds to give the rest of the team a little bit of breathing space. When they had possession, they kept moving forward because that's how the game was played, in what today seems like a rather cavalier attitude but back then was simply how everyone approached football. You went out to win, nothing else.

That started to change in the mid-60s, with the main catalyst being the appointment of Helenio Herrera as Inter Milan coach. Herrera had come across a tactic adopted by the Austrian coach Karl Rappan, whose system known as *riegel* or *verrou* focused attention on defence, with Rappan instructing all players in the backline to man-mark their opponents, while a ball-playing midfielder ahead of them helped keep the play flowing. This safety-first approach appealed to Herrera, who decided to use it as the basis for all his teams. Crucially, however, he made one tweak by pulling back the midfielder into defence, thus creating the role of the sweeper – a player who was tasked with clearing anything that managed to make it past his fellow defenders.

Attacking-wise, Herrera demanded that the ball be moved towards the strikers as quickly as possible. He drummed into his players the need to avoid retaining the ball in midfield since that increased the possibility of possession being lost in an area close to his defence with players out of position, which, in turn, opened up gaps that could be exploited. Jonathan Wilson, in *Inverting the Pyramid*, explained this belief in simple terms: 'In attack, all the players know what I wanted: vertical football at great speed, with no more than three passes to get to the opponent's box. If you lose the ball playing vertically, it's not a problem – but lose it laterally and you pay with a goal.'

The revolution that Herrera brought about was not only tactical but also a philosophical one that focused primarily on not conceding goals. A team went into a match at 0-0 and on par with the opponent, so, the thinking went, the minimum they should take going out of it was that same scoreline. Any team with a strong defence would manage to do just that, and if it happened that the opposition backline wasn't as talented, solid or attentive, then they might manage to score at least once to swing the result in their favour.

Herrera had tinkered with the system in the early days of his managerial career before finally perfecting the formula when he moved to Inter, where, across the city, he came up against another great believer in defensive pragmatism in AC Milan's Nereo Rocco.

Once Herrera coached Inter to play according to his defensive vision, they won three Serie A titles, two

European Cups and two Intercontinental Cups over a period of eight years, as the team came to be referred to as *La Grande Inter.* Basic statistics highlight how Herrera's teams evolved: in his first season Inter scored 73 goals and conceded 39, but by his third season the goals against had gone down to 20, while goals scored stood at 56. The big difference was that the parsimony of the third season won him his first Serie A title.

In Italy Herrera was nicknamed *Il Mago* (the magician), thus acknowledging that there was more to him than his tactics – he was a great motivator who used psychological tricks to push his players to do better, and a visionary when it came to coaching techniques. Overseas, however, his fame was largely limited to the new style he'd championed at Inter. That defensive approach that he helped popularise also earned its own nickname – *catenaccio* – after the iron bolts used to lock doors. In time, that word would come to represent all that was negative in the game, a byword for an attitude that focused exclusively on not losing, rather than winning.

That would probably have amused Herrera, who throughout his career was accused of the opposite, of wanting to win at all costs. For him, the formation that he adopted was down to pure pragmatism. At Inter he'd become the highest-paid coach in the world but he knew that if he wanted to keep earning that money he needed to win. Winning was his main motivation, rather than some ideological footballing belief. A defensive formation was the one he felt best suited Inter, just as a more adventurous system had brought him earlier success with Atlético Madrid and Barcelona.

The root of *catenaccio*'s bad reputation doesn't lie with Herrera and the other early innovators who dreamed it up.

It was when others began to look at it as a solution to their own problems that it began being sullied.

*Catenaccio* soon had many admirers who realised that while they didn't have the talent to be as efficient as Herrera's team when going forward, their less talented players could defend as assiduously as Inter. A solid, well-organised and well-coached defence could keep stronger teams at bay, which might get them a point from a league match. Or if they were lucky and one of their strikers managed to escape attention, they might even scrape a win. Either way, the chances of getting something increased by being cautious.

Gradually at first, but increasingly soon after, coaches started to live by the gospel of doing everything possible to avoid defeat. *Catenaccio* was the basic template that was needed, one that was easy enough to understand and replicate at any level of the game. And so most did. Yet, as with most copies, these lacked the brilliance of the original and the basic notion of using a strong defence as a better platform to gain a win. These new prophets of *catenaccio* cared little about that. What they were looking for was the comfort of not ending on the losing side as that provided the best guarantee of keeping their job.

Once such a mindset took hold, other aspects started creeping in: ideas of how to stop others from playing by bending the rules. Play-acting to get free kicks had always been part of the game but for many years it had been frowned upon. It simply went against football's ethos. Or, at least, that's how it *had* been, because now it began to be viewed as simply a tool to help your team gain an advantage, be it a penalty, a free kick in a promising position or even a booking for the opposition player. Results were all that mattered, not how you got them. And it was at this juncture of football's history that a goalkeeper's ability to pick up the ball began to be abused.

The best way of stopping your opponent from hurting you is by preventing them getting hold of the ball. You could do that by passing your way around them as the 'total football' of the Netherlands tried to do. Not everyone was as talented, however, so many simply found a slyer way of achieving the same objective. All it involved was for a defender to pass the ball back to the goalkeeper, who would pick it up, bounce it a couple of time while looking up to see whether any of his team-mates had managed to get into interesting positions before … rolling it back to the same defender who had given the ball to him in the first place. After this the routine would keep on being repeated until someone from the other team trudged forward to put enough pressure on them to bring the sequence to an end. Naturally, the charade would be resumed at the next possible opportunity.

It was, at least from a cynical point of view, a brilliant tactic that used up precious minutes while giving the rest of the team some moments to catch their breath. If you were ahead – or holding on to a draw, as for many it was the same thing – and wanted to wind down the clock, there was nothing better.

There was even the potential added benefit of frustrating the opposition enough that they made a slip. The back-pass became like a hypnotising motion that could lure opposition defenders into dropping their guard and leaving the man they were marking a bit of extra freedom that could be exploited. In other words, it was the perfect tactic if you didn't care about the aesthetics of the game, just the end result.

And an increasing number of people were focusing only on that. As the years went by more coaches were being seduced by the idea of setting up with systems that caused their teams as little pain as possible, making it clear that they had to gain any advantage they could. Having goalkeeper and defenders pass the ball like a particularly slow game of pass the parcel became a duty.

Of course, all this paid little attention to whether the match people were paying to watch was any good. In keeping with the over-riding views of the time it was felt that fans wouldn't complain about the quality of the football if their team were getting results. Football was a sport; if people wanted entertainment they were free to go to the cinema instead. In fact, most of those running clubs – the same people who chose the coaches they wanted to lead their teams – felt that fans would keep on attending regardless of practically anything. One only had to look at the state of stadia across Europe to see just how true all of that was.

Yet the signs that people were falling out of love with football were there. More importantly, some of those entrusted with running it were willing to not only admit that but actually do something about it.

\* \* \*

In 1981, English football had introduced the idea of three points for a win to address the increasing negativity in the game. Just one point difference between a win and a draw wasn't seen as being enough of an incentive to push forward, so the gap was increased to two points. It was a simple move but, in a conservative sport, a controversial one. Other leagues considered it but opted to pass, and for more than a decade no one else chose to copy that idea.

Elsewhere, other changes had taken place. A decade after *L'Equipe* had set up the first European Cup and the idea of cross-continental cup football was welcomed enthusiastically almost universally, UEFA had in 1965 made its own move to encourage teams to be more adventurous by introducing the away-goals rule that saw goals scored away from home counting double if the result after two legs was a draw. Again, the idea was to make it more attractive for teams playing abroad to go into the match looking for something more than a goalless draw to take back home.

That rule came to be part of the football fabric and it certainly contributed to heightened drama. Whether it achieved what it had set out to do and make teams more willing to adopt an attacking stance isn't as clear-cut. Indeed, the idea of attacking football didn't seem to have too many supporters at the highest level of European competition, particularly by the 90s. The scores for the European Cup finals from 1980 till 1988 were two goalless draws, five 1-0 wins, a 1-1 draw and the most goals came in a 2-1 result. Most of those matches were as dour as the scorelines suggest.

As the former Netherlands defender Berry van Aerle told UEFA's official website two decades after PSV's success over Benfica in 1988, 'It wasn't a particularly good match, with both teams very cautious,' which is something of an understatement – there had been only one shot at goal in the first half – but ultimately that was the philosophy. Or, as he added, 'It does not matter how you win it, just as long as you do.'

Tellingly, the sterility of those cup finals was broken in 1989 by Arrigo Sacchi's AC Milan, who smashed Steaua Bucharest 4-0. Sacchi, the antithesis to his country's footballing tradition and one of the greatest innovators in European football history, preached attacking football that put opponents under constant pressure. Yet, for all their success, Sacchi's Milan were an anomaly. It wasn't really surprising that most of the teams at the 1990 World

Dubbed a spaceship by architect Renzo Piano, Bari's San Nicola stadium still looks futuristic three decades after being built. Not that it hasn't experienced its fair share of problems.

That of Toto Schillaci with outstretched hands and bulging eyes became one of the most iconic images of Italia 90. Crazy to think that there could have been another Schillaci with him.

*Roger Milla could have stayed on Reunion sipping beers by the beach. Instead he went to Italy to change the course of African football.*

*Germany's iconic look.*

*Hounded but not broken, Italia 90 was a turning point in fan culture.*

*Sly Stallone: the original American actor and goalkeeper. But not the only one.*

*Tomas Skuhravy was unbeatable in the air as Costa Rica found out.*

*The win over Sweden was the highlight of Scotland's 1990 World Cup. However, Andy Roxburgh was building a team for the future.*

*John Byrne scored the winner to take Sunderland into the FA Cup Final in 1992. What could have been had he been given a chance at the World Cup?*

*Sergio Goycochea went from unknown to hero back home in Argentina whilst bringing to an end Italy's magical nights.*

*Only a handful of England players turned up to record their part of 'World in Motion'. Those who didn't missed a shot at immortality.*

*Lessons from the 1990 World Cup helped shaped Oscar Washington Tabarez and deliver World Cup success 30 years later.*

*Claudio Taffarel: the first of a new breed of Brazilian goalkeepers.*

Cup sided with the tradition of adopting a safety-first approach.

And no one was really prepared for the levels that they were willing to go to. The opening match between Cameroon and Argentina quickly provided a taster. The brutality and levels of tactical fouling that Cameroon were willing to dish out (although the Argentines were no slouches in this department) was shocking, even allowing for the laxer refereeing views of the era.

As Matthew Engel, writing in *The Guardian*, brilliantly summed up the main tactic: 'Cameroon neutralised Maradona mainly by kicking him. He spent much of the game horizontal despite wearing calf pads as well as shin pads. His ten team-mates seemed too stunned to make any trouble but they were kicked as well, if they got in the way.'

At least the brutality provided some entertainment in that encounter. Other matches weren't so pleasant. Consensus has it that the nadir came in the match between the Republic of Ireland and Egypt. Both were aware that a draw might be enough to see them go through to the next round, so from the off there was the realisation that this wasn't going to be a classic. And so it proved. The Irish, playing in their first-ever World Cup, played a very functional style of football that was aimed at maximising their chances. On this occasion that meant giving the ball to goalkeeper Packie Bonner whenever possible. By the end of the match, for six out of the 90 minutes the ball had actually been in his hands.

Even so, they did try to win. The Egyptians had no such ambitions. They were set up in an ultra-defensive mode, with defenders passing the ball back to the goalkeeper at every opportunity, at which point he'd pick it up, eat up a bit of time by taking a few steps with the it, then hoof it upfield.

Over and over (and over) across 90 minutes this killed any hope of anything interesting happening.

Even Jack Charlton, who wasn't one to shy away from adopting results-focused tactics, was somewhat stunned by what he saw and let rip after the match: 'I hate teams like that. I've seen results that were amazing over the years but I've never played a team that never created a chance in 90 minutes. I didn't like the game. I didn't like the way Egypt played. I didn't like their time-wasting. I didn't like anything.'

Italia 90 wasn't the first World Cup to see such antics. One of the most memorable matches of the 1982 World Cup – indeed of World Cup history – was the one that saw Italy take on Brazil. It's remembered for the breathtaking action and the five goals that ultimately saw the Italians edging the match. But those memories have somewhat overshadowed the slower moments, particularly the ones where the expert Italian goalkeeper Dino Zoff broke the flow of play while giving his team-mates some moments to catch their breath by resorting to back-passes with his central defenders.

But the reliance on back-passes and other time-wasting tactics in Italia 90 was widespread at an unprecedented level. When the final ball was kicked, the tournament had registered an average of 2.2 goals per match, which remains the lowest recorded. Five matches ended goalless, while 15 were 1-0, including the final, which is widely regarded as one of the most boring ever.

The impact on entertainment of all this was so drastic that something needed to be done, particularly as FIFA were eyeing a lucrative new market that football had failed to penetrate up to that point. In 1988 they'd assigned the hosting of the 1994 World Cup to the USA, with the setting up of a professional league one of the pre-conditions. It was crucial for football to get a footing there, not least because it would make it easier to increase advertising revenues once American eyeballs were added to the list of the sport's global spectators. Yet alongside this desire there was also an awareness that for the American public to accept the game it needed to be more entertaining. The sight of goalkeepers and defenders endlessly passing the ball between them to eat up time was hardly likely to achieve that.

Indeed, in the years following Italia 90, numerous suggestions far more outrageous than the elimination of the back-pass cropped up, with calls to introduce penalty shoot-outs to decide drawn matches or to increase the size of goals to make scoring easier among those considered. It all betrayed a certain air of desperation to make sure that the US World Cup was attractive enough to win its way into the locals' hearts.

Despite the incentive, however, many were irritated by the revolutionary zeal underlying these proposals, and while football was indeed struggling, it didn't need such a radical overhaul.

That had long been football's stance, including when the option of eliminating a goalkeeper's ability to pick up a pass from a team-mate had already been discussed a decade earlier. Indeed, in 1981 a proposal to do so had been put in front of the FIFA technical committee. Back then it hadn't been considered to be enough of a problem to test out the idea. This time, however, the feeling was completely different.

After the 1990 World Cup, Sepp Blatter – then the general secretary of FIFA – decided to set up a committee named Task Force 2000, where notable former players and coaches such as Johan Cruyff and Bobby Charlton were asked to come up with solutions to make football more attractive. The name of the committee suggests that they were being tasked with allowing the game to survive in the new millennium, which might seem a stretch but, given how things were going and how boring football was becoming, in hindsight perhaps it wasn't too exaggerated to think that, had things remained the same, new generations might start being attracted to other sports.

Regardless of how drastic the members felt the situation was, it was based on the thoughts of the task force that, ahead of the 1991 Under-17 World Championship, the International Football Association Board recommended that a new law be tested during the youth tournament:

'To prohibit the goalkeeper from retrieving the ball with his hands after it has been passed back from a team-mate. If this rule is breached, the referee shall award an indirect free kick to the opposing team at the point where the goalkeeper touched the ball with his hands …'

Originally the competition was set to be held in Ecuador but a cholera outbreak forced a hasty relocation to Italy. It proved to be a happy return to the *bel paese* for FIFA, thanks also to the success of smaller footballing nations – Ghana won the tournament, while the likes of Qatar, Australia and the USA made it through the group stages – which was used as proof of the effectiveness of its various grassroots programmes. More importantly, the tournament lacked the time-wasting mentality that had dominated during Italia 90.

It's impossible to gauge what sort of an impact it truly had but the overwhelming feeling was that the experiment with the back-pass rule had worked. In the technical report written after the tournament, it was claimed: 'Delegates, players and experts were all very positive about the no back-passing rule. In particular they praised FIFA's efforts to make the game more continuous and to eliminate time-wasting by players passing the ball back and forth with their own goalkeeper,' before concluding, 'The positive response to the tests carried out in Tuscany should be continued whenever possible at the professional level.'

That seemed to decide it. Soon after, the back-pass began to be phased out of the game. When the decision was finally made, FIFA were scathing in their criticism of the actions that had forced them into the decision. 'The goalkeeper has a rare privilege in football,' claimed the press release issued to announce the decision. 'The use of his hands to keep the ball out of his goal, which would otherwise be virtually impossible. But it is a privilege that should not be abused. After all, football is essentially a game of skill and there is no skill in simply standing there, holding the ball in one's hands.'

The change didn't come in time to save European football from one last great heist built at least in part on the ability to exploit the goalkeeper's freedom to pick up the ball. Today, Denmark's success in Euro 92 is viewed in romantic terms; an underdog that hadn't even managed to qualify for the tournament but ended up winning it. And, obviously, there's much to admire in the triumph of determination and teamwork over objectively stronger opponents, especially when most of the Danish players were on holiday when they were told that they were going to be replacing Yugoslavia just days before the tournament started.

This lack of preparation showed in their opening two group matches, where they failed to score, drawing one (0-0 against England) and losing the other (1-0 against Sweden). Indeed, they only came to life in the final group match against France but that was all they needed as a 2-1 win sent them through.

The Danes had two standout stars. Striker Brian Laudrup was one of the most talented players in Europe at the time and was the one who shouldered most of their creative efforts. At the other end of the pitch there was Peter Schmeichel, the giant goalkeeper who was on his way to becoming a legend. The other players, although not close as far as quality was concerned, made up for the gap with hard work and stepping up at the right moment.

They were also conscious that there were others who were stronger than them, which meant a need to use every trick in the book to overcome them. So when they not only found themselves in the final against world champions Germany but managed to grab an early lead, they resorted to the tried-and-tested back-pass to help them manage the match.

In reality, they used and abused the back-pass. Time and again, the Danish defenders passed the ball back to Schmeichel, who waited until a German striker had run up to him before picking up the ball. Every time they did this, they managed to eat up valuable seconds while also breaking up the rhythm of an opponent who was fiercely trying to get the equalising goal.

This tactic, along with Schmeichel's ability to save everything thrown at him, wore down the World Cup winners, who by the time the Danes scored a second ten minutes from time had probably realised that it wasn't going to be their day. One last hurrah for the goalkeeper's liberty to pick up a back-pass.

\* \* \*

As the years passed, views on the changes brought about by the elimination of the back-pass evolved such that it's now almost universally seen as a positive innovation. Back in

1992 that was hardly the case. Understandably, goalkeepers, present and former, were highly sceptical of the change that was going to massively alter how they did their job. But they weren't the only ones.

The game has always been dominated by people of a highly conservative bent who, in this instance, didn't necessarily see back-passes as a means of wasting time but more of a tactic that teams could adopt. This view was largely centred around the philosophy of 'that's how it has always been and that's how it should always be'.

All of this was highlighted in the first match in English football in which back-passes weren't allowed: the 1992/93 Charity Shield between Leeds and Liverpool. Early on, a Leeds defender pushed the ball back to his goalkeeper, John Lukic. What had been a routine action until a few weeks earlier was suddenly transformed into a high-pressure moment, especially as the Liverpool striker Ronnie Rosenthal sensed an opportunity and made his way towards the goalkeeper. There was still plenty of time for Lukic to scan the pitch and hit it towards a team-mate but the only solution he saw was to boot it with as much ferocity as he could muster across the sideline for a throw-in.

Commenting for Sky Sports, Andy Gray expressed his irritation at the change in law. 'I just think that is the perfect example regarding it … is that making the game any better, when you see the goalkeeper under pressure like that, just lumping the ball out of play? I don't think so,' he ranted, before scoffing when his co-commentator Martin Tyler suggested that goalkeepers might get better at dealing with those situations as the season went on.

Worse was to follow. In a match between Spurs and Sheffield United, a back-pass towards United goalkeeper

Simon Tracey's weaker left foot saw him hilariously run with the ball towards the sideline, so uncomfortable was he on that side. Even more comically, he then tried to snatch the ball away from the ball-boy who was looking to put it back into play and, when that failed, rugby-tackled the Spurs player to prevent him from taking the throw-in. For his efforts, Tracey ended up being sent off.

The problems weren't limited to England. The former Italy goalkeeper Luca Marchegiani was more adept with the ball at his feet than many of his contemporaries but even he found it difficult. 'We found ourselves blown away,' he said. 'We did not immediately understand the extent of the change and getting used to it was not easy.'

Carlo Mazzone, the much-loved and well-travelled Italian coach with a reputation for over-achieving at lesser lights, had to change his whole approach. 'It [the back-pass] was a typical strategy of the small sides,' he said. 'I changed my training sessions, it was necessary to learn to play the ball backwards in a certain way, on the goalkeeper's right foot, to avoid getting into trouble.' Perhaps he too had seen Tracey's comedy of errors and learned from them.

Some even tried to find creative ways to get around the new rule. Early on there were those who chose to head the ball back to the goalkeeper, even if that meant lying down to do so. Apart from it not being nearly as effective as they perhaps imagined, it was quickly stamped out as the law stated that, 'No trickery may be used to get around the terms of the amendment to Law 12.'

Ironically, however, the most damning commentary on the back-pass came from the kind of teams who were quickest to adapt to it. AC Milan, the pressing machine built by Arrigo Sacchi, were one of them. 'We had been training on systematic pressing for some time and so we found ourselves ready for that revolution,' their legendary defender Franco Baresi explained.

Ajax, another team known for their open approach to the game, were also ready for this change. Particularly as in Frank Hoek they had a visionary goalkeeping coach who had long preached about the need for goalkeepers to be good at using their feet. Unsurprisingly, he 'loved the back-pass rule'. 'Everybody hated it but I loved it,' he said of the change. 'Really loved it. It fitted perfectly with our way of thinking at Ajax. We had a big advantage. Firstly, if we had the ball, but also if the opponent had the ball because if they passed it back to their goalkeeper he did not know what to do with it. From the start, we had a big advantage.'

It was these sorts of teams – and their success – that helped football evolve to make the most of the new changes. The fundamentals of all that's positive and taken for granted in the modern game lay in that rule change.

There are still coaches who preach the credo of defensive football but this is a very different game to that of 1990, as evidenced by the almost universally adopted strategy of playing the ball out of defence even from a goal kick, something that would have been considered unthinkable in 1990.

\* \* \*

For all the negative football and time-wasting, there's obviously still much that's worth remembering fondly from Italia 90. Even so, with the benefit of decades of hindsight, the rule change that the tournament helped usher in and the positive impact it indirectly had on football might be the most influential outcome of any World Cup competition.

# Scottish Stepping Stone to Glory

SOME PLAYERS are born to wear their nation's shirt. They're identified as stars from an early age and when their names are mentioned it's together with knowing nods, a signal of certainty about their future. Often these players come through at one of that country's bigger clubs, so they're in the spotlight as soon as they make the first tentative steps in adult football. This means added pressure yet it also allows for greater rewards. Those who can transfer their promise from youth football to the adult game are immediately exalted as the next big thing. If their countries are at the top of the footballing table, continental competitions inevitably follow, thus further spreading word of their ability.

All this only happens with the finest of talents, those blessed with a combination of skill, mental fortitude and luck. Very few players manage to enjoy such a smooth transition but those who do tend to be the ones that become the most familiar household names. For these individuals, national call-ups come at a very early age, further affirmation of their talent and setting the scene for them to lock down their place for years to come.

Most players' paths to the top are more circuitous than that, however. They take in one or two smaller clubs where they gain experience, improve and sometimes fail before working their way up gradually. It takes time and hard work for their talent to fully emerge but eventually it does and they too start being considered as fundamental players, both for their club and internationally.

So when national team coaches come to name the squad they want to take with them to major tournaments, they often go for a mixture of the two groups – the precocious talents and those who make the most of their talent through hard work. They know that no team in the competition is strong in all areas but, ultimately, it's the one that can come together at the crucial moments that tends to win.

Perhaps it's this specific thought that causes those managers to make certain choices that, to an extent, are surprising to the outside world. They go for a player who isn't getting regular club football because they see in them an ability that's missing from the rest of their team. Or for someone who hasn't yet played for the national team, in the hope that their freshness adds an element of unpredictability.

Often, however, it's the player who manages to hit the right patch of form at the right moment that gets their attention. Many in the game still value momentum, the belief that recent good form has a quasi-physical weight that keeps pushing the player or team onwards to achieve further success almost regardless of talent. In those moments, the confidence is so high that players don't obstruct their own talent by doubting themselves. There's no questioning of whether they deserve to be achieving this success, just the certainty that they can do it. Unrestrained by any psychological holdbacks, they start hitting levels they'd never achieved before.

Sadly those runs eventually come to an end and, when that happens, players return to their true level. Yet when it's ongoing it's as if they've managed to capture lightning. It's unsurprising then that when managers see something like that on the eve of a major international tournament they opt to take a shot on that individual. If, somehow, they manage to tap into that energy and the momentum carries over, then the bet is well worth it. And the history of the World Cup is littered with instances of such gambles paying off spectacularly.

That's the case today, even if the game is guided by statistical models that tend to force football people to look at cold facts more than anything else. And it was certainly the case back in 1990 as the world's leading coaches were finalising their squads.

\* \* \*

For the Netherlands, the European champions, the need back in 1990 for someone to come in with something extra – from a footballing sense – was more vital than most other nations. Following their continental success in 1988, manager Rinus Michels had been elevated to a role with the national federation, with the former Feyenoord coach Thijs Libregts tasked with taking over. He'd won a league title at Feyenoord but in most people's view that success had more to do with the presence of Johan Cruyff, who had opted to take revenge on his former club Ajax by joining their rivals when he returned to his homeland. That wasn't Libregts' own view, obviously. He felt fully capable of taking the supremely talented Dutch to World Cup glory.

The players themselves felt otherwise. They didn't appreciate his arrogant attitude and, damningly, some of his views verged on the racist. Even though the Netherlands had made it through from a tough qualifying group that included West Germany, most of the players weren't happy and made their views very clear.

This wasn't just any group of players; not only was it composed largely of the same individuals who had won the nation's first international trophy but it also contained the trio that many felt were the best on the planet at the time: Marco van Basten, Ruud Gullit and Frank Rijkaard. When they demanded that Libregts had to go, there was no refusing them. Similarly, when they asked to be given a voice in the selection of his replacement, the Dutch federation had little choice but to fold, particularly after Michels opted to support the players.

What happened next, however, has become part of Dutch national team infamy. Some of the players went for the tactician Aad de Mos, while others supported a motivator such as Leo Beenhakker. The majority, however, wanted the man who excelled at both aspects: Johan Cruyff. This was always going to be the most likely outcome but it was also the most problematic. As a player, Cruyff had clashed with the national federation and any attempt to persuade him to accept the job would have required the federation to accept his demands, whatever they were. This is rarely something that those in power enjoy doing.

It didn't help that Michels himself wasn't too enamoured with the choice. Having earlier backed the players' right to vote for the next coach, he now lobbied against their choice, arguing, with some justification, that Cruyff was both too inexperienced as a coach and had a tendency to fall out with authority figures, something that would inevitably lead to headaches for his bosses at the federation.

Michels had coached Cruyff to great success. Yet as the star of the great Ajax team of the 70s, Cruyff dominated attention and was seen as the main reason for their success.

Some felt that this embittered Michels as it took away from the merit of the tactical revolution that he'd brought about that changed the way football was played. Now, having finally emerged from Cruyff's shadow with the European Championship triumph, Michels was reluctant to put him in charge and risk being eclipsed once again.

So when the KNVB announced the name of the new national team coach in late April of 1990, it wasn't Cruyff whom they presented to the public but instead the players' number-two choice, Leo Beenhakker.

Understandably, the players weren't too happy. They felt let down by the association and betrayed by Michels. In a group where the level of talent was matched only by the size of their egos, this was always going to cause problems, with many players regularly going to their favourite journalists to air their grievances.

It was into this cauldron of unrest that Beenhakker entered. Successful both domestically, having won league titles with Ajax, as well as abroad, where he'd led Real Madrid to a domestic sweep a year earlier, he had all the credentials. Yet there was scepticism around him from the very start and not just because of the players' unrest.

In 1985 Beenhakker had stepped in for Michels as Dutch coach when the latter had to undergo heart surgery. The situation hadn't been rosy when he took over, so when the Dutch failed to qualify for the 1986 World Cup, not many fingers should have been pointed at him. Unfortunately, in sport, emotions tend to overrule common sense, so not everyone was as objective about Beenhakker's part in the overall failure. He was left holding the package when it exploded, so he was the one hit by the blast.

Perhaps that should have warned him off from retaking the job. No one would have blamed him, especially with so many players close to mutiny. The reality was that under the circumstances, no one apart from Cruyff would have mollified the players enough for them to focus on the World Cup. Beenhakker was experienced enough to know the odds were against him and should have let someone else drink from the poisoned chalice. Then again, for the coach who hadn't had much of a career as a player, the opportunity to coach in the World Cup was just too big of a dream to simply give up. Passing the offer could have meant declining his only opportunity to test himself at that level and he wasn't about to let that happen. After all, he'd managed big characters and doubters throughout his career. Given his successes over the span of decades, he probably had enough confidence in his ability to believe that he'd eventually win over the rebelling players.

Yet even someone with such a history of success requires a dose of good luck when faced with such a situation. Perhaps that's why, when putting together the list of players he wanted to take with him to Italy, he felt the compulsion to include a striker who a few months earlier had been written off as washed up but who had suddenly rediscovered his goalscoring form in spectacular fashion. A player who was enjoying the kind of form that seemed to overturn all that had been known about him, whose luck of late was blessed far more than most.

That player was Hans Gillhaus and his circuitous road to redemption had been heavily re-energised by a surprising move.

\* \* \*

For most of their history, Den Bosch had been an Eerste Divisie – Dutch second tier – club. At the start of the 80s they'd taken a gamble on former player Hans Verel, appointing him as coach when he was just 27. Verel first laid the foundations before gradually putting together the team that eventually achieved promotion in 1983.

Despite the pressure to retain their place in the top flight, Verel still had an eye on the club's future, giving the 20-year-old Gillhaus his first-team debut on the opening day of the season. And what an introduction it proved to be! Played out on the wing, Gillhaus popped up in the second minute to score Den Bosch's first goal in the Eredivisie in more than a decade. However, his debut came to a premature end when he was forced off in the 24th minute, but it was still quite an introduction for the young man.

His injuries and the regular availability of more experienced players limited his game time but he still made 12 appearances, scoring two further goals, including one in a 4-2 defeat at the hands of eventual champions PSV Eindhoven. His contribution helped Den Bosch retain their place in the top flight, but they still opted for a change of management, providing the former Feyenoord and Netherlands defender Rinus Israël with his first senior job in charge. For all Verel's achievements at the club that made his dismissal a harsh one, it proved to be the right move as Israël added tactical discipline and made Den Bosch harder to play against.

Israël also began using Gillhaus in a more central role rather than on the wing, which proved to be the right move as he scored nine times in what was Den Bosch's finest-ever season, one that saw them finish sixth in the Eredivisie. For him it was only the start because the following year he hit 16 goals, a phenomenal total that made him the club's highest-ever scorer while in the top flight as they registered another sixth-place finish. A year later he went one better, scoring 17 times, despite the team not doing as well. To this day, no other player has managed to overcome Gillhaus's record while wearing Den Bosch colours.

As often happens in the Netherlands, promising players don't stay too long with smaller clubs and, given his record, it was clear that Gillhaus had outgrown his surroundings. When top Dutch talents are lured away by richer clubs in Europe, the local big boys look inward to fill the gap. That had happened before and remains the case, just as it was in 1987 when Gillhaus finally got the opportunity to head out.

PSV had just sold Ruud Gullit to AC Milan for £6m and, while in the long term the move would prove to be fundamental in making the Italians the finest team in European football, that kind of money was in those days transformational. Conscious that there was no direct replacement for a talent as mercurial as Gullit, PSV opted to spend their windfall on a collection of players who would make their team even stronger than it was before.

It was the Gullit money that enabled them to bring the experienced Danish midfielder Søren Lerby back to the Netherlands, where he'd built his reputation with rivals Ajax. Another former Ajax graduate, Wim Kieft, also returned home after four largely underwhelming years in Italy with Pisa and Torino. These additions helped strengthen a squad that was already brimming with some of the best players of their era, such as Hans van Breukelen, Ronald Koeman, Berry van Aerle, Eric Gerets, Jan Heintze, Gerald Vanenburg and Frank Arnesen.

Still, PSV wanted to add some youthful verve so that's when they turned to Den Bosch's star man. The previous season they'd won both league matches against Den Bosch but on both occasions had fallen behind to Gillhaus strikes. He'd even scored against them in the Dutch Cup when Den Bosch caused a major shock by winning on penalties.

If any further proof of his readiness for the big time were needed, it lay in his track record against the other members of the traditional big three of Dutch football – Ajax and Feyenoord – both of whom were on the receiving end of a Gillhaus goal. This was a striker who could hurt the best of teams despite playing in a side with far less resources.

Even though he knew that for the sake of his career he couldn't remain at Den Bosch and the opportunity to play for a club like PSV was one that couldn't be missed, it was still 'a very big transition', as he later admitted. In particular, he wasn't used to the intense schedule that PSV players had to live with as they went hard in all competitions, including the European Cup.

By early spring, this intensity became too much for Gillhaus, who had to miss some fixtures due to injury. But a little bit of rest was all he needed, and in April he was back in action just as things were heating up.

Throughout the season, Gillhaus had often filled in for Frank Arnesen, which was lucky, because when the European Cup Final came round it opened a path to the squad in place of the injured Arnesen. Shifted to the left wing, rather than up front supporting Kieft, Gillhaus was tasked by PSV's coach, Guus Hiddink, to stop Benfica's full-back, who tended to move forward in support of their attack. It meant a final spent running up and down the pitch to add defensive cover while also trying to create a threat himself. By extra time he was completely exhausted, which is probably why Hiddink opted to replace him in the 107th minute.

Despite the tiredness, Gillhaus would still have preferred to be on the pitch to take a penalty kick. Thankfully, his replacement, Anton Janssen, scored to avoid any regrets on that front. In fact, all spot kicks by both teams were pretty much faultless until Van Breukelen saved Benfica's sixth attempt to put PSV at the summit of Europe. The man who missed – Antonio Veloso – was the player Gillhaus had spent the match tracking.

\* \* \*

For someone who had spent his entire career at a mid-table club where avoiding relegation was the best they could hope for, Gillhaus's debut season at PSV had gone beyond his wildest dreams. A treble of trophies, including the most prized one in European football, suddenly placed him among the greats of Dutch football. Yet, paradoxically, that unexpected success would eventually lead to the end of his time in the Netherlands. 'When the European Cup was won, a little bit of the hunger was maybe gone,' he admitted later. 'We were never at the same level after that.'

The mark of a great player doesn't lie in their ability to do well one season, but to keep doing so year after year, regardless of how successful the previous season was. Perhaps Gillhaus wasn't mentally there at that point of his career and couldn't find the motivation to push himself as he had the previous season. It's an unsurprising reaction but not one that could be easily accepted at a club as used to success as PSV.

That, however, is only part of the story. In the summer following their European Cup success, PSV had signed a young Brazilian striker who had just topped the goalscoring charts of the Olympic tournament. That striker was Romário who, over the space of the next couple of years, would become one of the best in world football.

It was a stunning move by PSV, who had managed to grab themselves such a talent before anyone else had even really woken up to his potential. For Gillhaus, however, it didn't bode well. He was still scoring crucial goals but not at the rate that Romário was putting them away. As the months progressed he found himself increasingly on the sidelines. This was problematic, not only because Gillhaus hadn't been in such a situation since he'd first broken through at Den Bosch, but it was also hampering his chances with the Dutch national team at the worst possible time.

Gillhaus had received his first call-up soon after joining PSV, when he played in a couple of friendlies. From then on, he was a regular in the squad, even if rarely a starter. Given the quality of talent available, that was hardly an embarrassment. Still, as a European Cup-winning striker of the strongest Dutch team of the era, he had every reason to hope for a place in the national squad that travelled to Italy. The problem, however, was that the longer he was out of the team, the less likely that became. As he later acknowledged, 'I was happy there, but there was not enough game time. I was behind Romário. The rest of the world was probably behind Romário. I just needed a fresh start.'

PSV realised as much and expressed a willingness to consider any prospective offers. Yet when one eventually came it was from a somewhat unlikely source: Aberdeen. At the time, Aberdeen were still trying to live up to the heights reached by Alex Ferguson. In their efforts they'd gone down the strange route of appointing Alex Smith and Jocky Scott as co-managers in 1988, with the latter taking care of training while the former handled the more administrative tasks.

Indeed, it was a conversation between Smith and Ferguson that would end up significantly affecting the manner in which Aberdeen's squad came together. The chat between the two resulted in the Manchester United boss providing the contact details of a Dutch football agent, which in turn allowed them to sign goalkeeper Theo Snelders and rangy forward Willem van der Ark.

Both Dutchmen proved to be big hits at Aberdeen, albeit in different manners, which opened the management team's eyes to a new market of talented, affordable players that could help them bridge the gap with Rangers and their rich imports from south of the border. Such transfers also sent a signal of their ambition to the established core of the team that were always being tempted with moves elsewhere.

One of those was the striker Charlie Nicholas, who had got his career back on track at Aberdeen after a disastrous ending to his time at Arsenal. Although grateful for the opportunity that Aberdeen provided him, Nicholas was constantly being linked with a move back to former club Celtic, who were tempting him with promises of further trophies and honours.

Aberdeen, in a bid to show him that he could fulfil his ambitions with them, went shopping. There was a belief that they relied too much on Nicholas and without him they struggled to score. So, eager to relieve some pressure on their star forward, they went looking for another striker to shoulder the burden in attack. Understandably, they turned once more to the trusty Dutch agent, who immediately pointed them in Gillhaus's direction.

\* \* \*

Today the thought of a Scottish club that isn't either Rangers or Celtic managing to attract a European Cup-winning striker seems rather ludicrous. Back in the late 80s, however, Aberdeen were still seen as a strong club whose reputation on the continent had been enhanced by their Cup Winners' Cup success over Real Madrid in 1983. Despite Ferguson's departure they'd remained one of the top Scottish teams –

by the time they made the move for Gillhaus in late 1989 they'd already won the League Cup – who played offensive-minded football that was bound to appeal to any striker.

So when they made the move to sign Gillhaus, it didn't sound preposterous. Indeed, within a couple of weeks both club and player had agreed to a transfer for the relatively modest fee of £650,000. 'Aberdeen were very eager,' Gillhaus said. 'They did a good job of making it interesting to me. They were a good team, but the type of football they played also helped.'

Gillhaus's impact in Scotland was immediate. His debut came at Dunfermline, where within the opening half-hour he'd already scored twice to effectively kill the match. Particularly memorable was the first of those two goals. A free kick lumped into the Dunfermline penalty area was headed in Gillhaus's general direction by a team-mate and the Dutchman launched into an overhead kick that looped the ball into the back of the net. It was a breathtaking combination of skill and audacity that allowed him to make the most out of what had been a hit-and-hope action that most others would have let pass.

A few days later he followed that up with a goal in his first home match, scoring against the despised Rangers with a long-range effort. He'd not even been in Scotland a week but his hero status had already been cemented. It wasn't just the goals that excited the fans, although there were to be many of them. His ability with the ball at his feet and capacity to go past players added another dimension to Aberdeen's play. With the clinical Nicholas alongside him, they could hurt most teams, and often did.

Unfortunately, Aberdeen didn't turn their dominance into wins frequently enough and too many draws in the run-in cost them a shot at the league title. That was disappointing but Gillhaus had done his part, hitting another purple patch towards the end of the season, while also scoring crucial goals in the Scottish FA Cup as they reached the final. There they faced Celtic in a dour match in which neither team could fashion the killer punch. As with the European Cup, it went to penalties but this time Gillhaus had stayed on to the very end and got to take a penalty (which he scored) as Aberdeen ran out winners.

Any season that ends with a new trophy in the cabinet can be counted as a good one but for Gillhaus it was doubly so. At PSV he'd become a bit-part player in an admittedly dominant team that was too restrictive for someone of his talent. Moving to Scotland might have been seen as a backwards move but it had given him the impetus he needed to push on.

Which he'd done. He'd scored important goals, which is what strikers are often judged on, but beyond that he showed how much he'd matured in his performance, using his running and technique to open up space for his team-mates. Those months in Scotland – and away from the shadow of a talent as brilliant as Romário – had not only reminded people of what he could do but also marked him out as one of the most in-form players in Europe.

It certainly meant that when Beenhakker included him in his squad for Italia 90, no one objected; it was a fully justified inclusion. But there was probably more to the inclusion than purely form. Gillhaus was a player who was outside of the cliques that had formed in the lead-up to the start of the tournament. The coach needed as much help as he could get.

\* \* \*

On paper, the Netherlands had an ideal start to the tournament. They were heavy favourites to win the first match against Egypt, and they would have done were it not for a late penalty that brought the scores level. Understandably, the failure to win what was supposed to be the group's easy match didn't go down well with the media back home. Already heavily criticised for the bickering before the competition, this raised the pressure a couple of notches higher.

For Beenhakker, however, it provided the perfect opportunity to bring in some new faces, ones that were friendlier to him. Gillhaus was in. His World Cup debut was a drab affair, however. Two years earlier, the Dutch had thrashed England 3-1, and Bobby Robson wanted to avoid a repeat at all costs. More concerned with not conceding rather than scoring, the English defended resolutely and kept the Dutch as far away from their penalty area as possible. Truth be told, the Dutch weren't particularly effusive in their play either.

Still, a draw in the group's toughest fixture wasn't a poor result. Gillhaus had done well enough in creating space for Van Basten to keep his place for the crucial match against Ireland. That the Netherlands needed a win helped his case, with Beenhakker opting to play three up front to force the issue.

It worked to a degree. The Dutch seemed to be cruising following an early Gullit goal but a late mix-up earned Ireland an equaliser to seal a third draw for the Dutch. Thankfully for them results elsewhere still allowed them to go through but, rather than a more comfortable tie, they were now due to meet bitter rivals West Germany.

This proved to be one of the most infamous matches of World Cup history, a 2-1 defeat for the Dutch that saw both teams go a man down midway through the first half after a spat (literally) between Rudi Völler and Frank Rijkaard.

Gillhaus only played the final ten minutes of that match, thrown on as the Netherlands tried to force extra time. Sadly, he was unable to make much of a difference.

With all the talent that they fielded, the Dutch should have done much better in Italy. Not enough players gave their utmost and too many focused their energy on fighting ego-driven personal battles. Not Gillhaus, however, who appreciated more than anyone in that squad just how precious and fleeting success can be in football.

It's only right, then, that he has largely positive memories of the tournament: 'Even though we didn't do as well as we wanted to it was great to play in a World Cup in Italy, which is a real football nation.' He was even philosophical about the manner of their elimination: 'It is probably less painful to go out of the World Cup to a team that actually went on to win the tournament. We went out against the eventual world champions and that can happen.'

\* \* \*

While the tournament hadn't gone as well as he might have hoped, Gillhaus had confirmed his status as a top player. His strike partner Nicholas, the player he'd been brought in to help convince to stay, had opted to return to Celtic after all but this added responsibility seemed to embolden the Dutchman.

Having won two trophies the previous season had a similar effect on Aberdeen, who went into the campaign confident that they could win the title from Rangers. It took them some time to find their most consistent form but from the start of the new year they were devastating. A run of seven consecutive wins put them in pole position and they went into the final match of the season knowing that a draw would give them the title. Unfortunately that match was at Rangers and, deprived of the injured Snelders, Aberdeen simply couldn't gain the result they needed, losing 2-0 to see the title going to the Glasgow giants once more.

It was a huge blow, arguably the beginning of the end. The following season didn't kick off as expected and the club parted ways with the two co-managers as a result. Club legend Willie Miller took over and one of his first actions was to sell Gillhaus to Dutch club Vitesse Arnhem for £300,000. It was a surprising decision that was caused, as rumour goes, by a falling out between player and manager, even though the reason for it has always been shrouded in mystery. That Aberdeen had two highly promising youngsters, Eoin Jess and Scott Booth, coming through probably played a part as well, making it a less risky decision for the new manager.

Regardless, it was a sad end to Gillhaus's Scottish experience. Yet he still had plenty to give as a player, as he showed back home the following season, in which he scored 22 goals to propel his new club to fourth place and UEFA Cup qualification.

He stayed at Vitesse for another season before moving to Japan for two goal-filled seasons with Gamba Osaka. His career then wound down at AZ Alkmaar, FF Jaro in Finland and then a return to Den Bosch, where he rounded off his playing days by helping them return to the Eredivisie. Den Bosch therefore bookended his career but, in between, he achieved the kind of success he'd only have dreamed of when he was starting out.

Managing to carve out space for himself in one of the most talented squads ever and play at the biggest stage of them all has to be the crowning achievement, one that wouldn't have been possible had he not made the move to Scotland. 'I was at Pittodrie for little more than half a year and then I was playing at the World Cup,' he said. 'I left PSV in order to get playing time. My performances at Aberdeen got me into the international squad again. I had been in the international squad before but the generation of strikers ahead of me were world class. We had Marco van Basten, Ruud Gullit and Wim Kieft up front, so it was always difficult to get into the squad. Thankfully after moving to Aberdeen I played a few games at the World Cup.'

Thankfully indeed.

# The Making of El Maestro

WHEN THE disappointment began to fade away, it was replaced by an overwhelming feeling of pride. Uruguay, a country of just over three million people, had played its way to the brink of a World Cup Final. After decades of obscurity, the 2010 World Cup had finally re-established *La Celeste* as one of the leading nations in the game. This was thanks to an emergence of talent that undoubtedly deserved the world-class adjective: Edinson Cavani, Luis Suárez, Diego Forlán. But there was more to their success than that.

Regardless of the level of talent, there were no prima donnas in the team. Everyone knew their strengths but were also well aware of their weaknesses, so they relied on old-fashioned hard work and team ethic to make sure they were more than the sum of their parts. A spirit of sacrifice coursed throughout the team, with everyone willing to do what was necessary to make sure they moved ahead.

The apex of this mentality came in the quarter-final against Ghana when a last-minute shot would have eliminated them had it not been handled on the line by Luis Suárez. Not many other star strikers would have been back defending so deep, much less be willing to risk dirtying their name to stop a goal. But Suárez didn't even flinch for a second. He realised it was the best decision for the team and was willing to sacrifice himself.

It paid off and Uruguay made it to the semis. Of course, it could easily have gone the other way had Ghana scored the resultant penalty. Suárez would have vilified himself for nothing. Yet this is what the team was hard-wired to do. Everyone supported each other; when one fell, another stepped in to close the gap.

A year later, the same team would finally regain the title of South America's best when they won the Copa América. Again, their football was a mixture of hard work, sacrifice and flashes of brilliance. It was the epitome of a vision that had been decades in the making. The vision of Óscar Washington Tabárez. And one that had its roots in Italia 90.

\* \* \*

Uruguay has a long history of success at the FIFA World Cup, dating back to the tournament's inception in 1930. As the hosts and one of the 13 countries that took part, Uruguay had a strong showing that ultimately saw them emerge as the tournament champions. It was a true show of force; only Peru managed to put up something resembling a challenge before going down to a 1-0 defeat. Otherwise, the Uruguayans scored four or more goals in each match, including the final against Argentina, which they won 4-2.

Sadly – albeit understandably – they refused to defend their title in Italy four years later in response to the many European nations that had opted not to take part when the competition was held in Uruguay. Similarly, they opted not to make the trip to France in 1938 in protest over another European country being chosen to host the tournament even though most South American nations thought that the competition's hosting would alternate between the two continents. Although both if Uruguay's decisions were justified, it's hard not to wonder what might have happened had they chosen to compete in either one of those tournaments.

Still, their stance said much about the Uruguayan character – of their stubbornness, true, but also of a determination to stand up for what they saw as their right and an unwillingness to bow at the feet of bigger nations.

Just how unyielding they were would be witnessed by the rest of the world in 1950, when the tournament returned after the forced hiatus due to the Second World War. Played in Brazil, the hosts were widely expected to win their first-ever world title due to their advantage as hosts but, largely, to the talent within their team.

That edition of the World Cup didn't have a one-off final but rather a final round in which four teams played one another, with the one ending with most points being the winner. In their opening two matches, Brazil further confirmed their status as the overwhelming favourites by demolishing the two European finalists Spain (6-1) and Sweden (7-1) before they went into the final match. Uruguay, on the other hand, had been held to a 2-2 draw by Spain before needing two late goals to defeat Sweden 3-2. This meant that, mathematically, they were still in with a chance of winning the competition but in the eyes of anyone but themselves stood little chance against the might of the Brazilians.

What followed is a match that has become a myth, one in which the Brazilians were heralded as champions before a ball was kicked and an incredibly partisan local crowd of more than 160,000 cheered wildly when they finally broke the deadlock upon the restart of the second half. Surely, they felt, the floodgates would now open and Brazil would go on to claim their pre-ordained destiny.

Amid the cacophony of joy and expectation, the Uruguayans kept their composure. They also kept probing the Brazilian defence for weaknesses they knew were there, an effort that finally paid off when Juan Schiaffino and Alcides Ghiggia found the net within ten minutes of each other. A deathly silence descended on the Maracanã as the possibility of anything other than a Brazil win began to dawn on the home crowd.

In the minutes that followed, the Brazilian attempts raised only howls of desperation as the Uruguayans raised a shield-wall behind which no opponent was allowed to go. The seconds ticked away until the referee looked at his watch for one last time before blowing his whistle. Uruguay were world champions once again. The 11 men wearing light-blue shirts had found strength in one another when faced by a seemingly unbeatable opponent and had used that inner strength to achieve the seemingly impossible, while traumatising Brazilian football for generations to come.

As they celebrated their triumph both on the pitch and back home, those Uruguayan players didn't realise that their country would never reach those heights again. Four years later, they exited the World Cup at the semi-final stage, beaten by the Hungary team of mighty fame. And they experienced another semi-final defeat in 1970 when the Brazilians enjoyed a modicum of revenge by winning 3-1 en route to their third World Cup success.

That defeat signalled the end of Uruguay at the top table of world football. While they had the passion, and the talent continued to emerge on a regular basis, they simply couldn't match their bigger neighbours or the European strongholds. As the years progressed, Uruguay stopped being considered a great footballing nation, especially after they failed to qualify for the World Cup on two consecutive occasions in 1978 and 1982. For a country of such rich history, it was an abject humiliation.

Things improved slightly midway through the 80s. In fact, in 1986 Uruguay had gone into the World Cup tagged as one of the possible outsiders. In Enzo Francescoli and Jorge da Silva they had two strikers of genuine class and quality, which they'd shown in winning the Copa América. Yet they had no real intention of relying on the silky skills of their forwards, opting instead for an aggressive approach. Within 25 seconds of their opener against West Germany, Nelson Gutiérrez hacked down Rudi Völler to set the tone for the rest of the match. And their tournament.

In the second match, against Denmark, they went in hard from the first minute; too hard. Miguel Bossio was sent off after just 19 minutes and Uruguay were lucky to end with ten men as they futilely tried to stop the Danes, who emerged 6-1 winners. Same again against Scotland, when it was José Batista who received his marching orders early on. Undeterred, and knowing that they needed a draw to qualify for the next round, they took gamesmanship to an all-new level as they wasted as much time as they could to grind out a draw.

Eventually they went out to Argentina in another brutal affair. Few were sad to see them go, their unyielding approach and win-at-all-costs attitude having earned them no fans. Although publicly they portrayed themselves as victims of a conspiracy and a target of harsh refereeing, there was the realisation that they needed to bring in someone who had more forward-looking ideas about how the game should be played. Not necessarily someone who frowned on the aggressive nature of the Uruguayan approach – that was part of their footballing character – but perhaps a coach for whom that wasn't the only feature of his game. Fortunately, they had just the right man for the job.

\* \* \*

From early on in his coaching career, Óscar Washington Tabárez had the nickname of El Maestro – the Teacher – because that's what he was. His first calling was as a teacher, a job that he enjoyed among the kids of Montevideo, also the city where he'd been born in 1947.

Tabárez, however, was also good at playing football and opted to follow that passion in his early 20s as he played in defence for several mid-table Uruguayan teams, such as Sud América, Deportivo Italiano, Montevideo Wanderers, Fénix and Bella Vista, with a brief spell with the Mexicans of Puebla in between. He probably reasoned that he'd be able to return to the classroom when he was older, while a playing career was open only to young men – an eminently justifiable way of reasoning and one that anyone who loves the sport would take had they the talent.

While that dream came true for Tabárez, others were to remain unfulfilled. He'd dreamed of playing for one of the country's bigger clubs and perhaps the national team but that never came to pass. He didn't have enough talent and, in any case, suffered too many injuries to really make a mark. It was one of those injuries that, in late 1979, forced him to make the tough choice of ending his career. Still only 32 and with a young family to support, it was a hard decision but he didn't have the luxury of time to feel sorry for himself. Instead, it was back to the classroom and teaching to put food on the table.

By then, however, football had taken over as his main passion, so he embarked on the coaching courses needed to remain in the game. Again, a fortuitous choice because a year after retiring he was asked by Bella Vista – his last club as a player – to return as coach of the youth team.

His big break, however, came when asked to manage the Uruguayan Under-20s at the Pan American games in Venezuela. Football in South America is always fiercely contested, regardless of the age category, and so it was on this occasion. Tabárez's Uruguay cruised through the competition before beating Brazil (who else?) 1-0 in the final.

That success gave Tabárez credibility and opened doors. The following season he was named as manager at Danubio, before moving to Montevideo Wanderers, whom he led to a second-place finish. They were beaten by Peñarol to the league title but the new champions appreciated the work that Tabárez had done at their rivals so much that they promptly offered him the coach's job. It meant that he'd achieved as a coach what had always escaped him as a player: moving to one of Uruguay's traditional big clubs.

He'd stay there for just one season but it would prove to be a memorable one. While domestic honours had always been important for Peñarol, they took particular pride in their standing as one of the most successful clubs in continental competitions. Five years earlier, they'd won their fourth Copa Libertadores and it was this competition that they coveted most of all.

Yet Tabárez almost never got to lead them in that competition. His start at the club was rather uncertain and when Peñarol lined up against historical rivals Nacional at the start of April, there was talk among those running the club of sacking their coach.

Fortunately for him, Peñarol not only won (2-1) but showed great character in doing so, despite ending with eight players. The players themselves had no idea of how vital that match had been for their coach. 'The players found out a few days later and we couldn't believe it,' striker Diego Aguirre commented – but that made the grittiness of their display all the more commendable.

That the idea had even been entertained was risible. A year earlier, when club legend Fernando Morena retired from football, he was still owed four months' wages by the club to whom he'd dedicated so many years. The club agreed to a series of friendlies in Mexico to generate some funds but still couldn't honour their commitments to a legend. Peñarol's financial crisis was such that they were forced to adopt a very cynical approach. It had also forced them to put their new coach in charge of a squad brimming with fresh faces. Even Tabárez himself was just 40 years old. And, in keeping with their new mindset, he'd been chosen because his salary expectations were modest.

Tabárez also had the disadvantage of lacking experience at the highest level, particularly when it came to continental competitions – he'd never made it to the Libertadores as a player – but the draw for the first round was fairly benevolent, putting them in the same group as fellow Uruguayans Progreso and Peruvian teams Alianza Lima and San Agustín. Peñarol made easy work of qualification, but the next round (another group stage that served as the semi-finals) was less straightforward.

There they faced two Argentinian sides in Independiente and River Plate, with the latter the competition's holders. By that stage, however, Tabárez's work of integrating a group of young players with the more experienced core of the team was paying off. The ease with which Independiente were beaten at home (3-0) proved this but the match that truly ignited their belief was the return between the two in Argentina.

Independiente is a club that has experienced more success on the continent than at home, and they'd never lost a home fixture in the Libertadores. Yet that record was swept away by a tactical masterclass as Peñarol sat deep, absorbing Independiente's attacks before using the speed of their strikers to exploit the gaps in their opponents' defence. They went 4-0 ahead before two late goals gave the score a bit of respectability for the home team.

Even so, Peñarol were lucky in that the Argentinian rivals cancelled each other out, allowing the Uruguayans to top the group despite a defeat in their final match against River Plate. Yet no club has ever won anything without a piece of luck. Colombians América de Cali, their opponents, could attest to that, having lost the previous two finals despite being the stronger team. They were determined not to make it three final defeats.

At the time, Colombian football was fuelled by drug money, which allowed the top clubs to recruit talent from all over the continent. The team that made it to the final in 1987, along with some of the best Colombian talent of the era, featured two Argentines (goalkeeper Julio César Falcioni and striker Ricardo Gareca), two Paraguayans (winger Juan Manuel Battalia and midfielder Roberto Cabañas) as well as the former Peñarol midfielder Sergio Santín.

The first leg in Cali was a rude awakening for Tabárez's team as the home players' determination to win was demonstrated both off the pitch (to rile their opponents, some América players wore shirts of Peñarol's hated domestic rival Nacional before the match) and on it (Peñarol's most creative players were on the receiving end of heavy tackling that went unchecked by the referee). América de Cali won 2-0 without really impressing. It was an ominous sign.

Not that this deterred either Peñarol or their fans, who packed their stadium from the early hours of the day of the second leg in the hope that their singing would help their team overturn the result. Yet even that hope seemed to be extinguished in the 19th minute, when Cabañas put the visitors ahead.

It all seemed to be over. While Tabárez had given his team shape and motivation, they were simply being beaten by a more talented team. Fortunately for them, that team was human and probably felt that the hardest part of the job was done. América forwent attacking from that point on, opting instead to protect what they had.

Even when Aguirre equalised for Peñarol, América kept on playing with the same mindset. And it almost worked until Tabárez looked to his bench and put Jorge Villar on. It says a lot about Tabárez that he was willing to put an inexperienced 20-year-old on in the biggest match of his career. Villar wasn't some precocious talent whose skill demanded that he play; he'd go on to enjoy a lengthy career, but not a particularly notable one. Yet the combination of his youth and the coach's faith was exactly what Peñarol needed in the 42nd minute of the second half, when they were awarded a free kick midway in their opponents' half. Villar placed the ball, shooed away his team-mates and hit a powerful shot that sailed over the wall and into the top corner of the goal.

Peñarol had survived. At the time, the final wasn't decided on aggregate but on which team first managed to get to three points, with two points for a win and one for a draw. Therefore they had to play another match, in a neutral venue, in the knowledge that only a win would do. Yet in managing to make a comeback at home, Peñarol had also managed to break an invisible mental barrier. Before the final, their opponents, with their big names, seemed almost invincible. There were no such thoughts now.

The tie-breaker, played in Chile in front of a half-empty stadium, was a match of two halves. América Cali dominated the first half and had the clear-cut chances that should have won them the match. Their profligacy then cost them as Peñarol reversed the tide in the second half and pushed on to get the goal they needed. Two minutes before the end of extra time, Peñarol should have scored when a loose ball reached midfielder Ricardo Viera, whose free header went just wide of goal, to the horror of his team-mates, who in that moment must have felt that the title had slipped away.

Similar thoughts were had by the América fans, who surely felt that, having survived that moment, the title would be theirs. But just as the most positive among those fans were beginning to celebrate, Diego Aguire took the ball from a team-mate's feet, entered the América penalty box and unleashed an unstoppable shot into the bottom corner.

It was, in the words of most newspapers, a miracle. It was also Tabárez's miracle. Not only had he retained his job when the vultures were circling but he'd managed to forge a young team with an average age of just 22 into continental champions. It wasn't the most creative of teams but he adopted the tactics that fit the needs of the team and, above all, worked on the mental side to ensure that his players compensated for their failings with the traditional Uruguayan grit.

Not that he was willing to accept the praise that came his way, opting instead to focus on building a bigger narrative. 'The players of Peñarol are instilled with an almost historical motivation which pushes them to transcend themselves,' he said in the aftermath. 'This is how our club forged its glory.

This is how we keep winning. It is the energy of a small country used to adversity in all areas and which is proud to compete with the greats in football.'

Midfielder Carles Muñoz echoed similar thoughts:

> How incredible that we Uruguayans are, by God, how incredible. I want to scream and I can't. I want to jump and I can't. I want to cry and the tears don't come out because that's how we Uruguayans are, because that's how we are, because that's how we Charruas are. We fight.
>
> As in 1962, as in 1966, as in 1982, [references to previous Libertadores triumphs] we Uruguayans won because we are like that, because we put in until the last moment, because we never give up, because we fight against adversity, because the more difficult it is, the more we like it.

For all of Tabárez's pride, their victory wasn't universally popular. The Argentinian newspaper *Clarin* wasn't impressed by the functional tactics adopted by Peñarol (and also América de Cali), and after the final commented, 'We [South Americans] always run more and more quickly but where we play less and less, and where there is always an increasing of a lack of football.'

Still, the victory transformed Tabárez in the eyes of many. No longer was he the failed player trying to make his mark on the game but a coaching genius who understood to perfection the Uruguayan soul so much that it was like another member of the team. He was, in other words, the ideal candidate to take over the role nationally. His first task was to lead Uruguay at the 1989 Copa América held in Brazil. As with his time at Peñarol, the start was difficult and Uruguay risked elimination in the first round. It was only when a result elsewhere went their way that they managed to qualify for the next round.

Then, as if freed from the pressure that had been haunting them, they seemed to click. Paraguay were dispatched 3-0. They then beat Argentina 2-0 in the semi-final. That opened a path to the final against Brazil that ended in defeat. Yet the standard had been set.

* * *

Soon after, Uruguay launched into a series of World Cup qualifying fixtures, followed by a tour of friendlies that was demanding on the players but allowed the coach to really shape how they played.

The star was still Enzo Francescoli and, even though he wasn't always released by his club, Olympique Marseille, he could see what the new manager wanted to do:

> Fundamentally, he has changed the team's style. That has always been maestro Tabárez's great concern. Since the beginning of this cycle, he has wanted Uruguay to show that it is not all that was said about them in the World Cup in Mexico. It was the first big challenge for the group and they have assumed it with absolute responsibility.
>
> Uruguay has played in Europe and is showing, with its game, that we play hard but we are not dishonest, bullies, as was said in the '86 World Cup.

Indeed, the Uruguayan squad that Tabárez had at his disposal at the 1990 World Cup was filled with promise. Many back in Uruguay believed it was as good, if not better, than the squad that had gone to Mexico four years earlier. Importantly, and unlike his predecessor, Omar Borrás, Tabárez was willing to trust his players; he wanted them to take risks and play offensively.

With such a talented team, it seemed like everything was in place for a great campaign. However, expectations were once again dashed, just like four years earlier.

\* \* \*

Spain, the first opponent, were completely dominated by the Uruguayans, who couldn't convert any of their chances, including a missed penalty. A draw against a strong European team might not have seemed like a bad result, yet somehow it seemed to drain the players of confidence, and the team's fortunes took a turn for the worse when they lost 3-1 to Belgium. At that point, qualification hung on a victory against South Korea, which would secure a spot among the best third-placed teams.

It was a tense affair, with little football played, but Uruguay eventually prevailed with a late goal from a young Daniel Fonseca. It was the first victory for the national team in a World Cup in 20 years, and it would be another 20 before they repeated the feat.

Despite the victory, the players still appeared to lack confidence. This was evident in the way they approached the round-of-16 match against Italy. It's never easy to play against the hosts in a major tournament but, with the talent available to them, Uruguay should have shown a little bit more adventure than the doggedly defensive tactics they ended up using. It worked for an hour, before Schillaci finally managed to find a way through their defence. Aldo Serena then scored a second in the closing minutes to mark the end of Uruguay's tournament. And with that came the start of criticism from the soccer community back home.

* * *

Although there was no dishonour in elimination against the hosts and one of the favourites for the competition, those charged with running Uruguayan football weren't best pleased and Tabárez was sacked on their return home. His biggest failing, it seemed, was his moralising about the need for his team to play fairly, which had, supposedly, caused his players to lose their traditional grit.

Foreign-based players also came under scrutiny, being accused of not putting in enough effort, while the squad had disagreements with the federation and some journalists. To make matters worse, the presence of football agent Paco Casal at the team's base in Italy added another layer of tension and provided further proof that the players had other matters on their minds. Some even went as far as implying that he put pressure on Tabárez over who to pick, forcing the coach to use those players he was looking to sell to European clubs. Such was the distrust that a poll found that the majority in Uruguay felt Casal hadn't wanted Uruguay to beat Italy – then home of the richest league and a source of transfer riches – and this had somehow filtered down to the players.

This fed into demands for the exclusion of foreign-based players. For years, the feeling of distrust of those playing abroad would linger, an easy excuse every time something went wrong. And they often did. With hindsight, it's easy to determine just how wrong the dismissals and criticism were. Once Tabárez left, things got even worse for Uruguay. Criticism of their best players – the ones playing in Europe – destabilised the squad and they failed to qualify for the

1994, 1998 and 2006 World Cup finals. Víctor Púa did manage to lead them to the 2002 edition, but once there they failed to progress from the opening group stages.

The irony is that all of that might have been avoided had the penalty against Spain gone in. And what an irony it is. For here's what happened: a José Herrera header was handled on the line by striker Francisco Villarroya. Rubén Sosa stepped up and sent the ball over the bar. In other words, almost exactly the same sequence of events that would occur 20 years later against Ghana, albeit the other way round.

Who knows the chain reaction that would have unfolded had Sosa's kick gone in. For sure, Uruguay would have finished in the top two, avoiding the hosts in the next round. Perhaps their confidence wouldn't have suffered such a big hit, and they'd have overcome either Yugoslavia or England in the next round. From then on, anything could have happened. Instead, Uruguayan football endured almost a decade of civil war.

\* \* \*

As for Tabárez, the experience didn't seem to have any lasting negative impact on his career. A two-year spell at Boca Juniors paved the way for a European experience, landing in Italy at lowly Cagliari. There he achieved another minor miracle, guiding them to ninth place in Serie A. This earned him a move to AC Milan, arguably the biggest opportunity of his career.

It was the right move but at the wrong time. His attacking brand of football would have fitted in well with the club's culture, and indeed it was one of the reasons why owner Silvio Berlusconi hired him. The problem was that he was coming in to replace Fabio Capello, who had won four leagues titles in five years, along with a Champions League. Big shoes to fill. Too big, even for someone of Tabárez's ability. His time in Milan started with a defeat against Fiorentina in the Italian Super Cup and never really recovered, ending by December after a defeat to lowly Piacenza.

After a year's break, he moved to Real Oviedo, where he only avoided relegation by narrowly beating Las Palmas in the play-offs. A return to his beloved Cagliari followed but that, too, was a brief experience: four matches, one point and another dismissal. Hoping to find the right club, Tabárez moved to Argentina, taking over Vélez Sarsfield, but left after a year with the club struggling towards the bottom of the league table. Boca Juniors welcomed him back soon after but, yet again, the reunion wasn't a happy one, with Tabárez unable to repeat the success that he'd achieved there.

Once his time at Boca ended, the offers stopped coming. The momentum that he'd built early on in his career had completely come to a halt. Despite being just 55 years old, Tabárez's ideas no longer seemed relevant for the world of football. It looked as if retirement for the former teacher had come early.

That lasted for four years. Then came November of 2005.

\* \* \*

Uruguay had finished fifth in the CONMEBOL qualifying group for the World Cup finals, edged out not only by their historical rivals of Brazil and Argentina but also by Ecuador and Paraguay. Still, there was confidence that they'd make it through a play-off against the winners of the Oceania group, Australia, just as they'd done four years earlier. Yet the tie proved to be anything but the formality some thought it might be. At the end of 210 minutes the aggregate score was tied at 1-1. On penalties, the Australians proved to be more clinical. Uruguay, once more, were out of the World Cup.

Inevitably the defeat to Australia brought about a period of deep introspection. Something different needed to be done or the Uruguay national team was doomed to international oblivion. Tabárez was the man to deliver that. Not only because he was the last man to deliver a victory at the World Cup finals for Uruguay but also because his exile had allowed him the time to reflect on what was needed. El Maestro had a masterplan for Uruguayan football.

This was based on four ideas. The first focused on young players but went beyond the mere identification of talent. Tabárez put in place what was referred to as *'proceso de inferiores'* (the youth process), where from an early age players were coached to not only learn the preferred style of play but also the values that the national team represented. The latter was crucial for Tabárez, for whom the criticism back in 1990 that his players weren't focused on the national team but on earning transfers had bitten deeply.

Therefore the second idea that he set about fostering was a culture among players in any age category that there was nothing as important as putting on a Uruguay shirt. Along with that idea, he drilled into his players the notion that sacrifice and dedication were musts to succeed, that anyone playing for Uruguay was to serve as a role model and representative of their society. This, his third key insight, served many purposes, not least ensuring that the Uruguayan people identified with the players who were wearing their colours. Again, a lesson from 1990 had been absorbed by the master, who then used it to build what he saw as the fourth and final belief: a team can best be shaped if the players all share a similar set of beliefs.

His was an all-encompassing vision and one that needed time to grow roots. Once it did, Uruguay started to feel the benefits. Going into 2010, they weren't particularly fancied and yet they almost made it all the way. At each step the players showed the values that Tabárez had been drumming into them for four years, none more so than in the key moment against Ghana. What the rest of the world took as proof of more Luis Suárez villainy, for Uruguay was merely the exemplification of a spirit of sacrifice for the greater good, just as Tabárez preached.

That was to be the high point of Uruguay under Tabárez at the World Cup as far as results were concerned. Yet he hadn't gone into the job looking for one great tournament but to build a system that kept developing great players and even greater teams. His and Uruguay's presence in subsequent World Cups was the true culmination of that vision.

To say that Tabárez had transformed Uruguay into a footballing nation that neutrals loved would be an exaggeration. The spirit of sacrifice and hard work he preached was often interpreted as dour and vicious by outsiders. Yet his teams also generated respect both for their cohesiveness and the talent of their individuals.

This was his biggest success, as he said:

> We used to be known for our violent play – whether it was a legitimate accusation or not – and not being known for our fair play. We have responded to that by creating great footballers. We have worked hard at youth level and we only have a little over three million inhabitants. When you produce one great player in Uruguay, that's equal to 20 in Brazil and ten in Argentina. Therefore,

we have had to approach the game differently compared to everyone else.

Rubén Sosa, who starred in Italy, is one of many who speak fondly of his former coach, yet he acknowledges that the man who led the team in South Africa in 2010 had learned a lot from the Italian experience:

The Tabárez of today learned, and that is why the word 'teacher' fits him so well. I believe that he learns day by day and that he does not rest. Although I am not going to tell you that this is the best version of him, he is constantly improving.

That of 1990 was one of the great Uruguayan teams and deserved more. We went 40 days before on a tour of Europe, where we played friendlies with Germany, England and we arrived at the World Cup already exhausted mentally.

In Italy we were based in Veronella, a small town that had a hotel and many vineyards. We hardly ever saw a car go by. We wanted to see people! So, we got physically and mentally very tired, and we felt like the World Cup lasted two months.

He [Tabárez] realised that this was not the method and as a great teacher he learned and for South Africa 2010 he changed the course. That is why in 2010 El Maestro went to South Africa a week before. And Uruguay came out fourth.

What Tabárez did with our team is incredible.

\* \* \*

When Uruguay returned home from the 2010 World Cup, they received a heroes' welcome. Amid the celebrations, Tabárez gave one of the most powerful speeches ever. 'Success is not only results,' he said, 'but the difficulties that we go through to obtain them; the struggle and the spirit to face challenges, and also the courage to overcome them. The journey is the reward.'

He didn't make reference to the Italia 90 World Cup, but he didn't need to. His career, and the manner in which he approached his second spell in charge of the Uruguay national team, was a lived example of his words.

For the wider world, Uruguay's Italia 90 was an abject failure. Yet not for Tabárez, who saw it as just another passage in his journey, one that helped shape him into the man who would lead Uruguay to glory once more and shape himself into a legend.

# How Milla's Second Act
# Shaped a Continent

ON SUNDAY, 4 January 2020, Jeunesse Sportive Saint-Pierroise pulled off the upset of that year's Coupe de France. The amateurs overcame the four divisions separating them from Ligue 2's Niort, beating them 2-1 to make it to the last 32 of the French Cup. It was a fantastic achievement, one that was celebrated well beyond French borders as underdog stories always tend to be.

But this wasn't just any underdog. To get to their match against Niort, JS Saint-Pierroise had to travel 6,000 miles from their home in Réunion, an overseas French territory in the Indian Ocean, on a journey that took 11 hours. They'd voyaged from the other side of the world, almost literally, having to endure a drop in temperature of some 25 degrees. By the time they arrived back home, not only had the draw for the next round been made but the Niort coach had been sacked and a replacement appointed.

To further underline the magnitude of the achievement: only once before in the competition's 100-year history had a team from an overseas territory managed to make it through from this stage.

Two weeks later they almost made history once more. The players had dreamed of a tie against a Ligue 1 club but instead were drawn against fourth-tier SAS Épinal. Disappointment on the one hand, hope on the other; although not as glamorous, these opponents were perhaps more beatable. And it almost happened, keeping the score at 0-0 before conceding what proved to be the winner in extra time.

Defeat in such a manner tends to be heart-breaking. But once the pain started to fade away, the overwhelming sentiment was of pride at the odds they'd managed to overcome. It was an incredibly valiant effort from the minnows.

\* \* \*

Ironically, while JS Saint-Pierroise are indeed small fry in the greater realm of French football, they're giants back home. Founded in 1950, the same year as the formation of the Championnat de La Réunion de Football – the Réunion Premier League – they've been the island's most successful team. They've won the league over 20 times, more than any other club on the island, and the domestic cup on more than ten occasions.

They can even boast of the three instances where they could call themselves champions of all clubs from French foreign territories thanks to their wins in the Coupe des Clubs Champions d'Outremer (Cup of Champion Clubs from Overseas), a competition that brought together the league winners from French Guiana, Guadeloupe, Martinique, Mayotte and, naturally, Réunion. The tournament ran for 15 years from 1989 before evolving into a league format that clubs from Réunion – who had dominated the competition, with nine overall successes – didn't join.

Nor has that been their only international experience. Clubs from Réunion can play in the continental competitions organised by the African Football Confederation, something that JS Saint-Pierroise have managed several times, although rarely going beyond one round. If anything explains the footballing equivalent of the twilight zone that's the game in Réunion, it's precisely that ability to play in European and African competitions in the same season.

For all of their achievements, JS Saint-Pierroise have one claim to fame that beats all others. It's one that put the spotlight on football in Réunion far earlier than their Coupe de France run. Precisely three decades earlier. For that's where Roger Milla was seeing out his career when he received the call that would change the course of the 1990 World Cup and the identity of African football.

\* \* \*

Milla was born on 1952 in Yaoundé, the capital of what at the time was French Cameroon. In 1961 his family moved to Douala, the largest city and economic capital of the country that a year earlier had achieved its independence and become a sovereign nation.

As the son of a railway worker, Milla was one of the lucky ones. His family was part of the middle class and could provide him with a good education. Yet that also meant they had certain expectations of him. So when his parents noticed that he was spending too much time playing football after school and coming home late, they weren't too pleased; the child was supposed to come home on time, help with the housework and study.

Still, nothing could keep the young Milla away from the game. Facilities in 1960s Cameroon were lacking and those who wanted to play football had to make do with whatever they could. This often meant playing barefoot on a dusty field, with improvised goals and a patched-up ball. Coaching was non-existent.

That's how Milla grew up. Unsurprisingly then, even though he often went against his family's wishes by playing, he never entertained the thought of becoming a professional; it was too unlikely for a boy like him. Football was simply a matter of spending time with friends and having fun with a ball.

Yet all those games in rough conditions helped refine the raw talent that was there from the start. When he was 13, he received the opportunity to replace the chaotic games on dust fields with something played on a proper pitch when he joined Eclair de Douala. It would be a move that shaped his future, and that of his nation. Although this wasn't a major club, it provided him with his first taste of competitive football with their youth teams.

Goals, many of them, followed. Within two years Milla was simply too good to play against his peers. So at the age of 15, he made his debut with Eclair de Douala's senior team. Playing in the second tier and against men twice his age was the ultimate test but, yet again, the transition came easily to him. Goals started flowing from the start; once again he was simply too good for those around him.

At the time, Milla was still in school and dabbling in other sports. This included athletics, in which he was talented enough to win the national junior high jump championships. It was a result that underlined his athletic prowess and convinced the young Milla that he could make a career out of sports. Just as importantly, by that point even his parents had to agree that there was something special about their son.

It was with their blessing, then, that in 1970 the 18-year-old Milla signed a contract with top-tier club

Léopard Duala. Within a year he was celebrating his first national title and by the time he left in 1974 he'd won the Cameroonian championship three times, while scoring a breathtaking 89 goals in 116 matches.

In search of another challenge, Milla moved to Tonnerre in his native Yaoundé, where he won the African Cup Winners' Cup in 1975. He was the standout player of that team and of the continental game, something that was reflected in him being named African Player of the Year the following season. With Tonnerre he scored 69 goals in 87 matches, another impressive haul, particularly as he wasn't playing in title-winning teams – he failed to add to his domestic honours during the time spent with them.

For all the success he enjoyed with Tonnerre, Milla's motivation for making the move there wasn't purely athletic. The club had closer links with French football, meaning that it could provide him with a pathway to Europe. Those links, allied to his impressive statistics, meant that in 1977 Valenciennes decided to take a chance on Milla. At long last, here was the opportunity to prove himself in a competitive European league.

\* \* \*

Milla was by then 25 but, suddenly, he found himself in a completely alien environment. Valenciennes weren't a major club and could only offer him small accommodation that lacked everything but the basics. And yet that wasn't the hard part. Milla had to get used to a new culture, where everything from food to weather was new to him. So was the level he was now playing at and the demands that the coaches put on him.

Even so, Milla did as he always did when faced with a new challenge: he thrived. In his first full season in

French football he scored seven times in 29 appearances, which proved to be crucial in keeping Valenciennes in the top flight. His debut season went well enough to capture the attention of Monaco, French champions just two years earlier. It was a move that ended with his first big European trophy: the Coupe de France, won at the end of his first season at Monaco.

Yet it would be his first and only season at a club with big aspirations. Milla's record was very similar to the one at Valenciennes – five goals in 25 matches – yet that didn't meet the heightened expectations of his new team. On top of that, he'd been plagued by injuries that often kept him on the sidelines and that discouraged the Monaco management. Rumours that he was a bit too fond of partying also began doing the rounds. Eager to cut their losses with someone they considered a dud, Monaco quickly accepted an offer from Bastia, so Milla was on the move once more.

Contrary to Monaco, Bastia were often more preoccupied with the lower end of the league than the top. They'd barely avoided relegation the season before and were looking at Milla to help them fare a bit better.

It proved to be an inspired move. By the time he moved to Corsica, Milla was at the peak of his powers. Finally free of the injuries that had dogged his time at Monaco, he quickly imposed himself in his new home, reading the game to perfection, athletic, capable with both feet, with good speed and good technique.

He elevated the team to unexpected heights, including an unhoped-for domestic trophy. Once more it was the Coupe de France that he could hold aloft. Whereas the previous season he'd been a bit-part player in a final in which he came on as a substitute, this time he was the main attraction. And the match-winner: his goal – Bastia's second

– proved to be the crucial one as the plucky underdogs beat the royalty of French football, Saint-Étienne, 2-1. That triumph opened up a route to European football, although it proved to be a brief experience – Bastia were eliminated in the second round by the holders Dynamo Tbilisi – but at least there was the consolation of three goals in four matches for Milla.

The more he matured, the better Milla seemed to become. After Bastia he joined Saint-Étienne, who had just suffered the humiliation of relegation after being caught up in a massive bribery scandal. Financially crippled, the club was forced to sell its best players to survive and rebuild as best they could.

Milla scored 11 goals in his first season with them, a decent return but not good enough to help push them to promotion. It was better a year later, when he scored 20 times and Saint-Étienne won the league, along with a place in the top flight. Not that Milla got to enjoy that. For all his goals, Saint-Étienne decided they needed better players and promptly sent him back to the second tier with Montpellier.

By this point Milla was 34 years old, yet despite his age he was still the equal of younger players. Apart from that single season in Monaco, he'd never struggled for fitness, and whatever speed he lost with age he more than made up for with his natural guile, now sharpened by experience.

That was precisely what Montpellier were looking for when they convinced the veteran striker to join them. Determined to gain promotion after several seasons in the second tier, they had a good core of talented young players who needed a bit of guidance. Milla helped deliver that. Despite a poor start – they lost their first two matches of the season – they quickly took command of Group B of the division (at the time the league was split into two groups) and never let go. Their dominance was confirmed in the title play-off, when they twice beat Niort, with an aggregate score of 4-1.

For Milla it was the second championship win in a row. He also finished the league as Montpellier's leading scorer, with 19 goals, just one more than his young colleague Laurent Blanc, the future World Cup winner, who at the time played as an attacking midfielder.

Satisfying though that triumph was, it paled against what Montpellier managed to achieve a year later. While most promoted clubs' main aim is to avoid an immediate return, Montpellier faced the 1987/88 season on the front foot. Unlike Saint-Étienne two years earlier, they put their trust in the veteran Milla, while surrounding him with willing runners.

The results were scintillating. Montpellier scored 68 goals – by far the most of any club that season and 15 more than champions Monaco – as they finished in third place. Milla was once more their top scorer, with 12, which included a hat-trick against fourth-placed (and previous employers) Saint-Étienne in a magnificent attacking display. That league finish opened up a route back to Europe for Milla, a fantastic result for a 36-year-old who some had dared write off. Admittedly, their European adventure didn't last long – they were eliminated by Benfica in the first round – and their second season back in the French top tier wasn't nearly as successful, even if a mid-table finish was hardly a bad result.

It was also not a bad place for Milla to end his career. He could have stayed on in France, perhaps going down the leagues once more in search of a fitting opportunity. Yet he didn't, arguing instead that he'd spent enough time in the game. Even though it was still as fun as it had been all those years earlier when he'd played with his friends, he needed to slow down.

A friendly match was held in Cameroon to commemorate his retirement. More than 150,000 people turned up for that, proof of how iconic and popular Milla was to his people. Some valiantly tried to get him to change his mind, but he wasn't to be convinced. His time as a player was over and, as with the heroes in old movies, all that was left was for him to ride off into the sunset. Or, in Milla's case, to move to the idyllic paradise of Réunion to play out his final days.

Not that the move had been planned out. Milla had been invited to visit the island by a friend and enjoyed their laid-back way of life, so he decided to spend some more time there. Although he'd retired from the professional game, football remained a big part of his life. Inevitably, the news that a former international had moved to the island captured the imagination, with many looking to involve him in the local scene. Which is how he came to play for Jeunesse Sportive Saint-Pierroise.

Overall, however, pretty laid-back as twilights to successful careers go, it was one that still delivered silverware in the form of a domestic cup. It was the perfect combination of a relaxed lifestyle and the possibility to have some fun playing football. For Milla, it was a return to the idyllic days of his childhood.

His only concern, as he thought about things at his beachside home, was the manner in which the Indomitable Lions – as Cameroon have traditionally been known – were preparing for the upcoming World Cup.

\* \* \*

The man leading Milla's former team was Valery Nepomnyashchy, who had been appointed as Cameroon national coach in 1988. Initially he'd been earmarked for a minor role – training coaches or heading one of Cameroon's youth teams – but the sudden departure of Claude Le Roy meant that there was a vacancy to fill and he was in the right place at the right time to do just that.

Nepomnyashchy had been an average player who had never risen above the Soviet third tier before retiring at just 25. He'd then embarked on a coaching career but, even then, he was hardly a household name back home, with his main coaching experience coming at Kolhozchi Ashkhabad in the third tier of Turkmen football. Before his posting to Cameroon, he'd been leading coaching courses in numerous developing football nations as part of the Soviet attempt to exercise soft power. It was that programme that led him to Cameroon; in the right spot to land a mighty promotion when Le Roy surprisingly opted to move to Senegal. So unexpected was his elevation that it proved a struggle to find suitable translators to help him carry out his job. In the end, an office worker at the Cameroon embassy in Moscow had to be called in to support the new national team coach.

Still, Nepomnyashchy passed the first major test when he guided Cameroon to the World Cup finals. This was no easy feat, with the African continent only having two slots back in 1990. But the next test didn't go as well. Indeed, that he was still in charge by the time Cameroon played at the finals was perhaps even more surprising than him getting the job in the first place! Just two months before the tournament kicked off in Italy, Cameroon had gone to Algeria to play in the Africa Cup of Nations. As holders and one of the teams who had made it to the World Cup finals, they were among the favourites for the tournament. Instead, they failed miserably. Defeats in their opening two matches meant an early elimination. Even more worrying was their failure to score in those two matches. A 2-0 victory over Kenya in the final fixture was too little, too late.

Whatever hopes there had been, that Africa Cup of Nations dashed them. True, there was a level of over-confidence among the players, and no one wanted to get injured so close to the World Cup. Yet these were seen as excuses that papered over the reality that there was something missing from the squad. That was the public opinion and that was how the Cameroon prime minister, Paul Biya, saw it.

Milla had been at the Africa Cup of Nations, albeit only as a fan and a part-time consultant to the association. Earlier he'd made a trip to Cameroon to play in a former team-mate's testimonial. Despite his age, many felt that he'd retired too early and let him know.

Again, Biya shared those views. So a few days after the end of the disastrous tournament in Africa, he called key people within the Cameroon FA for a meeting at his office, during which it was agreed that Milla had to be in the squad for the World Cup. Once that was decided, Biya himself picked up his telephone and called Milla, urging him to reconsider his decision to retire. The plea worked; Milla was in.

\* \* \*

Milla's career with the national team had been filled with glory. He'd been there when they last played in the World Cup in 1982, when they'd suffered elimination without losing a match. Twice he'd led them to the title of African champions. He was, to all intents and purposes, a national team legend.

Even though Milla's inclusion was a boost, the doubts about Cameroon's prospects remained. That much was evident in the Cameroonian federation's choice of pre-World Cup base, what the players described as soldiers' barracks in Sarajevo. Conditions were sparse and equipment basic. Apparently green-lit by Nepomnyashchy, who was more focused on ensuring that his men were well prepared physically for the coming challenge, the players found themselves doing drills typically reserved for soldiers.

Milla had his own, different doubts. Asked whether he felt that he had the legs to play in such a competition, he replied candidly, 'Not really, to be honest, but football's not just a physical game. I'd always been an intelligent player, so I knew if I got into shape, I had a chance. My first aim was to get fit, and then it would be up to the coach to decide whether I was good enough.'

He wasn't the only one with doubts. Nepomnyashchy didn't feel that Milla was up to it. Not only had the striker been imposed on him but there was constant pressure to pick him. 'When I wasn't playing, they wanted him to put me through some really hard training sessions to get me into shape,' Milla confirmed. 'But fortunately I was one of our best players in the pre-tournament friendlies, so I won him over on my own.'

If Nepomnyashchy had been forced by higher-ups into picking Milla, he found their backing when he faced criticism from within the team. Bordeaux's Joseph-Antoine Bell was arguably the best African goalkeeper of his generation and had just been chosen as the second-best player in the French league. He was also highly vocal in his opinions, regardless of who they may offend. Asked about their prospects on the eve of the World Cup, he replied that Cameroon had 'no chance of coping with Argentina, or any other team'.

Understandably, this wasn't well received. Bell, who had been widely expected to be the regular goalkeeper, was unceremoniously dropped from the starting XI. Fortunately for them, Cameroon had a fine deputy in Thomas N'Kono. Indeed, when the International Federation of Football History & Statistics came to choose the best African goalkeeper of the 20th century, N'Kono came in second, Bell first.

In a 2020 interview, N'Kono shared his belief that he was ahead of his time. He's right, and his performance against Argentina in·the opening match of the World Cup proved that. A match that's more remembered for the tackles and physicality, as well as Cameroon's surprising victory, would probably have had a different outcome without N'Kono in goal. Not because he made any breathtaking saves – he didn't – but simply because of how he played.

With Cameroon concentrating on making it impossible for Argentina to play through the centre and pushing them to the flanks, the only option left for the South Americans was to fling in crosses, where, inevitably, they found N'Kono willing to come out to catch the ball. His speed and agility gave him the courage needed to go against the convention at the time of goalkeepers staying on their line as much as possible. N'Kono wasn't like that. He could read the game and was willing to use that to his advantage, which sometimes meant rushing off his line to snuff out danger before it had the opportunity to develop. One of the reasons why Argentina didn't have clearer shots at goal throughout was N'Kono's ability to prevent opportunities. It was a different way of goalkeeping, one that inspired a young boy called Gianluigi Buffon to pick up the gloves.

Milla played the final ten minutes of that match as Cameroon, 1-0 ahead, hung on with ten men, which became nine in the final minute, yet his involvement was minimal. That wouldn't be the case in Cameroon's second match.

The opening exchanges had been rather lacklustre, with Romania cautious not to open themselves up, knowing that, having won their opener, a draw could be enough to go through. Cameroon also weren't willing to go on the offensive, so it resulted in a rather staid affair.

Nepomnyashchy, however, felt that his team could get more than a draw, so early in the second half he put Milla on. The move paid off almost immediately. Milla had been on the field for just a few minutes when a ball was flung into the box in desperation more than anything else. The ball seemingly hung in the air, which made it hard for the Romanian defender beneath it to clear. Milla saw his opportunity. As the ball fell, he barged in to gain control and fired past the goalkeeper.

It was a magnificent display of opportunistic attacking play. Minutes later, Milla showed another side to his game. He'd managed to win the ball just outside the penalty area and lobbed it towards a team-mate on the right-hand side of the box. A Cameroon striker rose with a Romanian defender but neither could get to it. Milla, however, had continued running and latched on to the loose ball before shooting with such accuracy and ferocity that the Romanian keeper couldn't do anything. A beautiful mix of skill and finishing.

While the goals were wildly different, the celebration wasn't. In both instances, Milla went to dance in front of the corner flag in what was to become an iconic image from that World Cup. With good reason. Celebrations at the time were often muted, consisting of nothing more than raised fists, enthusiastic cheers and maybe a jump to signal exuberance. Not Milla, however, who celebrated the goal for what it was, a moment of pure joy and ecstasy. In doing so he became a trailblazer of the modern goal celebration. He single-handedly injected a sense of confidence and flair on to the football pitch, forever changing the way goals were celebrated. From that point, the sheer ecstasy brought forth by scoring would be expressed with even greater fervour and emotion.

The goals had taken everyone by surprise – the television graphics listed the scorer as 'Miller' – except those back in Cameroon who had exhibited such faith in Milla when they called him out of retirement. Now they could prepare for the knockout phase, since their two wins guaranteed qualification regardless of what happened in the final group matches. In fact, they actually finished top of their group despite a 4-0 thumping at the hands of the Soviet Union. Milla came on midway through the first half with Cameroon already two goals down but he could do little to influence proceedings.

The reward for finishing top of Group E was a tie against Colombia. The South Americans had been some people's dark horses for the tournament but had barely scraped through as one of the best third-placed teams. Still, they were hard to beat, favouring a patient build-up that kept opponents at bay.

Unsurprisingly, after 90 minutes it was 0-0, with very few moments to excite the fans. The same went for the opening half of extra time, at which point thoughts automatically started shifting towards the possibility of penalties.

Milla had other ideas. Soon after the restart, he took possession of the ball outside the penalty area, gracefully adjusting his body position. His swift movement caught a defender off guard as he embarked on a mesmerising sprint towards the box. Skilfully evading a challenge, he looked up briefly before curling the ball into the top corner of the goal.

More was to come. Rene Higuita, the Colombian goalkeeper known for his flamboyance, ran out of his penalty area to sweep up a directionless pass played forward by the Cameroon defence. Unfortunately, his own attempt to pass the ball to his team-mate Luis Carlos Perea went awry. Under pressure from the relentless Milla, Higuita failed to control the return pass. Seizing the opportunity, the appreciative veteran effortlessly placed the ball into an unguarded net. It was the killer blow in a 2-1 victory. More significantly, it was the goal that for the first time ever put an African team in the quarter-finals of the World Cup.

There was an element of serendipity in Milla's crucial goal. 'I was lucky because I played with Carlos Valderrama, the Colombia captain, at Montpellier,' he said. 'We had a great team, including Júlio César, the Brazil defender, and a young Laurent Blanc, who had come through the ranks. Through Valderrama I'd seen videos of Higuita dribbling the ball out of his area. I knew if I was quick enough I might be able to take advantage of a mistake. It worked.'

Next up were England and what would turn out to be one of the most iconic matches of the competition, one where the goals flowed almost as much as the heavy tackling. Almost.

Again, Milla came on as a substitute at half-time with England leading by a goal. Again his introduction was pivotal. A swing of the hips allowed him to break free on the right of the England box. He'd almost certainly have scored had Paul Gascoigne not scythed him down. Emmanuel Kundé made amends from the resulting penalty to equalise.

Just four minutes later, Milla was at it again. Gaining control a couple of metres outside the England penalty area, he used all his experience to draw defenders towards him before slotting a perfect through ball to fellow substitute Eugène Ekéké, who fired in. Suddenly, Cameroon were ahead and, possibly, on their way to the World Cup semi-final. As the England team seemed to tire, the Cameroonians kept on running, enjoying the fruits of Nepomnyashchy's harsh training.

Their dream lasted for 18 minutes, when Lineker was felled in the penalty area. He scored the resulting penalty and did so again in extra time to secure a 3-2 victory.

The defeat stung because it felt like such a missed opportunity, as Milla explained:

> Looking back now, you have to say that. We went 1-0 down, but Paul Gascoigne committed a foul in the penalty area and Emmanuel Kundé equalised from the spot – and then Eugène Ekéké put us 2-1 up. We kept going forward because we wanted to entertain people. For us, first and foremost, football was about entertainment, so we wanted to win spectacularly. But it wasn't to be.

However, it didn't sour the mood for long. 'We were happy. England knocked us out, but we were happy because we'd had such a great tournament and gone so far,' Milla continued. '1990 was an unforgettable experience.'

Equally unforgettable was the return home, where thousands flocked on to the streets to welcome their heroes – so many that they needed a military escort to make it through. Such was the welcome that it made people wonder what would have happened had Cameroon won. 'It would have been crazy. An indescribable joy if we had won the quarter-final. I don't even dare to imagine what it would have been like if we had gone further in the competition,' was Milla's view. 'I've the feeling we could have got to the final if we had beaten England. And in the final anything can happen.'

After the World Cup, he returned home to play for Tonnerre, where he stayed a further four seasons, scoring 89 goals in just over 100 appearances. Such was his form that Cameroon picked him once more for the 1994 World Cup. Their experience there was decidedly less happy – they failed to win or make it out of the group stages – but there was further satisfaction for Milla, who not only made it on to the pitch at 41 years of age but even scored again.

He carried on playing, staying for a season with Pelita Jaya and then another with Putra Samarinda, both in the Indonesian league. He finally retired – for real this time – in 1996 at 44 years of age.

The 1990 World Cup helped reignite Milla's career, and it won him his second African Footballer of the Year award. It also made him a global icon, which, in turn, helped make him a very rich man. For Milla proved to be a prodigious talent even as an entrepreneur, investing his earnings to build a real estate portfolio, opening several restaurants in Yaoundé and also having a perfume in his name.

Yet Milla's impact extended far beyond his own personal achievements. Before 1990, African football was viewed in a condescending, quasi-racist manner; everyone agreed that there was talent but that no African team was tactically capable of excelling at the highest levels. Milla and his team-mates changed that. They were tactically astute, knowing when to defend but also possessing the flair to carve up defences. There was more to them than raw strength. After all, Milla's goals were down to his skill and speed, not power. All of this opened people's eyes. It made them question their preconceptions.

It would take years for African players to become as prevalent in European football as those from South America. Other successes were needed along the way to eradicate the misconceptions – Nigeria's scintillating football at the 1994 World Cup, their dream team winning gold at the 1996 Olympic Games, George Weah's rise to being the best player on the planet – but it was Cameroon in 1990 that really shook up perceptions. It was their success that made it impossible for anyone to argue against increasing the number of qualifiers to the World Cup finals from Africa, which increased from two to three soon afterwards. As Milla said later, 'We've made an impression. Our performance allowed Africans to be taken seriously.'

And none of that would have been possible if Roger Milla hadn't decided to leave his idyllic villa in Réunion to answer the call of his nation.

# A Costly Surprise

'YOU HADN'T a clue what we would do!'

It was a friendly conversation among two former coaches reminiscing about those moments when their careers crossed paths. But for one, Andy Roxburgh, hearing the other, Bora Milutinović, say those words still brought back memories of arguably the biggest disappointment of his career.

That comment took Roxburgh back to 1990, when he was in charge of Scotland as they went into the World Cup. His group lacked the world-famous names that had blessed previous Scotland teams but it was still a wonderfully talented squad. The possibility of achieving what every Scottish team had failed to do – qualify beyond the first round – was a real one.

Sadly, those dreams came crashing down in the first match against a nation, Costa Rica, making its debut on the World Cup stage and written off as the whipping boys in a group that contained Brazil and Sweden along with Scotland. While the Costa Ricans may not have had experience themselves, in Milutinović they had someone who knew his way around. Four years earlier he'd taken on the high-pressure job of coaching Mexico at their home World Cup and succeeded beyond their wildest expectations, carrying them to the quarter-finals, where they were eliminated on penalties by eventual finalists West Germany.

Milutinović imbued his players with great self-belief but there was more to it than motivation; he also managed to fuse their natural skill within a well-disciplined tactical system that relied heavily on a strong collective that worked tirelessly for each other.

Scotland had little idea of all this when they took to the pitch. Cameroon's surprise victory over Argentina had served as a warning against over-confidence, at least going by the players' comments before the match. Roxburgh himself stated that, 'I've always been confident that our lads are capable but we have to produce the goods and I think the team from Cameroon showed everyone what can happen. I think we have to be wary of that and we have to be at our best to win.' Ominously, he then added: 'Any team falls below par then they're in danger of losing a match.'

Or, at least, it sounds ominous knowing now what transpired. Scotland did dominate most of the possession, but this was mostly sterile with efforts on goal coming either through shots from distance or via free kicks.

The pressure increased a couple of notches just after the restart when a delightful backheel by Jara wrong-footed the whole Scottish defence, allowing Juan Cayasso the freedom to calmly lob over the onrushing Jim Leighton to put Costa Rica ahead. The shock of going a goal down seemed to energise the Scots but not enough to really cause panic among the Costa Ricans. Their best opening came when Mo Johnston managed to get himself free at the centre of the penalty box but his shot, although powerful, was too central to cause Luis Conejo too many problems.

Beyond that Scotland's efforts didn't amount to much, certainly not enough to deny Costa Rica a historic win on their debut. It was a huge shock; not as seismic as Cameroon's win over Argentina, but for Scotland it proved to be far more damaging.

The respected writer Brian Glanville, writing about the match in his authoritative book *Story of the World Cup*, noted: 'The Scots couldn't exploit Costa Rica's indifferent prowess in the air.' It was an astute observation – Czechoslovakia would rout the Costa Ricans largely by exploiting the height of Tomáš Skuhravý. But the Scots did have an excuse for this: they lacked enough information about their rivals.

This wasn't through any fault of their own or a failure to properly scout their rivals but rather because of a deliberate tactic adopted by Milutinović. 'We were meticulous until that game but couldn't get a proper look at Costa Rica,' Roxburgh admitted. 'The coach had months to prepare his team and never showed his hand. That was what killed us.' Just as Milutinović had planned. And at the heart of the decision, there was a friendly he'd seen the Scots play that had left a deep impact on him.

In March 1990, Scotland hosted a highly anticipated friendly against Argentina, the reigning world champions. With several players from Argentina's triumphant 1986 World Cup squad present, including goalscorers Jorge Valdano and Jorge Burruchaga, as well as the promising Claudio Caniggia, the absence of the iconic Diego Maradona left over 50,000 Scottish fans disappointed. Nevertheless, the spirits of the Tartan Army remained high.

Around the 30-minute mark, Murdo MacLeod delivered a lofted pass from the left of midfield to Alan McInally, who deftly redirected the ball into the path of the onrushing Stewart McKimmie. The Aberdeen right-back seized the opportunity, unleashing a thunderous strike that found the back of the net, marking his first goal in almost five years since his previous top-flight goal against Clydebank.

The match, although labelled as a friendly, was far from cordial. Scotland refused to be intimidated by their esteemed opponents, resulting in fierce tackles and escalating tempers. They had the backing of their fans in a national stadium that held a special place in the hearts of the Scottish players whenever they faced the world's best.

The unexpected hero was McKimmie, who scored the only goal of his 40-cap international career. It confirmed a historic trend of Scotland showcasing their strength at home, securing victories against formidable opponents and consistently drawing large, passionate crowds to their matches. The combination of a strong team and enthusiastic support created an electrifying atmosphere at the national stadium.

While the victory over Argentina had further ignited Scottish dreams of an extended run in the World Cup, it also alerted Milutinović. He'd been among the 50,000 at Hampden that evening and left impressed by what he'd witnessed. 'I came to Glasgow and saw a beautiful stadium, a full stadium,' he later recalled. 'Scotland won 1-0 against Diego Maradona's Argentina. I bought so many videos of the league and the cup games, everything. And you know what I decided? I decided to not show them to my players. Why? Because Scotland played so good, with intensity.'

Milutinović had just taken over as Costa Rica coach, after the local FA sacked the previous boss three months before the start of the tournament. That didn't mean he went in unprepared. Instead his knowledge of the team was such that he was comfortable in leaving out of the squad some of the country's biggest stars who had been pivotal in helping them reach the World Cup finals. His decisions weren't popular and were rendered even less so when he unceremoniously took the squad off to Italy five weeks before they were due to leave, thus depriving the sports-mad island from the planned party send-off.

All of that might have been forgiven had the news coming back home during that period been positive. Instead, it was anything but. The only high-profile friendly that they engaged in ended in a 1-0 loss to a decidedly average Wales team that had finished bottom of its World Cup qualifying group. That defeat had been witnessed by the Scottish media, who were decidedly unimpressed and reported as much.

Apart from that, Milutinović restricted friendlies to Italian amateur teams, where the only objective was to improve his team's match fitness. And even those often ended in either draws or defeats.

There was, however, method in his apparent madness. The Costa Ricans had qualified largely because Mexico, the regional powerhouse, had been expelled from the competition following a scandal involving the use of overage players in youth competitions. He knew that his players were inexperienced, with some of them never having been to Europe. By omitting the stars from his squad he was not only keeping it ego-free but also ensuring that it was filled with younger players who were also more willing to take on his instructions.

That's where the early departure came in. Milutinović had also deeply analysed all the opponents they were due to play against and identified a setup that was to be adopted against each one. During their extended stay in Italy, his players worked on those tactics on a daily basis, so by the time they came to play it was almost as if they were second nature.

For the Scotland match, that meant keeping it as compact as possible in the penalty area to deprive the Scottish strikers of any space. Meanwhile, all that Scotland had to go on during preparation was the Wales fixture, where Milutinović later admitted that he 'didn't play my full team' – for the Costa Ricans it was the opposite. He may not have showed his players the tapes that he'd acquired but Milutinović had analysed them enough to realise that if he kept the wingers wide and deprived the strikers of any space, the battle was won.

That's how it turned out. The days of constant training had prepared them on an almost cellular level for the typical Scottish game plan. Scotland, on the other hand, had no reply apart from pumping more crosses into the box, which still could have yielded results were it not for a mixture of bad misses and brave goalkeeping by Conejo.

As the Scottish players trudged off the pitch, the BBC commentator exclaimed that it was a 'shock for Andy Roxburgh. A disaster for Scotland.' And that was pretty much how the rest of the media, particularly those in Scotland, saw it. Costa Rica should have been beaten and the fact that they weren't was largely down to the manager. Roxburgh's choices were analysed in detail – the selection of striker Allan McInally instead of Ally McCoist, in particular, was roundly criticised – and doubts over his suitability for the role were raised.

That the Costa Ricans were better than anyone had expected them to be didn't seem to make any difference. This attitude frustrated Craig Brown, later Scotland manager himself and in 1990 one of Roxburgh's assistants. 'There was anger, there was disappointment,' Brown said. 'I still remember that vividly. The media did and still do influence fans. If they say things then supporters tend to buy into it. The fans were all told Costa Rica were a poor team; it was a black-and-white scenario where apparently they were only there to be thumped. The reality was different.'

While these might seem like the words of a man looking for excuses, they contain a lot of truth. The core of the Costa Rica team was made up of players who had excelled at youth level, having first qualified for the Under-16 World Cup in 1985 and then the Under-20 version in 1989. More significant than that is the fact that these supposed whipping boys went on to give the much-vaunted Brazil a hard time, losing only 1-0, before beating a strong Sweden 2-1 in the final group fixture to qualify for the next round. That they did so well in the group stage shows how well Milutinović had prepared them for the challenge they were going to face. Tellingly, lacking the time for similar preparation against Czechoslovakia, they were well beaten.

Even so, there's little doubt that Scotland had got at least part of their preparation wrong. As defender Dave McPherson said:

> Andy told us their keeper was a has-been who wouldn't come for cross balls and, sadly, nothing could have been further from the truth. We were lulled into a false sense of security as we settled for knocking the ball into the box for target man Alan McInally in the hope the keeper would spill something at the feet of our strikers. Who were we kidding? The guy was like a flying salmon. He came and picked everything out of the air. Andy had stressed the need to test the keeper early on and he came and caught a couple of balls easily. We should have taken that as a warning, but instead we thought he'd just got lucky.

Not that Andy Roxburgh needed others to criticise him to know that he'd got things wrong. That's why Milutinović's comment years later had stung, because Roxburgh knew that his team should have reacted better and taken something from the match.

McPherson admitted as much: 'It wasn't all on the coaching staff, by the way. As players, we were experienced enough and should have slowed the play down, shown greater patience and settled for getting the ball wide and delivering greater quality into the box.'

The reaction was predictable. There were immediate calls for Roxburgh's dismissal from the press and the fans. One of the banners hung at the next match said, 'Don't worry Andy, your P45 is in the post'.

Roxburgh described the days that followed as his 'most interesting week in football'. That loss to Costa Rica ended up colouring how he was seen, at least back home. For someone who devoted much of his life to elite coaching, that can't be easy.

\* \* \*

Football was the be-all-and-end-all for Roxburgh from a very early age. 'You played in the playgrounds or in the streets at night in those days,' he said. 'But my grandmother worked on the Balmoral estate and I would go there in the summer to play in the lush grass. Football was everything. That's what you did. The priority was to watch, play and talk about football.'

Roxburgh attended Bellahouston Academy, a Glasgow secondary school that boasts a long list of luminaries among its alumni, including former Rangers and Scotland midfielder Ian Durrant, as well as sports presenter Chick Young. It was there that Roxburgh received his footballing education, with his talent recognised when he was selected for the first team at the tender age of 15.

Roxburgh's talents were also noted at national level, where he was chosen to play for Glasgow Schools along with being a schoolboy and youth international. The highlight in his young career came when he played a pivotal role in the schoolboy international between Scotland and England Schools in 1961, scoring the only goal at Parkhead.

In that same year, Roxburgh joined the famous amateurs of Queen's Park. He already had a relationship with the club, established months earlier when he witnesses some of the game's legends close up. In 1960, their Hampden stadium was chosen to host the European Cup Final. Roxburgh hadn't managed to get a ticket for the game between Real Madrid and Eintracht Frankfurt but the groundsman helped sneak him in beforehand, allowing him access to the pitch, where the likes of Puskás, Gento and Di Stefáno were warming up.

His time at Queen's Park allowed him to play the game he loved without undue pressure. He stayed until 1963, winning the Scottish Amateur Cup and earning a cap from the Scottish national amateur team. For all his successes there, he wanted to make football his livelihood, which is why he joined East Stirlingshire for the 1964/65 season before moving to First Division club Partick Thistle, where he stayed until the end of 1968/69.

All the while, however, Roxburgh was thinking about the future. Perhaps he'd realised that he didn't have the talent to make it at the highest level of Scottish football. Or maybe he felt that there was more to the game than his talents allowed him to express. Whatever the reason, he took on and obtained his Scottish Football Association (SFA) coaching qualification in 1966, when he was just 25 years old.

In 1969 Roxburgh moved to Falkirk, where he teamed up with a certain Alex Ferguson. The two strikers helped Falkirk win the Second Division championship in 1969/70, leading to promotion to the First Division. There Roxburgh remained until the end of 1971/72.

He then rounded off his career at Clydebank, in the Second Division. It was there too that he had his start in management, appointed to act as player-coach from 1973 to 1975. The idea of a player being a coach seems a quaint one today but it used to be quite an attractive proposition in the past. Knowing that they couldn't afford the wages of top players – even ageing ones – as well as a manager, smaller clubs would offer them the combined jobs as an incentive.

For someone like Roxburgh, who had been thinking about the management side of things for so long, this must have been incredibly enticing. It opened for him a path that could keep him in the game. Yet it didn't prove to be particularly successful for him, with a lack of resources preventing him from making the impact he wanted. He hadn't earned enough during his playing career to retire off his savings, but as he also had a degree in physical education, he began to work as a primary school head teacher as his football career wound down.

That teaching career didn't last long either, since he was offered the role of the SFA's first director of coaching in 1975. The national team had just done well at the World Cup, going out despite not losing a match, and the nation could boast some of the best coaches in world football, with Jock Stein and Bill Shankly leading the way. Roxburgh's appointment was meant to ensure that such excellence in coaching would not only continue but increase.

With that appointment, Roxburgh's new home became the National Sports Training Centre Inverclyde, a training facility that over time was referred to by the name of the village in which it was located, that of Largs in North Ayrshire. Originally built as a home for a shipbuilder, the facility had first been converted into a hotel and later taken over by the army during the Second World War. The Scottish Council for Physical Recreation bought the building in the 1950s, and it became the location for coaching courses. As facilities go it was spartan, made up of bunk beds, a bell system for mealtimes and phone calls, and a gloomy lounge without alcohol.

Yet this was a key destination for any coach aspiring for greatness. The building's history and grandeur weren't what made it special, that was down to Roxburgh who, over the coming two decades, transformed it into one of the most prestigious coach development centres in Europe.

At the same time as football coaching in England was being shaped by the long-ball dogma, Roxburgh tapped into his country's rich coaching history by inviting the most talented coaches of the time to teach those working their way up. Among the latter there was Alex Ferguson – who famously opted not to go on his honeymoon in order to catch a training course at Largs and eventually became one of its most vocal supporters – Jim McLean and, later, Kenny Dalglish and David Moyes.

That success was largely down to Roxburgh's foresight. Contrary to many others in Britain, he'd realised that Scottish football couldn't prosper if it always looked inwards. He began inviting Europe's elite coaches to share their knowledge, including Arrigo Sacchi, fresh from winning the European Cup and revolutionising the face of European football.

The presence of such high-profile coaches boosted Largs's reputation to the point that coaches from all over

Europe chose it as the best place to gain their badges. Chief among these was a certain Jose Mourinho, who would go on to become one of the very best himself. But none of that would have been possible without Roxburgh being at the helm. He was the visionary who surrounded himself with some of the best minds in Scottish football and then used their input to help build a world-class programme.

Apart from shaping future generations of coaches, Roxburgh's role included forming those of Scottish youth teams; his job description included managing all Scottish teams, from under-21s downwards. Here too he showed an uncanny ability to get the most out of whatever resources he had without sacrificing his principles. Under his tutelage, the young players often did extremely well, reaching the semi-finals of the 1978 European Under-18 tournament and then the quarter-finals of the 1983 World Youth Championship.

Roxburgh's crowning achievement, however, came in the 1982 European Under-18 Championship, where Scotland could rely on several players who would go on to enjoy a stellar career, such as Bryan Gunn, Gary Mackay, Dave Bowman, Paul McStay and Pat Nevin. Roxburgh had them playing to their potential, overcoming each challenge as it came, until a 3-1 win over Czechoslovakia meant that they'd won the competition. It remains Scotland's only major international trophy success.

His vision, the knowledge gained by being in contact with so many greats, and his results made him the obvious choice as the Scotland manager in waiting. And yet when he did get the job, there was a lot of scepticism.

While Roxburgh had done well in his decade with the SFA, his achievements were nothing compared to those of his predecessors. Jock Stein was a legend at Celtic, leading them to become the first British club to win the European Cup, and when he passed away during qualification for Mexico 86 in came Roxburgh's own former team-mate, Alex Ferguson, who by that point had not only transformed Aberdeen into one of the country's leading clubs but also beaten Real Madrid to win the European Cup Winners' Cup. The apparent availability of another great in Jim McLean, as well as Billy McNeill – winner of three league titles as Celtic manager as well as being Stein's captain – contributed to the incredulity over the SFA's decision to go with such an unknown.

Beyond that there was also the state of the national team itself. Two of the all-time Scottish greats – Graeme Souness and Kenny Dalglish – called time on their international careers after the Mexico World Cup. Both had been bedrocks of the team for the previous decade but they were starting their own managerial careers, so Roxburgh was forced to fill the gaps that their absence created. Not an easy task for anyone but perhaps harder on someone like Roxburgh, who was in the critics' crosshairs from his early days.

It didn't help that his time as Scotland manager got off to a very poor start. Two disappointing 0-0 draws, against Bulgaria and the Republic of Ireland, immediately made qualification for the 1988 European Championship a tricky proposition. Indeed, any hope evaporated when a home victory over Luxembourg was followed by a defeat at Hampden to the Irish and then a 4-1 hammering away in Belgium.

At that stage, knives were being sharpened for Roxburgh, regardless of him seeming to find his feet with two significant victories, one in Bulgaria and another over Belgium, which, incidentally, proved to be crucial for the Republic of Ireland to qualify. Instead, focus was on a 0-0 draw away at Luxembourg in their final qualification match.

That seemed likely to seal Roxburgh's fate. Yet, crucially, he retained the support of Ernie Walker, the powerful and well-connected secretary of the SFA. Walker had been key in giving Roxburgh his coaching role back in 1975 and had worked closely with him as they sought to raise Scotland's profile. Walker trusted his manager and was secure enough in his role to persist with his choice despite the criticism.

Notably, Walker had astutely recognised that the team was going through a period of transition and that the manager needed time for his work to start showing results. There was no escaping that the qualification group for Euro 88 had been a disaster but in those matches Roxburgh had gradually been bringing in a new generation of players who would provide the basis for the national team for years to come.

Roxburgh himself admitted as much before a friendly against Hungary in September 1987, when he remarked in the programme notes that 'the next World Cup starts here'. Ally McCoist made his debut on that day, promptly scoring twice in a 2-0 win for a relatively young Scottish team.

Boosted by the faith shown in him by his boss, Roxburgh kept on building. He'd missed qualification for the European Championship – incidentally something that had eluded his predecessors – but he was going to be ready by the time qualification for the World Cup kicked off.

And so it was. Once more Scotland started their home commitments with a draw but this time there was praise for their performance in holding a very strong Yugoslavia. They'd already opened qualification with a win away in Norway and went to enjoy three successive victories following their home draw, including a crucial home win against France. Away defeats to Yugoslavia and the French dented their hopes but a 1-1 draw with Norway was enough to see them qualify.

Once qualification was over, Roxburgh embarked on a series of friendlies to fine-tune his team and experiment some more. In February he took his squad to a training camp in Italy, playing two matches in Genoa's Luigi Ferraris, where they were due to play two of their World Cup fixtures. He also tried to vary the type of opposition his team faced, playing East Germany, Egypt and Poland at Hampden. It was a way of seeing how they shaped up against varying styles.

Roxburgh's commitment not just to the immediate but also longer term saw him hand debuts to Bryan Gunn, Stuart McCall, John Collins, Gary McAllister and Robert Fleck. It further confirmed why the SFA had stuck by him. Yet those matches also held worrying signs. Scotland lost two of those home friendlies and drew the other. It wasn't the form to build enthusiasm and courage. A narrow 2-1 win against Malta at the latter's Ta' Qali national stadium at least boosted morale, although not much.

Fate, it seemed, was turning against Scotland and Roxburgh. His squad was missing two key players – Davie Cooper and Steve Nicol – through injury. Mo Johnston, who had scored six goals in qualification, was also struggling and only confirmed he'd be able to make it at the last minute. Even so, he wasn't in the best shape. The same went for Jim Leighton, although in his case there was no injury involved; the goalkeeper had simply endured a horrendous season with Manchester United, almost losing them the FA Cup through a series of fumbles in the final. That had gone to a replay for which he suffered the humiliation of being dropped.

There was more frustration when Scotland arrived in Genoa, where Roxburgh found out that Ally McCoist was also carrying a hamstring injury that he'd kept secret, such was his desire to be in the squad. All of this, on top of the pressure of starting off the World Cup against a supposed weak team, got to them. As did their inability to prepare properly. Still, the defeat was humiliating. Roxburgh made reference to the shot count – that stood 19 to 4 in Scotland's favour – but that had little impact apart from making him sound naive. The calls for him to quit or be sacked began once more.

He wasn't helped by a further injury to central defender Richard Gough. Yet Scotland didn't give up. And Roxburgh had something of a plan for their next match against Sweden, who had gone into the World Cup as a possible dark horse. They'd topped a qualification group that included England and had a team full of talented individuals who played across Europe. To counter this, Roxburgh added the steel of Murdo MacLeod and Gordon Durie to his line-up. The masterstroke, however, was the inclusion of Robert Fleck.

The striker had been handed his debut against Argentina but wasn't called on again after that match. He'd gone off on holiday after his season came to an end but Cooper's injury opened a space in the squad and he rushed from the beach to fill it.

Now this unexpected call-up was making an appearance at the World Cup. There was, however, a reason for Roxburgh's choice and it wasn't the criticism received for starting with Alan McInally against Costa Rica. That season, Fleck had tormented the Swede Glenn Hysén when Norwich played Liverpool, with the defender unable to handle his speed and movement, so much so that he was sent off. And while Hysén played it cool before the match with Scotland, Roxburgh knew that for all his composure he'd struggle against Fleck.

It proved to be a prescient choice. Fleck was too much for the Swedish defence. First, he won the corner from which Stuart McCall scored the opening goal and then he was involved in the action that led to a penalty ten minutes from time that Johnston scored. While Sweden pulled a goal back minutes later, Scotland held on for the win.

From calling for his head, now everyone was hailing Roxburgh for his choices. The win kept Scotland alive, even if it meant they needed a result against Brazil to go through. Of course, this wasn't the first time that Brazil stood in Scotland's way, having beaten them 4-1 in 1982 after going behind. And, while this iteration of the Brazilian team had much less flair, there was enough talent to frighten anyone.

Fortune was still not smiling on Scotland and Roxburgh. Craig Levein, whom the coach saw as his ideal sweeper, was forced out by injury and Gary Gillespie was struggling for fitness. Then with the first half petering out, MacLeod was knocked out trying to stop a Branco free kick and had to be replaced.

Still Scotland hung on, diligently closing all gaps and stopping the Brazilians as much as possible from playing through them. They almost made it, too. But fate, that cruel mistress, had other thoughts. With seven minutes remaining a fierce shot by Alemão from outside the penalty area was saved by Leighton at full stretch. The goalkeeper, however, could neither hold on to the ball nor parry it out of danger. Instead, it went straight into the centre of the penalty area, where Gillespie threw himself to push it out of the onrushing Careca's path. Unfortunately, Muller, on as a substitute, reacted faster than anyone else and slotted the ball in.

Defeat, coupled with Costa Rica's come-from-behind victory against Sweden, left Scotland in third place. It might have been enough – the best third-placed teams qualified for the next round – but results elsewhere didn't go their way. They were out of the competition.

Roxburgh was honest in his reaction, admitting that they'd lost to a better team, without being able to hide his disappointment at the 'cruel blow to lose out just at the death ... particularly to such a soft goal'. Indeed, he could argue that Scotland's whole participation was one cruel blow after another, with injuries not only preventing him from playing his preferred starting XI, but impeding any rhythm developing, with one problem cropping up as soon as another seemed to be fixed. Roxburgh also had to shoulder some of the blame, particularly for his indecisiveness over who to play in attack alongside Johnston. McInally, Fleck and McCoist started each of the three matches, respectively.

While it was of no consolation, the Scots could go home with pride. Pressure had clearly got to them against Costa Rica but they'd redeemed themselves against Sweden and then should have achieved a draw against the mighty Brazil, when, to Roxburgh's credit, they went out looking to play rather than purely defend.

During the tournament the 20,000 Scots who had travelled to Italy – with no arrests reported – sang about how they always did things the hard way. That was certainly true. Too hard. But Costa Rica aside, Roxburgh's tactics had been spot on, despite him struggling amid all the other duties he had to handle during a World Cup. 'None of this is meant to sound like bleating,' he said later. 'The intensity of it all was quite a shock. There were times when I simply thought I would not get any sleep.'

Yet the experience strengthened him, just as his blooding of new players was justified by the emergence of a new Scotland team. Over the next two years he achieved something that had eluded every other national team manager, when, despite being drawn in a strong group that featured Bulgaria, Romania and Switzerland, the Scots still managed to finish top to qualify for the European Championship for the first time in their history.

It was a fantastic achievement in an era when the competition was limited to just eight teams. That setup also made it tough for Scotland to expect to get out of the group stage in the finals, especially as they were drawn in a group that featured the Netherlands, Germany and the Commonwealth of Independent States (a collection of countries from the former USSR). Too tough, as it turned out.

Yet contrary to 1990, there were no recriminations, apart from those involving the pre-tournament loss to injury of influential captain Gordon Strachan. The Scots played well against the Dutch (a 1-0 defeat) and very well against Germany (a 2-0 loss) before rounding off the tournament with a resounding victory over the CIS (3-0), even though the latter were still in with a chance of qualifying. It was arguably one of the finest showings – performance-wise at least – by any Scottish team at a major tournament.

The praise that went Roxburgh's way did lighten the blow. It also finally properly established him as someone who deserved the role.

Of course, the career of a coach is one that more often than not ends in failure. So it was for Roxburgh. Scotland were drawn in a tough qualification group for the 1994 World Cup, one that featured (eventual finalists) Italy, Switzerland and Portugal. Despite the quality of opposition, the Scots went undefeated at home. Sadly, they also failed to win any of those matches, while also suffering some heavy defeats on their travels. They ended up fourth and a long way from qualification.

For Andy Roxburgh, this signalled the end of the road as Scotland manager. Tellingly, he'd put in place a succession plan, with Craig Brown stepping up from his staff to replace him. Brown led Scotland to qualification for the 1996 European Championship and the 1998 World Cup. Informed by what has happened since, those overseen by Roxburgh and Brown seem like a golden age for the Scottish national team.

At the time, public opinion wasn't of that view. Roxburgh was deemed a failure, facing harsh criticism for a conservative approach. That he'd neither played at the highest level nor been a club coach prejudiced him, with some even feeling that his appointment had more to do with his ability to network with high-ranking SFA officials.

Others didn't see it that way. Roxburgh received numerous approaches to coach in Europe and elsewhere but he always refused; the idea of one day having to lead a team against his beloved Scotland was one he wasn't willing to contemplate.

Eventually he did get an offer that was perfect for him when UEFA appointed him as the association's technical director. For the self-confessed 'teacher of football' this was the ideal role, assisting member associations in their development while always looking to innovate. The latter he did by setting up a forum that brought together the continent's elite coaches. That people such as Alex Ferguson, Marcello Lippi, Fabio Capello and Ottmar Hitzfeld not only took Roxburgh's call but also readily agreed to his idea shows just how much they respected him.

When he left that role after 18 years he carried on in football. First he spent some time working with the New York Red Bulls – his only coaching stint with a club – before moving to the Asian Football Confederation, where he once more filled the role of technical director. Again, he was being entrusted with improving the coaching infrastructure of a whole federation.

And he keeps on going. 'There's still too much to do,' he said. 'The best way to describe it is to say that football has been a way of life. I've been very fortunate that the mixture of football and education, because I had a background in both, has been literally a way of life ever since.'

\*\*\*

Andy Roxburgh's remarkable journey in the world of football has been one of unwavering passion, relentless dedication and profound impact. With boundless energy and an insatiable drive, his journey is far from over. His enduring belief in the transformative power of football as a way of life has propelled him forward.

His career provides an indelible legacy, a testament to the impact one individual can have on the beautiful game. The 1990 World Cup didn't reward him for his work, yet he did eventually get the deserved recognition. Ironically, that came when Scotland repeatedly failed to do what Roxburgh – and the team that he put in place – had shown a knack for doing: qualifying for major tournaments.

He did that through dedication and pursuit of progress that serve as an inspiration to all, reminding us that there's always more to be done in the perpetual quest to unlock football's full potential.

# Italy's Wasted Opportunity

AS THE camera panned over the 22 men lined up, it lingered slightly longer on Diego Armando Maradona. Not for nothing. The Argentine was considered the greatest player on the planet who four years earlier had dragged his country to a World Cup success virtually on his own. Now here he was, back in the same competition looking for more of the same, starting from the opening match against Cameroon.

It didn't turn out that way. Maradona was constantly marked by two or three Cameroonians who used every tactic possible to stop Argentina from playing. Players were hacked down unceremoniously with the objective of keeping them as far away from the Cameroon penalty box as possible. As the minutes ticked by, the world champions' frustration grew before turning to panic when Cameroon eventually went ahead.

What the Argentines didn't have to worry about on that day was the state of the pitch. That might seem like a small reason for comfort; this was the opening fixture of the World Cup, one of sport's biggest competitions, so of course the pitch was perfect and players didn't have to worry about it! But that hadn't been the case when 60 days earlier the same pitch that millions around the world were now looking at had been rightly compared to a 'potato field'.

Before every World Cup, FIFA delegates regularly visit the hosting stadia to ensure that everything is going according to plan. Often, they'll make recommendations on any improvements necessary, but rarely will their demands be as exceptional as the ones lodged on 3 April 1990, just weeks before the start of the competition. The pitch at Milan's Stadio Meazza was in such a pitiful state that there was no way it was going to be fit to host the world's finest players. The delegates may or may not have been the ones to draw the analogy with a potato field – probably many journalists, players and supporters beat them to the punch – but it was an apt description of a pitch that was badly cutting up and in key areas had more mud than grass.

Ironically, it was the World Cup itself that had created the issue. As with all host cities, the already majestic stadium had undergone restructuring work to make it suitable for football's premier competition. A third tier had been built to increase the capacity to 74,559 but this had come at a huge cost, not just financial (although that too, as with everything associated with Italia 90), as the grass suddenly found itself deprived of the light needed to grow properly. The additional build also inhibited the circulation of air and placed the grass under too much stress, creating a harsh microclimate that made it excessively cold during the winter and too hot in the summer.

That this was the reason would only be identified later. Back in April 1990 the priority was fixing up the pitch as quickly as possible. It was re-laid and, over the course of five weeks, grounds people tended it night and day to make sure it would be ready for the competition's opener. The work paid off and for the six matches when the eyes of the world were fixed on the San Siro, no one saw anything other than an immaculate playing surface.

A month later, however, and everything was dug up once again, this time for the foolhardy idea of selling tiny chunks of the turf to fans eager to have a souvenir from the tournament. Lamentably, it was all for nothing – most of the pitch ended up in a rubbish dump as no one was really interested in buying chunks of soil and grass. If anything exemplified the huge waste that Italians would eventually come to see as the main legacy of their World Cup, that image of a pitch on which so much money and energy had been spent being literally thrown away surely has to be it.

For the San Siro pitch, it was just another in a long list of disasters; the start of an odyssey that would never truly be over. By September of the same year, the newly re-laid pitch – the second in the space of three months – was being criticised for the divots that made it practically unplayable. Experts were called in, the worst parts of the turf patched up temporarily and then the whole area replaced at the end of the season. Yet it was all for nothing; by the start of the 1993/94 season it was in a pitiful state once more. This time, it was only repatched to try to limit the cost. It wouldn't be enough.

It got even worse in September 1994, with missing chunks of the pitch being filled in with sand that had the nasty side-effect of increasing players' injuries and once more making it virtually unplayable. Another re-laying was carried out in the summer of 1995. More misfortune was around the corner, however, and in 1997 a fungal bacteria attacked the grass, preventing roots from reaching the depth they needed to get a good enough hold. In 1998 the whole pitch was completely dug up, with new drainage laid and a different soil mixture used. It still wouldn't prove to be enough.

Everything was dug up once more in 2014 and replaced by a hybrid of synthetic turf stitched into real grass that gave the pitch added resilience. This, 15 years after the works that had created the whole mess, would at last prove to be a more durable solution, even if the fight would never be truly won. Not a season passes by without criticism over the state of the San Siro pitch, an incredible situation for a stadium that hosts two clubs that have been European champions on multiple occasions.

All this wasn't predicted when improvement work started on the San Siro in 1987. Back then, the only objective was that of presenting an image of architectural grandeur that would reflect positively on the host nation. Wowing visitors during the four weeks of the tournament seemed to be all that mattered. Assessments on the long-term benefits of all the work done were academic at best. In that way, Italia 90 was the template that future World Cups would come to follow.

\* \* \*

Italy's dream of hosting the World Cup had begun in the early 1980s, when the country was going through an economic boom. It was one of the architects of that financial growth, Prime Minister Bettino Craxi, who had first mentioned the idea in public and then pushed to see it come to life. Tellingly, given all that eventually unfolded over Italia 90, Craxi would eventually die in Tunisia, where he'd fled to avoid charges of political corruption, of which he'd become a symbol.

The Italian bid was voted as the most favourable one in May 1984, edging out the rival proposal of the USSR. Not only was Italy historically a country with rich footballing traditions but, with the memories of the political drama and boycotts that had overshadowed the Moscow Olympics still fresh in peoples' minds, it was a much safer choice.

It was only once planning started in earnest, however, that the scale of the challenge began to emerge. In a bid to ensure that as many benefitted from the competition as possible, the organising committee had identified 12 cities across the Italian territory in which matches would be held. This didn't mean there were 12 stadia that were good enough to host a World Cup. Quite the opposite. While many were architectural marvels, they'd also been built before or around the Second World War and had benefitted from only minor modifications since. Not one had fully covered stands all round. They either needed to be built, rebuilt or heavily modified. Both the host country and FIFA had severely underestimated just how much work was needed.

Some saw this as an opportunity. Among them was the man chosen to oversee the organisational efforts of Italia 90, Luca Cordero di Montezemolo, a Bologna-born member of an aristocratic Piedmontese family that had served the royal House of Savoy for centuries. He was 39 at the time but had long been considered something of a golden child, having been Enzo Ferrari's assistant at his motor company.

At the time, Montezemolo had been tasked with focusing on the racing team. Despite being very young for someone bearing such responsibility – he was 26 when he took over – he delivered immediate results, overseeing Ferrari's three consecutive Formula 1 titles between 1975 and 1977. Later, he managed Team Azzurra, the first-ever Italian yacht club to take part in the America's Cup, a participation that captured the Italian public's imagination. In between, he'd worked at the highest levels of FIAT, managing several of the conglomerate's companies.

Montezemolo's choice, then, was an understandable one. In his first press conference he portrayed a very strong vision of what he wanted to achieve with the World Cup, claiming,

'My dream is to make the 1990 World Cup a showcase of Italian technology and industry geared to the 20th century.' That would come to be the blueprint for anything associated with Italia 90.

His first major task was to find some money to get things started. That he did by roping in some of Italy's biggest companies, most of which were public utilities, as sponsors persuading them pay some of the costs. He'd also looked at the last time Italy hosted a major tournament, the European Championship of 1980, to see what had gone wrong there. What he took away from that review was that those matches had been confined to a few major cities and had left little impact on the nation. The World Cup needed to be different, reaching all corners and modernising as many stadia as possible.

In that way, Montezemolo was a visionary with big dreams. His real talent, however, was the capacity to navigate complex political intricacies, never offending anyone that mattered while still managing to accommodate those with the strongest pull.

Nowhere would that be expressed better than at the foot of the Italian peninsula. The obvious candidate stadium to host the World Cup was Lecce's Via Del Mare. Although not an iconic destination, it could hold 55,000 and had been almost completely rebuilt in 1985 to celebrate the local club's historic first promotion to Serie A. Of all the stadia in Italy, few needed as little work as this one.

The main problem was that Bari, not Lecce, is the capital city of the Puglia region. More than that, AS Bari's owner, Antonio Matarrese, also happened to be the president of the Lega Calcio – the body that manages Italy's leagues – and he wanted his club to benefit from all the investment that was being poured into the World Cup.

There was only one way that Bari could edge out Lecce's claim and that was by having an even better stadium. Which is precisely what happened. The famous Genoese architect Renzo Piano was brought in to design a fantastic facility that he nicknamed 'the Spaceship' for its unmistakable modern aesthetic form. The original project envisaged a football stadium with a 45,000 capacity, all covered, arranged in two concentric rings: the lower ring inside a specially created artificial hill, with the upper ring built with the impression of being suspended in the air. The architect also had the idea of separating the upper tier into 26 sections (in the shape of petals) to aid security. With each petal being eight metres away from the next, fans would be kept away from each other, thus eliminating any possible clashes. Similarly visionary was the idea to have lights all around the roofing perimeter, which to this day is a unique concept that leaves no shadows on the San Nicola pitch.

For all Piano's innovative ideas, they began to be polluted when opposing demands were agreed to in order to maintain the diplomatic equilibrium. The Italian Olympic Committee (CONI), which had agreed to bear some of the infrastructural costs, pushed for the inclusion of an athletics track around the pitch. It was the only way they could justify spending money on football stadia, but no one seemed to care that this would come at the cost of the stands and fans being pushed further away from the field of play. Even less thought was given to the delicate balance that the architect had striven for, ruining his careful planning so much that his beautifully designed cover no longer shielded those seats closest to the pitch, which were now left open to the elements.

Work on the new stadium began immediately, with a consortium of local building magnates headed by Salvatore

Matarrese – who happened to be Antonio's brother and perhaps the main reason for the manoeuvring to get a new stadium built – managing to deliver it within three years. The result was as spectacular as both Piano and Montezemolo had dreamed. Even though it never came close to reaching the 58,000 capacity that the final build provided, anyone who witnessed any of the five matches it hosted during Italia 90 was amazed by just how futuristic it all felt.

Underwhelming visitors was never going to be the problem with this or any other stadium in Italy. Even though the financial boom years had begun to transform into a recession as the decade wore on, no expense was spared for the World Cup. Initial projections had estimated that the San Nicola would cost around £44 million, but when the expenses were finally tallied the final figure was around £10 million more than that.

What the initial projections had never really cared for was what happened after the World Cup. As with practically all stadia in Italy, the San Nicola was handed over to the local government to administer, in this case the Municipality of Bari, responsible for managing the city. Yet they weren't given the funds necessary to maintain the stadium, which, unsurprisingly, started to fall apart as the years went by.

In October 2009, part of the Teflon roofing covering the visitors' section was blown away in a storm. Over the next five years practically all the remaining roofing followed suit. None was replaced, leaving fans at the mercy of the elements. The electronic scoreboards suffered a similar fate and, although these were replaced when they first broke, they weren't the second time round. The athletics track that the Olympic committee had foisted upon the stadium has also been worn away and is unusable. Not that the latter was a big loss, as apart from hosting the Mediterranean Games in the early 90s, it was rarely used.

Yet the biggest problem with the San Nicola was its size. There were big dreams and hopes for the club when the stadium was being designed. Indeed, for the decade that followed the World Cup, AS Bari were a regular member of Serie A. Since the year 2000, however, they've been back in the top flight only once, spending the rest of the time in lower leagues, just as they have for most of their history. They even suffered the ignominy of two bankruptcies that forced a restart from the bottom tier. During this period, average attendances hovered between 11,000 and 24,000, meaning that even in their best years Bari struggled to fill half their stadium.

As if to validate the stadium's existence, there have been instances when the Italian national team played in Bari, while the final of the Champions League was also hosted there, although that was way back in 1991. Most of the time it lies empty or underutilised.

Quite simply the San Nicola is too big, the pitch too far away from the stands and the stadium is too costly to maintain. But no one has the money needed to tear it down and rebuild a replacement that's fit for purpose. Not that anyone would have the temerity to suggest that a stadium that's just 30 years old should be pulled down, particularly not in a region that has historically been economically disadvantaged and has a higher unemployment rate than the Italian average.

That same compunction wasn't felt elsewhere.

\* \* \*

In 2008, demolition crews moved into the Stadio Delle Alpi to start tearing it down, just 18 years after hosting its first match. Even more damningly, at that point it had been unused for two years.

If a 60,000-capacity stadium for a minor club like Bari was always going to be excessive, one holding almost 70,000 for Juventus and Torino, two of the country's most decorated clubs, didn't seem to be such a big stretch. There was never any doubt that Turin wouldn't be among the host cities. Yet when Italy was given the right to host the World Cup both clubs still played in the Stadio Comunale that had been built in 1933 on the last occasion that the world championship had been hosted there. Again, the feeling among the organisers was that this wasn't good enough. Despite vocal opposition, the eventual decision was to build a bigger, grander ground.

That's what was delivered. Architecturally, the stadium that was named Delle Alpi by public vote, was another majestically imposing build with a flourish at either end in the form of huge wing-like covers. Two sets of drawings were presented at design stage, one with and one without an athletics track around the pitch. As with elsewhere, the organising committee went for the latter, which was the opposite of what should have happened had the decision been solely based on the long-term needs of the clubs. The inclusion of those athletics tracks wasn't incidental.

In those years the Italian Primo Nebbiolo was the head of the International Amateur Athletic Federation and it's rumoured that he exercised his considerable influence to ensure that as many of those tracks as possible were built. Crucially, the possibility of stadia hosting more than one sport was a way of ensuring the financial support of the Italian Olympic Committee that held members who harboured political aspirations. They wanted to be seen to be contributing to this national effort.

Yet, like elsewhere, this inclusion was an afterthought, which meant that, apart from some events hosted there in the stadium's first two years, it didn't became an athletics venue. The absence of a warm-up track – a basic and fundamental necessity for any athletics meet – made it inadequate for that particular purpose as well as reinforcing just how little thought had been given to this.

Still, first impressions were positive. Giovanni Agnelli, Juventus's owner at the time, exclaimed, 'The Delle Alpi is beautiful. I had never seen it before, it looks truly excellent.' While club president Vittorio Chiusano enthusiastically said, 'The Delle Alpi is certainly spectacular. People have already shown that they love this stadium. Just a few matches will be enough to get fans used to it. It's a beautiful stadium.' Beautiful it certainly was, as was everything else associated with Italia 90. It had certainly cost enough for that: the final bill exceeded the original plans by a staggering £117 million.

Functionality was another thing. Not only was the running track unusable for hosting athletics, but it also created big problems. As with Bari, it pushed fans away from the action, making it difficult for them to create any kind of atmosphere or establish any connection with the team. The reality of this situation began to unfold with the passing of years, and thoughts about the new stadium were quick to change. 'At the Delle Alpi it is as if we're always playing away from home,' Agnelli said, expressing his disgust with the stadium, before concluding that, 'You see very little and poorly.'

The respected Italian journalist Marino Bartoletti picked up on the theme: 'There were points in the stadium where you could not see the pitch. The Delle Alpi is a cathedral in the desert; there was too much compromise in its design.'

Those references to poor views weren't spurious but rather brought about by the infamous lack of visibility from the highest tier of the stadium, where fans claimed that they could barely see the action. For all the grand designs, it too proved to be unfit for purpose and fans began to show this in the only manner that truly makes an impact: their absence. As the years went by, the number of Juventus fans attending declined. The combination of bad views and rising ticket prices to make up for the ever-increasing maintenance charges made sure of that, despite the club enjoying some of its most successful years.

As early as 1994, Juventus had been looking at ways to escape from the Delle Alpi to a stadium of their own, with several plans drafted over the years. Finally, the perfect opportunity arose when Turin was chosen as the host city for the 2006 Winter Olympics. Juventus were given a 99-year lease on the land on which the Delle Alpi stood.

Few tears were shed when they announced that the Delle Alpi was to be torn down. No one went there to claim treasured mementos, to recall cherished memories. Instead, the demolition was widely celebrated.

As for Torino, theirs too was a happy ending as they ended up at the old Stadio Comunale – the one that had been deemed not good enough for Italia 90 – which was modernised to host the Winter Olympics and now provides them with a home that fits their needs.

The perfect epitaph to the Delle Alpi was delivered by local journalist Maurizio Crosetti, who, writing in the Turin-based *La Repubblica*, said, 'We had fun with Brazil against Argentina, and then when Juve won quite a few things, but always feeling like they were guests in someone else's house, inside a stadium that was too big, too cold (in every sense: environmental and climatic, because in winter freezing cold, there were draughts everywhere) and too empty.'

\* \* \*

Crosetti could have written the same words about the Friuli in Udine. Built in the mid-70s with a futuristic design that featured a 200-metre-long arc from one end to the other supporting the covering to the main stand, from the start the stadium had grander ambitions than the football played in it, with Udinese languishing in Serie C at the time. Those aspirations were kept up in later years, with one owner expressing them by installing a gigantic scoreboard that was the third-biggest in the world when it went up.

Their grand designs were rewarded when Italia 90 came around, as the Friuli was selected as a host stadium. A further back-handed compliment was the lack of work that the stadium itself was subjected to. Apart from new parking spaces, offices and some new facilities for other sports, not much was done. Indeed, in a rare example of efficient use of public funds, the money that was saved was diverted to rebuilding another stadium in the region, that of Trieste.

Apart from the athletics track that, as elsewhere, was barely used, the Friuli stadium could claim to be the model of how a publicly funded building should be; it provided adequate facilities for the team, office space for various organisations and a suitable host for non-sporting events, such as a historic Bruce Springsteen concert in 2009.

Even so, this wasn't enough for the Pozzo family, who have owned the club since the mid-80s. They pointed at a stadium that was too big for their needs, one lacking in basic facilities that fans in other countries expect. After decades of pressure to be granted ownership of the stadium, in 2012 they finally managed to secure a 99-year lease. This kicked off a series of projects that effectively knocked down and then rebuilt every side of the Friuli. The only element that survived this rebuild was the historic arch.

Once more, the work that took place in Udine ended up being extremely efficient. Even though costs were high, the result has proven to be worthwhile, with every stand now covered, the athletics track removed and a sensible capacity of 25,000 being what the club needs.

\* \* \*

For all the desire to include as much of Italy as possible in the hosting, Rome was always going to be the focal point. Here, initial talks over a new stadium were quickly dismissed, with the decision falling on modernising the Olimpico, built to host the 1960 Olympics. A good idea – it would have been a shame to lose what was seen as Italy's national stadium – but one poorly executed. The original plans were drawn and then redrawn countless times. In the end almost the whole stadium was torn down and rebuilt at a massive cost: refurbishments that had been projected to cost a few million ultimately ended up costing more than £110 million!

Yet, despite the dizzying cost, the end result was poor. Rome could boast one of the biggest football stadia in the world but for spectators the whole experience was inadequate. The various redesigns had paid little attention to visibility – a common refrain of multiple Italia 90 projects – so it proved to be hard to follow what was going on from various spots in the stadium.

\* \* \*

Those complaints, however, paled when compared to what happened in Cagliari, the scene of England and Ireland's matches in the first round. Built in 1970, the Sant'Elia also underwent extensive modernisation, although this largely involved building a stand to cover the VIP area (a request by the organising committee for all stands to be covered was rejected) and new floodlighting. Adjacent to the ground, a ball-shaped building was built with the aim of hosting the press. The latter was used for the duration of the World Cup and barely ever after that. Despite the works not being overly grand, costs amounted to 40 per cent more than budgeted.

All that investment barely lasted ten years and by 2002 the situation was so bad that the Sant'Elia risked being closed by the authorities for health and safety reasons. That threat was dodged – although two stands remained shut down – after the club invested some of its own money in temporary stands set up over the athletics track. The reprieve was just as temporary, since a few years later more sections were closed off, limiting maximum capacity to 14,000, lower than Serie A's minimum of 20,000, forcing Cagliari to obtain special dispensation.

By the early 2010s a stand-off between Cagliari owner Massimo Cellino and the local authorities resulted in the club moving away from their historic home. It was a brief and unhappy period as there were no other facilities that could really host them adequately, but it achieved the intended objectives. In 2015, the whole stadium was torn down and rebuilt.

\* \* \*

It wasn't simply with the stadia that there was a problem. The air terminal at Ostiense in Rome followed a familiar pattern. On the outside, it's yet another architectural post-modern marvel, designed by Julio Lafuente and Giulio

Rocci. The roof is supported by a magnificent arched metal structure. Sunlight pours in through the expansive windows and portholes, evoking the feeling of adventure. On the exterior, a brick-textured portico extends at an angle, deterring graffiti artists.

Designed as a point of arrival for the train shuttle to Fiumicino airport, it proved to be a colossal failure. Rather than the 30,000 passengers expected to pass in transit, only around 3,000 used it. Soon it was decided to decommission it and transfer the terminus to another line. It would come to be seen as another cathedral in the desert or, as the local press labelled it, a temple of waste. For almost two decades the building that had cost almost £12 million to build lay disused and abandoned, taken over in parts by refugees and the homeless before eventually being turned into a shopping arcade.

Calamitous as that was, it wasn't even the worst of Italia 90's excesses. That title could probably be assigned to the train station in Farneto that was meant to provide easy access to the north stand of Rome's Olympic stadium. Built over a period of four years – although it was never actually finished – the station cost around £18 million and was used for just the handful of days during which the Olympic stadium was in use at the World Cup.

Once the final match was played, the station was closed and remained that way for over 18 years, before it was definitively removed from the metropolitan line map and then demolished. In this instance, eight people were charged with misappropriation of public funds but no one was found guilty.

But not even that can beat the story of the Hotel Mundial, a building halfway between Rome and Milan that was started but never finished – £12 million was poured into that doomed project that never accepted a visitor before it was knocked down.

\* \* \*

When it was first conceived, the idea was for the 1990 World Cup to project all that was good about Italy. The economy was booming and Italian design was still the epitome of greatness.

Instead, what it achieved was to highlight the everyday corruption and stultifying nature of petty politics. Luca Cordero di Montezemolo said:

> I laugh when somebody thinks that a soccer ball can change tradition, mentality, procedure, bureaucracy. We will be ready, as usual, but my opinion is that in the work up in Italy, a miracle happened.
>
> This is a very provincial job; it is not international. I have been in this office 12 hours a day for four years, focusing on the problems of Bari, Turin, Naples ... I'm a curious guy and this is a fantastic moment in the world, not only in the east, but all over. And here I was working in the stadiums, working with problems like lights, discussing with city and government officials. I couldn't go on a holiday anywhere – the States, Russia. Believe me, it was a prison.

In 1990 Italy had the best and richest league in world football; it was where every player dreamed of playing, if just to prove their worth. The World Cup that Montezemolo's team delivered matched the standards set by Serie A, with majestic-looking stadia and a futuristic presentation that truly broke the mould. Even the graphics used during the televising of matches were ground-breaking, going beyond what anyone else was doing in any sport.

Yet the cost of all of this was horrific. The total spend came to around £3.2 billion, more than was spent on three subsequent World Cups. Italians were still paying Italia 90's debt 25 years later and all they had to show for it was a host of stadia that not only weren't fit for purpose but were now owned by municipalities that didn't have the finances to maintain them, stadia used by clubs that couldn't really make money from them.

Maurizio Crosetti reflected on this:

> How much waste, though? Someone paid for this pile of now-useless things. The memory returns to the 'magic nights' of Italia 90, to all the ruins that were then abandoned in remote corners of the city, for example the 'press centres', which were like enormous balloons and which have all fallen into disuse, sooner or later.
>
> That colossal, wasted opportunity, the cascade of public and private money swallowed up by the event. Yet, after less than 20 years we have the oldest stadiums in Europe, uncomfortable, dangerous.

There wasn't even the comfort of lessons being learned. In 2009 Rome hosted the World Aquatics Championships. Once more it was a fantastic event that, sadly, was quickly overshadowed by appalling stories of wasted money. The main pool, built at a cost of €18 million, was used for a month and then abandoned, left unfinished and unusable.

\* \* \*

Italia 90 is often considered to be the first World Cup of the modern era. It came at a time when FIFA was beginning to realise just how lucrative football could be, and in pouring so much money into organising the competition, the Italians set the standards for how a country could use the stage offered by the World Cup to flaunt its status or prove how well things were going for them.

Eventually that's what FIFA came to look for when organising a competition, that willingness to go to extremes. Perhaps also because those were also the countries willing to do anything needed to accommodate FIFA's demands. In the decades that followed, such excesses have been witnessed over and over, in Brazil, South Africa, Russia and Qatar. In most of those cases, the legacy has been as much of a failure as it was in Italy.

Perhaps it would have all been worthwhile had Italy managed to win the tournament. Instead the whole nation woke up from the hangover of those magical nights to find themselves faced with the reality of a wasted opportunity – sporting and non-sporting – with a massive bill that somehow had to be paid.

Three decades on, a new generation of owners, influenced by the growth of the Premier League, are trying to reverse the damage. They want to tear down the massive vanity projects of Italia 90 to build stadia that can attract fans back. Yet that isn't easy when those same buildings are owned by municipalities and regional governments who feel that they have other priorities. The slow pace at which Italian bureaucracy moves doesn't help, nor does the political implications that have to be considered before a decision is made. Too often, it ends up being too much, with owners opting to sell up rather than keep on throwing money at a project that they don't see going anywhere.

All this time Italian football has been regressing. For it's there that Italian football's slide from the very top of the game began. Arguably that's the one true legacy of Italia 90.

# Twist of Fate that Disrupted
# the Magical Nights

AS FAR as World Cup opening matches go, few have been as memorable as the one that kicked off Italia 90. Decades later, those who witnessed it still recall the defend-at-all-costs approach adopted by Cameroon, their unforgiving tackling that resulted in two players being sent off and, above all, their astounding, unexpected win.

What's less remembered is the nature of Cameroon's winning goal. They'd just won a free kick on the right side of the pitch. The ball was drilled into the penalty area, even though only a couple of players had ventured forward. No one could gain possession the ball, which looped up high into the air before dropping towards the edge of the six-yard box. And while the Argentina defenders stared at it as if frozen, the tall striker François Omam-Biyik leapt high to head the ball towards goal.

It was a good, downward header from close to the goal but, still, the goalkeeper, Nery Pumpido, should have at least parried it. Instead, he went down awkwardly – as if he was undecided on how best to deal with it – and allowed the ball to trickle into the back of the net.

Pumpido had been Argentina's goalkeeper four years earlier when, driven by Maradona, they managed to win their second World Cup. That made him the obvious choice to keep goal in Italy. At least in his and manager Carlos Bilardo's mind. Others had a different opinion.

Luis Islas had been Pumpido's deputy in Mexico in 1986 but now he was no longer happy to be a back-up. Even though a move to Europe with Atlético Madrid hadn't turned out to be successful – he ended up on loan at Logroñés – he felt that he deserved to start the competition as Argentina's No. 1. When told that wasn't to happen, he decided that sitting on the bench for a month wasn't for him and vociferously told everyone what to do with the No. 12 shirt.

It was an understandable reaction. That of a back-up goalkeeper has to be one of the worst positions to fill during a major tournament; there can hardly be any playing roles as unrewarding as that. You have to train as hard as anyone else in the squad to keep yourself in peak condition in case you're called into action, while knowing full well that the likelihood of that call coming is almost non-existent. And, in the meantime, you have to support as best you can the person who's blocking your path.

So while the manner of his exit was unnecessarily dramatic, Islas was justified in feeling as he did, especially after Pumpido's poor performance in the opening match. But what he didn't anticipate is what happened in the 11th minute of Argentina's second match, against the Soviet Union.

After Argentina had dominated the opening exchanges, the Soviets made their first foray, with a cross by striker Igor Belanov. Pumpido rushed out to gather it before any of Belanov's team-mates could react but, as he did so, he collided heavily with one of his defenders, Julio Olarticoechea. The keeper was unable to get to his feet. The impact caused a visible deformity in Pumpido's leg, and it was immediately clear that the injury was severe. The medical team rushed on to provide assistance, yet there wasn't much they could do. Pumpido was eventually stretchered off and taken to the hospital for further examination and treatment. It was the end of his World Cup.

Had Islas been patient enough, he'd have had the opportunity he felt he deserved. Instead it was Sergio Goycochea, nominally the third keeper in the original Argentina squad, who stepped up in Pumpido's place.

\* \* \*

That Goycochea was even in the squad illustrates just how weak the 1990 team was. He'd come through at Club Atlético Defensores Unidos, a small multisport outfit from the Villa Fox district in Buenos Aires. There Goycochea played in the lower leagues, often against semi-professional teams. He did well enough that in 1981 he was chosen to represent Argentina in the FIFA World Youth Championship. That brought him to the attention of bigger clubs, which, in 1983, resulted in River Plate stepping in for him. At River, he received his top-flight debut but not much more beyond the role of back-up goalkeeper.

Even though he stayed at River for five years, he barely played more than 50 times. Instead, he was very much an eternal deputy to whoever held the No. 1 shirt, which, ironically, also included Nery Pumpido for long stretches. Still, he was relatively young – just 20 when he signed for River – so it was all about gaining some experience. The occasional appearance gave him hope and, in the meantime, he was learning.

After five years of this, however, he felt that the time had come for him to go in search of more regular playing time.

River couldn't offer him what he wanted so he looked for an alternative. That meant a move abroad, with Goycochea opting for the Colombian league with Millonarios. There, for the first time in his career, Goycochea was a regular, and a decisive one at that. In his first season he helped them win the league title, which opened the path to the Copa Libertadores, which offered the opportunity for more heroics in front of a bigger audience. He delivered, first by playing a key role in helping them get out of the group phase and then into the quarter-finals, winning plaudits for saving the final, crucial penalty in a shoot-out against Bolívar.

Millonarios failed to go beyond that stage – knocked out by fellow Colombians Atlético Nacional in a hotly contested affair – but his excellent displays in the continent's leading club competition did get him noticed back home in Argentina. That, along with his experience as a back-up, made him the ideal choice as a substitute goalkeeper for Argentina, especially after the whole Islas incident. As far as Bilardo was concerned, Goycochea ticked all the boxes. He might have been a bit green, with barely two seasons as a regular, but he had experience of high-pressure international knockout competition and also a relationship with the pre-chosen No. 1. After all, his job was going to be more focused on helping Pumpido stay sharp than anything else.

All that changed in the 11th minute of the match against the Soviets. Argentina needed to win following their defeat to Cameroon and, led by Maradona, they did eventually run out 2-0 victors. For Goycochea, the introduction had been a bit shaky – he'd parried a couple of shots that he could have held on to – but ultimately there was no damage done. One down, and no goals conceded.

His second appearance was just as shaky. Although it would be harsh to blame him for Romania's equaliser in a 1-1 draw, he hardly covered himself in glory when he was dragged out of position by a looping cross that he was never going to get to. The result meant that Argentina were through – given the start they'd had it was already a significant result – but they'd finished in third place, making their path significantly harder. That included having to overcome Brazil in the following round. And although the Brazilians hadn't been brilliant, they'd still won all their group matches and conceded just one goal.

Goycochea enjoyed the ideal start to the match against Brazil, when an outstretched leg stopped Careca from scoring in the opening seconds. Yet it didn't seem to have a beneficial impact on his game, and he was lucky when a Dunga header hit the post. The second half passed in similar fashion, with Argentina defending deep to keep out Brazil, something that they did to great effect until Maradona managed to set Caniggia through to score the winning goal.

For Goycochea that meant two clean sheets in three matches, a fantastic return even if much of the merit lay with his defenders and midfielders, who kept everyone at bay. Up to that point, however, he'd looked very much like a reserve. Blessed with great reflexes, which often got him out of trouble, for every good save he made there were as many instances where he rushed out too rashly or failed to handle a cross. Pumpido hadn't excelled against Cameroon but up until the Brazil match there was little to indicate that his replacement had been a boon.

All that was to change in the quarter-final. Not during the match itself, however, since despite there being many creative players both for Argentina and Yugoslavia, the quality of football was dire. It wasn't all the players' fault, since the match was played in energy-sapping heat and humidity that almost killed off from the start any hope of excitement.

That Argentina weren't built to attack didn't help. They even benefitted from being a man up as early as the 31st minute, when Refik Šabanadžović was sent off. Despite that, the Yugoslavs were still the most adventurous team throughout 90 minutes, led by a masterful Dragan Stojković, who at the time was called 'the Maradona of the Carpathians'. He lived up to his nickname that afternoon, although, unlike the real Maradona, he didn't have a player shadowing him wherever he went on the pitch. Even a man down, the Yugoslavs opted to sacrifice a midfielder in order to man-mark the Argentina captain.

For all Stojković's brilliance, Yugoslavia only had two good chances across the 120 minutes. One was saved by Goycochea and the other saw a bad miss by Dejan Savićević. The Argentines, on their part, thought they'd scored in the final minute of extra time but the goal was ruled out for a handball infringement. So, as had seemed probable from the very start, it all came down to penalties.

Ironically, the only player who had shone that afternoon was the first to miss. Stojković stepped up to take Yugoslavia's first penalty and promptly hit the crossbar. Any Argentinian celebrations proved to be far too early. Maradona stepped up to take their third penalty but his weak shot was saved. Matters were compounded when Pedro Troglio, the next Argentine to step up, also missed – his shot hit the bar – to put his team on the verge of elimination.

At that point Goycochea hadn't even come near any of the Yugoslav penalties, so when Branko Brnović stepped up not many would have had high expectations of the keeper. Brnović hit his shot well – low and angled – but didn't put enough strength behind it. Goycochea dived in the right direction and managed to palm the shot away. Reprieve for Argentina.

And he wasn't done yet. When Faruk Hadžibegić stepped up to take Yugoslavia's fifth penalty he knew that he had to score. And, like Brnović, he could hardly have done better with his shot, which was angled, powerful and reasonably high. Unfortunately for him, Goycochea guessed right once more and his athleticism provided him with the spring needed to claw the ball out of mid-air.

The replacement goalkeeper was suddenly the team's hero. Maradona was still the one who attracted all the journalists after the match as he limped out of the stadium – the punishment he'd received during the match evident in a hugely swollen ankle – and he spoke of luck favouring them. It was a view shared by many, who indeed felt that Goycochea had simply been lucky to guess right on those two instances.

In truth, Goycochea had made use of a mixture of preparation and psychology. 'From the position and the run-up he took, I knew Brnović wasn't going to hit it very hard,' he explained. 'It was just a question of waiting till the very last moment to see how he shaped to hit the ball.' The keeper's athleticism and lightning-fast reactions allowed him to do that.

'Gabriel Calderón had played with Hadžibegić in France and he told me that he usually put them to the keeper's left,' he continued. 'I weighed things up: it was the last penalty, he had to score to bring them level and it was a critical situation … I felt he was going to go for the side he felt more secure about.'

Regardless of how he'd done it, the Argentines were happy. Twice they'd faced teams with better players, and they'd come through on both occasions without conceding a goal. For all the criticisms and their obvious shortcomings, they were once again in the semi-final; the possibility of defending the title won four years earlier was still alive.

To do so, however, they'd have to overcome the biggest obstacle yet. Not only were Italy one of the favourites for the title, something that they'd underlined with an almost faultless progression to the semis, but they also had the backing of the home crowd. Argentina were once more the underdogs, which suited them well. Still, there was plenty of pressure on them. Back home, the country was on the verge of economic collapse thanks to irresponsible borrowing and a faltering employment market. An Argentina win at the World Cup was seen as a potential antidote to all those ills.

It's unlikely that the players were told of such hopes when the flamboyant president, Carlos Menem, who loved to be seen alongside famous sportspeople, made the trip to the opening match of the World Cup. That visit gave birth to the popular belief that Menem was a jinx, especially after he was pictured trying to shake Pumpido's hand, failing and tapping him on the knee instead – the same knee that Pumpido was to injure in the match against the Soviet Union.

Amid all of this tension, Maradona kept his mood light. He went to the Italian training headquarters for a friendly chat with his Napoli team-mates, who formed part of the Italian squad along with Salvatore Carmando, the long-time Napoli physio, who also worked with the national team. Maradona ended up joking with the Italian manager, Azeglio Vicini.

Whether that was all a psychological ploy is debatable. There's little doubt, however, that Maradona knew which buttons to press. The match was to be played in Naples, his home for the last few years but also a symbol of the impoverished south. For numerous historic and cultural reasons, the investment that had flooded into the northern half of the Italian peninsula to build an industrial base for the country was never matched with a similar flow in the south. This created an economic imbalance that has also mutated into a disdain by the richer north.

That's what Maradona referred to when he told the Neapolitans who were being urged to support Italy in the semi-final, 'After so much racism, now they hurry to remember that Naples is part of Italy. After being called *'terroni'* [derogatory term for southern Italians], plague-ridden, earthquake-stricken for 364 days a year. After slapping them in every possible way, now they say that Neapolitans are also Italians.'

It was a poignant observation and the reality of what he said was reflected by the number of politicians queueing up to remind the people of Naples that they needed to support their country, rather than their club. The fear that rather than having the backing of the home crowd the *Azzurri* would end up being jeered was a real one. Ultimately it was never in doubt. As one banner hung in the stadium stated, 'Maradona, Napoli loves you, but Italy is our country!' There were still plenty of cheers and songs praising Maradona before the match but when the two teams entered the pitch they were welcomed by a wall of Italian patriotism.

Boosted by the support, the Italians immediately took control from the kick-off. For the first time in the tournament, Maradona wasn't being man-marked wherever he went, with Vicini deciding not to sacrifice someone to do so. Later, defender Riccardo Ferri explained his manager's thinking: 'He wanted to stop Maradona from even getting the ball, so the ball carrier shouldn't be put in a position to give him the ball easily, but rather give it to him perhaps in a bad way.'

On his part, Maradona had sacrificed everything to make it to this tournament. He'd been assigned a special diet to reach his optimal weight; he also wore a shoe with a metal insole to protect a damaged toe. Even so, he'd played through excruciating back pain while enduring punishment in every match – he was the most-fouled player in the competition by a distance – that would force his knee to balloon afterwards. As the tournament wore on, a limp whenever he walked became increasingly noticeable.

Still, he was the architect of everything good for Argentina, as Italy found out early on, when he pushed the ball to Burruchaga, whose shot forced Zenga to extend himself. That brief flitter forward aside, however, the Italians were in charge, and in the 17th minute they were also ahead. Schillaci, receiving the ball with his back to goal, held off two defenders before passing to De Napoli, who promptly fed it forward to Giannini. The Roma midfielder lifted the ball over the head of an Argentina defender and nodded it towards the penalty spot, where Vialli was waiting. Aware that defenders would soon be on him, Vialli took the shot before the ball hit the turf; a brilliant strike that might have surprised Goycochea earlier in the tournament but not now that his confidence was riding so high. Even so, the shot was too close and hard-hit for the goalkeeper to do anything but parry. Luck favoured Schillaci, as it did throughout the whole tournament, as the ball bounced off the goalkeeper's gloves and on to his foot. He barely had to move before it was bouncing into the back of the net and Schillaci was wheeling away in joy.

No one knew it at the time but the best move of the whole match had come and gone. Initially, the goal visibly demoralised the Argentines, whose passing became increasingly erratic, and energised the Italians. The latter, however, failed to press home their advantage and gradually Argentina began to move the ball around better.

Once the second half kicked off, Argentina were the better team. The pressure of defending an advantage, which would put them into the World Cup Final, started to weigh on the Italians, who began making mistakes. Three times Argentina had half-chances from which they should have scored, before finally a floated ball into the penalty box was nudged just enough by Caniggia to push it past an Italian defender and the onrushing Zenga. It was the first goal the goalkeeper had conceded for the national team, not just during the tournament but that whole year.

As soon as the shock of the equaliser settled in, the Italians started playing once more. They seemed fresher than the Argentines and could bring on better-quality substitutes to influence proceedings. Three times they could have scored but on each occasion they found Goycochea in unbeatable mood. Whereas earlier in the tournament he'd relied on luck, now he was pulling off incredible saves. Which is exactly how you want your goalkeeper to be when you go into a penalty shoot-out, which is how things ultimately ended.

Of the two goalkeepers who stepped up that evening, Walter Zenga was by far the most famous and respected, as a Serie A winner as well as the best goalkeeper of 1989 according to the International Federation of Football History & Statistics. He was arguably the finest in the world at the time.

On that particular evening, however, there was no comparison. While the cocksure Zenga only got close to one kick, Goycochea had a look of conviction on his face that hinted at a higher knowledge over what was to come.

Every time an Italian stepped up to kick, he dived the right way, just failing to stop the first three kicks.

Then came Roberto Donadoni's turn. The midfielder was a vital, albeit often under-rated, player in the great AC Milan of that era, someone who could combine skill with work rate. He was solid with his penalty kick as well, hitting it at a good angle and height to the goalkeeper's left. Yet, as he'd done so far, Goycochea guessed right and this time his leap was enough to reach the ball.

When Maradona scored the next Argentina penalty – Zenga once again going the wrong way – all of Italy's pressure fell on striker Aldo Serena, who had come on as a substitute. The fear that Serena felt in that instance was all too visible on his face, while his eyes betrayed where he was going to place his kick. Goycochea guessed right – another dive to his left – and he caught the weak shot, before running to the centre circle, into the arms of his jubilant team-mates.

As the legendary commentator Bruno Pizzul put it on Italian television: 'Argentina is a finalist in the World Cup, these are images we never wanted to comment on.' Goycochea, the goalkeeper who should never have even made it on to the pitch, had killed the dreams of a nation that felt destined for ultimate success.

Again, the saves hadn't been simply fortuitous. 'With Donadoni, I changed my mind during his run-up,' he said. 'He was very talented and it was the fourth penalty, and I thought he was going to play it safe by hitting it to my right. But when I saw him walking up very slowly and stopping and looking at me, I did a little shuffle to put him off. I knew exactly what I was going to do with Serena. We were in the lead, he was tall, he was totally left-footed and I was logically expecting him to put the ball to my left. I went that way, knowing that I'd find the ball there.'

\* \* \*

If Goycochea was the Argentina hero, then Maradona was the villain, at least in the eyes of most Italians, who would never really forgive him. Within a year he'd leave the club where he'd reached his greatest success and the country where he was no longer welcome.

All that was in the future, though, as there was a final to be played. The Italian antipathy exhibited itself in the jeering of the Argentinian national anthem, with Maradona caught by cameras mouthing the words '*hijos de puta*' (sons of bitches) to the crowd.

Such a reception might have served to further fuel the Argentines. Yet by this point they were too tired and battered to really push much harder. The absence of the dangerous Claudio Caniggia, suspended for the final, made their eventual success all the more unlikely, especially against a West German team that had spread around the workload throughout the competition and thus came to the final fresher.

Even so, the Argentines defended with everything they had. The us-against-the-world mentality that had served them so well throughout the tournament helped them here too. Their ambition, clearly, was to take the final to penalties. Yet perhaps they'd made too many enemies with their rugged tackling. With five minutes to go, Nestor Sensini went in to tackle Rudi Völler in the penalty area. Regardless of how many replays were shown, it was impossible to tell whether he'd touched the striker. Not that it mattered, since in the eyes of the referee he'd committed a foul that merited a penalty.

Andreas Brehme stepped up and, once more, Goycochea guessed the right direction. This time, however, the shot was too well angled for him to reach. West Germany were ahead and Argentina, who ended with two players sent off, had nothing left in the tank.

\* \* \*

Even so, Argentina returned home to a heroes' welcome. The fighting spirit shown by the team against all odds had made them almost more well loved than the team that had won the competition in 1986. Goycochea eventually expressed the belief that, despite the final loss, 'To my mind, it was as if we were world champions anyway.' It was as if the rest of Argentina agreed.

In addition to moving to Racing in Argentina after 1990, Goycochea also assumed the No. 1 position in the national squad, helping Argentina win the Copa América in 1991 and 1993. The shot-stopper's club career was imbalanced; a run of matches with Racing was followed by a disappointing tenure in Brest, France, and then uneventful stays with Cerro Porteño and Olimpia of Paraguay.

Just in time for the 1994 World Cup qualifying, a return to River Plate in 1993 was exactly what the doctor ordered. Goycochea and River won the 1993 Apertura, but his days were numbered because Germán Burgos took his position. Goycochea's spot in the national squad then suffered as a result of his club troubles. He struggled during qualification and bore the brunt of the criticism following Argentina's devastating 5-0 loss to Colombia at home, going from hero to villain. He'd never play for the national team again.

Still, any disgruntlement was temporary. When fate had provided Goycochea with an unexpected opportunity, he'd stepped up to become a national hero. For that he'd forever be remembered and revered.

# Pride of the Nation

FOR PEOPLE who dedicate their lives to improving themselves, working hard in training every day to be in the best possible shape for the next match and feeling the results of their efforts on the pitch, footballers can be quite a superstitious bunch.

Despite the objective advancements in medical sciences, physical preparation and data analysis that should have diminished this attitude, it remains surprising that players continue to rely on superstitions. Instead of utilising the available technology to identify the true causes of a poor performance, they often insist on stepping on to the pitch with a specific 'lucky' foot or wearing particular items of clothing they believe bring them good fortune. These beliefs can take a life of their own, from dressing rooms that are considered unlucky to kits that are felt to attract ill fortune.

One of the most infamous incidents involving the latter came in 2012, when AC Milan lost to Arsenal 3-0 in the Champions League wearing an all-black kit. 'Never again shall we wear them,' their notoriously superstitious general manager Adriano Galliani stormed afterwards, blaming the result on the colour of their shirt while confessing that he'd lobbied hard against the team wearing such a kit in the first place. Eventually he got his way and the kit was dropped soon afterwards.

So when West Germany lined up for their opening fixture of Italia 90 against Yugoslavia wearing their all-white kit with a German flag criss-crossing their chests, they were going against the grain of received football wisdom. Two years earlier, West Germany hosted a European Championship that they were overwhelming favourites to win. The combination of home support and a wonderfully talented group coached by a living legend in Franz Beckenbauer seemed irresistible. Instead, they fell at the semi-final stage, conceding two late goals to the eventual winners, the Netherlands. And they did so wearing that same kit.

That disappointment should have been all the reason they needed to ditch the kit, if not for superstition then to forget the bad memories that it held. They didn't even need to make up an excuse, as national teams didn't tend to retain the same kit from one tournament to the next. Not back then and certainly not today. Yet Beckenbauer liked that kit and for some reason suggested to the higher-ups within the association that they continue wearing it. And what Der Kaiser wanted, he usually got.

\* \* \*

Today it might appear the most obvious requirement but in the very early days of the game of football players didn't need to wear clothes of a similar colour to those of their team-mates. It was a game to be played, not watched, and you were expected to know who was on your team regardless of what they wear wearing.

Like many other aspects, this need evolved as the game began to consolidate around a unified set of rules.

As football's popularity increased, so too did the calls for uniform shirts worn by players of the same team. In 1879, a reporter commenting on an FA Cup tie involving the Birmingham Association was flustered enough by the absence of identifying characteristics between the teams to comment:

> In football it is a most essential point that the members of one team should be clearly distinguished from those of the other. The only way this can be effected is for each club to have a distinct uniform as the diversity of dress displayed yesterday not only confused the members of the team but the spectators were quite unable to say whether a man belonged to one team or another.

Within a decade that would be the case and the distinguishing colours began to emerge. There were still problems. As the game became more organised, the onus to acquire the team's kits fell to the clubs, rather than the individual players, as it had been in the early days. Looking to save on costs, these clubs often opted for the most basic and commonly available kits commercially, which sometimes meant that two teams turned up wearing the same shirts.

To avoid such issues of colour clashes, in 1891 Football League teams were asked to choose the colours in which they wanted to play. Where two or more clubs went for the same colours, the choice was given to whichever had been a member of the league the longest. This is why some of the oldest established clubs such as Notts County, Preston North End and West Bromwich Albion stuck to the colours that they'd always worn. Others opted for change. Everton, who had previously played in a salmon pink kit, went for a blue one, whereas Burnley went in the opposite direction and dropped their navy-coloured shirt in favour of a claret-and-amber one.

Wolves, who had gone into a match against Sunderland wearing red-and-white stripes and thus causing the colour clash that had forced the league into action in the first place, were among the most gallant. Taking inspiration from the Wolverhampton motto of 'out of darkness cometh light', they dreamed up the gold-and-black shirts they still play in to this day.

Apart from a couple of early versions that included a prominent red band across the chest, the shirts of West Germany have always been white with a variable degree of black thrown in. That tradition was adopted when the Federal Republic of Germany came into being late in the 1940s. When the *Mannschaft* astonished the world and won the World Cup in 1950, they did so wearing a kit made up of all-white shirts with black trimmings and black shorts. That would remain their look for the better part of the next four decades.

Then came 1988. In hindsight, it was rather serendipitous that on the eve of the events that would eventually precipitate German re-unification that West Germany would be awarded the right to host a European football championship. For their brothers and sisters across the wall, this was another reminder of what they were missing, of the economic miracle in the western half of their nation and the apparent forgiveness by the rest of Europe over what had happened during the Second World War. There was no such reprieve for those in the east, only the inevitability of no prospect of ever being able to hold such a celebration of football. It was another slight to add to the list of frustrations that would eventually spill over into the demonstrations that led to a change in regime.

It was also something of a relief that the East Germans had missed out on qualification, even if that had been a closer call than many would have liked. Avoiding defeat to Russia in their away match would have swung the qualification group in their favour but they couldn't get the draw they needed. Rather thankfully so; their presence would have been awkward, like a guest attending a party they were invited to but weren't expected to join.

Perhaps because of all these factors, that European Championship turned out to be a celebration of fun and a riot of colour. And nowhere was this more visible than in the kits on display. From the Republic of Ireland's mix of green and white to Russia's geometry-inspired red shirts, via Italy's always-stylish blue – it was a tournament of bold choices. Fittingly, it was won by the team that made the boldest choice of all, with the Netherlands moving to a shinier and brasher shade of orange. Perhaps it was what they needed to psychologically overcome the mental barriers that had stopped them claiming the ultimate prize in the past.

Those kits pushed the limits of what had been previously accepted. But the kit that stood out most of all was the one worn by West Germany. Flowing across the chest of the traditional white shirts were the colours of the German flag, starting from the back of the right-hand sleeve and ending at the top of the left-hand shoulder. The inclusion of the sleeves in the design was revolutionary. To that point, even the more experimental kit designs tended to focus exclusively on the front of the shirt, with no attempt to integrate the sleeves, other than giving them matching colours. This was new. It broke the mould, enlarged the canvas and made the players themselves appear larger.

And it didn't stop there. The shirt didn't offer a subtle hint of the German flag. It was actually the opposite and there was nothing reserved in the manner that the flag was displayed.

Taken individually, each one of the three colours was substantial; together they truly dominated one's vision. They were bold and left you in no doubt. This was a shirt that screamed confidence. Opponents beware.

Then there was the geometric design, one that gives an impression of the square root symbol. Again, the sharpness of it all seemed to hint at inherent German characteristics; their fame for precision perhaps, even if the clinical abruptness with which the lines changed direction issued an unquestionable impression of power.

That this shirt gave off such notions of strength was a bonus, one that potentially might have influenced Beckenbauer when he asked to retain it. He wouldn't have been the first to be swayed by such factors. Football people have long felt that certain colours are better than others. In the 1960s, Bill Shankly changed Liverpool's strip that until then had featured white shorts and socks to an all-red kit. Writing about this in his autobiography, Ian St John recalled how Shankly:

> ... thought the colour scheme would carry psychological impact – red for danger, red for power. He came into the dressing room one day and threw a pair of red shorts to Ronnie Yeats.
>
> 'Get into those shorts and let's see how you look,' he said. 'Christ, Ronnie, you look awesome, terrifying. You look 7ft tall.' 'Why not go the whole hog, boss?' I suggested. 'Why not wear red socks? Let's go out all in red.' Shankly approved

the suggestion and like that the iconic all Red
Kit was born.

Even more famous is the instance in 1996 when Sir Alex
Ferguson ordered his players to change from their all-grey
kit at half-time, with Manchester United losing 3-0 away
to Southampton. Many assumed it was down to superstition
but in truth it was based on the work that had been done
with a vision specialist called Gail Stephenson from the
University of Liverpool. One of the topics discussed with
her revolved around the difficulty players may have picking
out certain colours during a match. Grey was on that list of
hard-to-identify colours and those 45 minutes at The Deli
were enough to convince Sir Alex that the kit had to go.
And, indeed, they never wore it again.

Instinctively, there seems to be merit to such a decision.
When you're on a football pitch trying to pick out your
team-mates, you want them to be wearing colours that are
easily identifiable, not just from opponents but also from
the fans in the background. All-red kits help you do that,
grey ones not so much.

Colour psychology refers to the behavioural phenomenon
wherein people's decisions and actions are influenced
by colour. In the relentless pursuit of even the slightest
advantage over their competition, top-tier clubs have
extensively explored this subject, making it a highly debated
topic that has sparked numerous research efforts. However,
despite extensive study, conclusive results have remained
elusive. Academic investigations into the influence of shirt
colours on a football match have produced conflicting
outcomes, leaving researchers without a consensus.

Not that any kind of research would have enabled
anyone to conclusively say whether the shirts that they

wore at Italia 90 allowed any advantage to the German players. What's beyond doubt is that, stylistically, they looked wonderful.

That's a view shared by John Devlin. A self-confessed football-kit obsessive, the discovery as an eight-year-old of *The Observer Book of Football* and its colour plate section that depicted the shirts of the Football League at that time caught his imagination, starting a lifelong fascination with the colours and designs of football shirts. This obsession has led him to write four zealously researched and beautifully illustrated books about the history of football kits, two of which focus on English clubs, while the others look at international kits. Few can match the depth of his knowledge of football kits from every corner of the globe. He says of the German kit:

> If you look at football kits of the time, they were all fairly regimental; they all followed the same pattern. This was the first one to break the mould. I believe that the brief given in designing the kit was to push a bit the boundaries of what was typically expected from a football kit rather than just do a straightforward, typical design and it certainly did that. There was nothing really like it. We'd had vertical stripes in the 70s and 80s but this was the first time that we'd had a deconstructed flag across the front of a shirt.
>
> From a British point of view, football was a bit in the doldrums in that era. This kit brought a touch of glamour. It was a bold, brave kit. And it was unashamedly German.
>
> The style was rolled out throughout all the gear, not just the shirt. It was rolled out through

the tracksuit with which players warmed up and
that too caught attention. But it just captured
the glamour that perhaps was missing from
British football.

It's hard to find fault with Devlin's assessment. Attendances
in English football were declining drastically all through
the 80s, as a combination of years of fan violence and lack
of investment in football stadia made attending matches a
non-option to all but the most hardened fans. People were
falling out of love with the game and little was being done
to attract them back.

Italia 90 changed all that. In large part this was down to
England's success during the tournament, which suddenly
made following football fashionable again. Combined with
the significant rebuilding and modernisation of most stadia
following the recommendations of the Taylor Report, the
inquiry into the Hillsborough disaster, the game's popularity
rebounded in exceptional fashion.

Although it was West Germany that brought the English
dream of World Cup success to an end, they did also provide
a glimpse of what could happen if a fresh approach was
adopted to the designing of something as basic to the game
as the football kit. That's why Devlin feels that 'my memory
of it is that it was very well received. The other ground-
breaking kit of the 1988 tournament was the Dutch one but
a lot of the players said that they looked like goldfish, which
is why it was dropped after the European Championship.
That wasn't the case with the West Germany one.'

In this case, however, memory is playing a bit of a trick
on him. While the Germans continued playing in the same
kit in Italia 90, this wasn't because of some widespread
public acclaim.

'At the time, it was not a universal success. They liked it and it made a big visual impact for sure, but it was not a huge success,' says Ina Franzmann, who, at first glance, seems an unlikely player in the story of the team's kit for Italia 90. A diminutive, soft-spoken woman with a quick smile, there's little about her that hints at the flamboyance typically associated with fashion designers. Yet she was the one who came up with what eventually became one of the most iconic football shirts ever. Even though, as she recounts, it didn't look as if it was going to be the case at the time.

'There were two reasons for that,' she continues, without pausing from her previous statement. Clearly, she speaks as someone who has given this a lot of thought. 'The first was the strong use of the German national flag which, at the time, was still something of an issue because of the recent German history.' The passing of time has perhaps dimmed this but it's undeniably true that there were many who in the late 80s still bristled at such an obvious sign of German nationalism. 'The second reason was that the design was very loud, very obvious. So it received quite a bit of criticism.'

Time, however, softened those views too. Actually, it did much more than that. 'The big success of this shirt came years later,' Franzmann says. 'I cannot really tell you when the success of this began. All I can say is that for the first few years it was not a big success. I don't have figures of how it did commercially but what I do know is that the immediate reaction from other companies or fans wasn't "Oh my god, what a design!"'

Then, suddenly, it began to shift. There's more than a hint of amusement in her voice as she says, 'Over the past eight years, I have had so many phone calls like yours, of people wanting to talk about the story of this kit! I've had so many invitations and done so many interviews about it!

But that is all in the last decade and this shirt was designed 30 years ago. So at the time it did not have a huge impact on my career!'

That career in fashion design began early, as Franzmann tells her story:

> My grandfather was a tailor, so I was influenced from a young age by cloth, patterns and colours. The visual aspects and design was very important in my house, even though neither of my parents were particularly creative. At the age of 13 I bought my first sewing machine and started to create my own designs. My friends encouraged me because they liked what I was doing so from this time it became clear to me that I wanted to go into the fashion or textile business.
>
> So after school I decided to start an apprenticeship as a tailor. In reality this was a decision taken by my father, who wanted me to learn a trade as a condition for financing my studies but, I have to say, it was the right decision because I learned all the basics of the job. Looking back, I was very lucky because it gave me a good base for all that I did afterwards. When people ask me for advice, I always tell them the same thing: start with a basic apprenticeship.
>
> I was always lucky because the little atelier that I worked for, the owner was very much art-driven, so we were working along with artists, sculptors, jewellers and designers. I did this for two years during my high-school education and, looking back, they were very important for my career.

All this was preparation for the big opportunity of her career: a job at Adidas. Even if at first Franzmann didn't see it like that. 'I have to say that I wasn't too excited,' she says. 'Sports companies played a different role than they do nowadays. This was 1984 and, although they were a big company, you can't really compare it with what it is as a company today.'

To understand her frame of mind a bit better, one needs to appreciate the kind of company Adidas was at the time. Founded in 1924 by Adolf 'Adi' Dassler, it had begun life manufacturing sports shoes – they developed the spiked shoes that revolutionised running and assisted US sprinter Jesse Owens to achieve immortality at the 1936 Olympics – and had never really ventured too far from those roots by the time Franzmann received the offer to join as an assistant designer. Their focus was on shoes and technical equipment. That's what they considered to be their core business; that's what Adidas did. Apparel, on the other hand, was seen as a minor interest of theirs.

Still, having mulled the opportunity over, Franzmann eventually decided to accept, thus becoming just the third member of the textiles division; the size of the team being another indication of the importance given to this at the time.

It was a fortuitous decision because she got in at precisely the right time. 'By the time I started I was very excited,' she says. 'And I became even more so when I actually began working there.' Particularly impressive was the breadth of international activity within the company, which made forming part of such a small team quite beneficial. 'Within a couple of years I started getting a lot of opportunities to travel,' she says. 'I went on sampling trips to China or licensing trips to America. As you can imagine, this was all incredibly exciting for me because I was still 26 or 27 at the time.'

Yet what truly won Franzmann over were the people who worked within Adidas. 'I met a lot of people who were extremely passionate about what they were doing,' she continues. 'In particular I was very impressed by the drive and vision of Horst Dassler. I consider myself very lucky to have been able to work closely with him because he was an excellent owner and a truly visionary person.'

The son of Adidas's founder, Horst was an impressive innovator on his own merit. He'd founded the Arena swimwear brand and made it one of the leaders in that sector before taking a role within Adidas's executive management team upon his father's death. At the time the company was falling behind its competitors, but Horst managed to turn the tide by betting heavily on sport sponsorship and tying many national football as well as Olympic committees to exclusive deals with Adidas.

It was one such deal that led to the birth of an icon. Although this is a story that she's told many times, Franzmann can't mask the evident admiration towards her former boss when she starts retelling it:

> It was Horst Dassler himself who told us that we had this opportunity to design the new Germany shirt. Up till that point it had always been a white shirt with trims in black. Sometimes there was more black than in other instances but that was the basic design.
>
> We started asking, 'Why not have something more colourful?' And we were told that we could add colour to the shirt. When I heard that then immediately I was thinking that for sure we

should start with the colours of the German national flag.

The graphic was a little bit the spirit of this time. Graphics at the late 80s were very aggressive, very bold, very visual and I tried to transfer this to the football shirt.

For sure I had always in mind the player, the athletes. I wanted to accentuate the bodies of the players, particularly the shoulders. I wanted to give a great impact to the shoulders and when you look at the design the lines end up at the top of the shoulder. That was done to symbolise victory.

It might not be Shankly claiming his players looked seven feet tall by wearing an all-red kit, but it's a fascinating behavioural psychology twist nevertheless.

'I have to say that at the time we did all the designs by hand,' Franzmann says. 'There were no computers to help us. We designed hundreds of shirts on paper and then tried to imagine how they would look on the bodies.'

That may have been the case, but Franzmann need not have worried; they looked great on the players. Proof of that lies in the lasting popularity of this kit and the number of people who still wear it. In this manner, Franzmann has left more of a lasting impression on popular fashion than if she'd rejected the Adidas offer in search of a more traditional career in the fashion industry.

Evidence of that lies all around her. 'If you go to Paris, to Milan you always see this shirt,' she says. 'Unbelievable!'

\* \* \*

Few aspects are as revealing about the direction football has taken as the importance that's afforded to teams' football kits. Each year marketing teams across the world of football compete in the unofficial contest to come up with the loudest way to launch their club's new kit. As with many other aspects of modern life, kit reveals must be spectacular to grab people's attention. This has reached a point where the launches of home, away and even third kits are staggered across a period of weeks to get as many people as excited as possible.

And, amazingly, it works. Social media, the ultimate modern test of what's important, tends to be aflame whenever there's a new launch. Many are willing to spend weeks trying to anticipate what the kit will look like, often poring over shaky images of possible leaks, and then put even more effort into debating every aspect of the gear once it does land.

Football kits have become big business. Each year the Premier League's 'big six' clubs sell a combined total in excess of seven million shirts. When Lionel Messi moved to Paris Saint-Germain, they sold 150,000 shirts within 24 hours. Kit manufacturers Warrior Sport even took Nike to court to contest the right to pay Liverpool millions of pounds to produce their shirts. Indeed, it has become something of a tradition for the biggest clubs to break each other's record for fees paid by kit manufacturers.

The irony of all this is that the kits themselves are rarely that special. Changes tend to be significant enough for fans to feel pressured into buying the new one but not sufficiently noteworthy to truly fire up anyone's imagination. There tends to be greater willingness to play around with the second or third kits but, even here, the major manufacturers tend to have a template that they copy from club to club.

Often the most interesting and innovative kit designs tend to be at the periphery of the game, at smaller clubs looking to impress a wider range of fans than their regular base. They're the ones willing to experiment, and while some do tend to go for the garish, those who do it well guarantee themselves cult status, which also means selling many more shirts than they'd normally expect to.

Adidas has been at the heart of that revolution. The boldness – along with the creative freedom – with which the design for the German national team was approached was reflective of the culture within the company. As football rebounded in popularity after the 1990 World Cup and new fans were attracted to it, the production of kits became attractive business, one for which Adidas had laid down markers for excellence.

Devlin captures how significant that kit was:

> In some respects, if you look at some of the kits in that World Cup, they went backwards. The Dutch dropped the kit they had won Euro 88 with and used a more muted one. Then you had the Russian and Czech that were all angles and geometry. There was no hiding place, no elegance with those kits.
>
> But the German shirt was pure elegance. It definitely changed the trope and said that you can do more with what a shirt can be. It influenced the industry massively. I don't think Adidas weren't flying pretty high but this changed everything for them. It almost gave them legendary status.

Of course, there's an element of nostalgia around the acclaim surrounding this shirt, as Devlin explains:

Football is an inherently nostalgic sport. We look back at times when we were younger or our lives were perhaps less complicated and the images associated with them bear these kits. So when you look at these shirts you also bring up these feelings.

That doesn't change the fact that it was a brilliant piece of design.

Franzmann is more circumspect about it:

I've asked myself why its success didn't come earlier and my main explanation is that it was ahead of its time.

It is always the same with revolutionary, new ideas. The initial reaction isn't great but eventually it becomes a success. And that's what has happened with this shirt. It has become an icon. It is like a piece of art. Of course, I would not dream of comparing myself with any of the great artists – I am just a designer – but the way that this shirt has worked and had an impact is a similar one.

Framed in Franzmann's office is her iconic shirt signed by all the players who won West Germany their second World Cup. She often finds herself looking at it, recalling both the night that Lothar Matthäus lifted the cup to the skies and also what the shirt has meant, to the football kit industry as well as people and herself:

I was very lucky. To have had the opportunity to work at such a big brand as Adidas, to get to try and design the shirt for the German national team and that, at the end of the process, they decided to go with my design. There were many other designs by some fantastic people that were not chosen.

Actually, I'm very proud of the success of the shirt that I designed.

# The Soundtrack of Italia 90

AMONG THE great musical artists of the 1990s there was a group of three men who made for unlikely stars. For one thing, they were all in their late 40s or early 50s when they began touring together. For another, their genre wasn't a popular one: classical music.

Yet the Three Tenors, as the Italian Luciano Pavarotti and Spaniards Placido Domingo and José Carreras called themselves, was a bona fide supergroup, one of the biggest acts of the decade who could command a television audience that exceeded a billion every time a concert of theirs was screened. By the end of their run, it was believed that more than half the world's population had seen one of their concerts either live or as a video recording. Only Michael Jackson could keep up with them for album sales. They were at the heart of what the *New York Times* called 'a global tenor mania'. And all that success began at Italia 90.

It was 1987 when, as all of Italy was working hard in preparation for the World Cup, José Carreras received the devastating news that he was suffering from acute lymphoblastic leukaemia. The prognosis wasn't good; he was given only a one-in-ten chance of surviving. Yet after undergoing rigorous treatment that included chemotherapy, radiation therapy and an autologous bone marrow transplant, Carreras recovered.

To show his gratitude, and share some of his good fortune, he set up the José Carreras International Leukaemia Foundation with the aim of raising money to go towards research that would make it a curable disease for everyone. What no one could have predicted when he did so was how this would be the spark for a whole new cultural phenomenon.

It was Mario Dradi, his manager and producer, who first had the idea of doing something with other stars of the operatic world. Pavarotti and Domingo were contacted, with both proving to be open to the idea of welcoming their colleague back from his sickness in a concert, while raising funds for his foundation. The opportunity to do so on the eve of an event such as the World Cup also immensely appealed to them, as all three were massive football fans.

The idea fascinated the World Cup organisers too. They saw it as another opportunity to show the world Italy's beauty. The Baths of Caracalla in Rome were chosen as the ideal site. Built between AD 212 and 217 during the reign of the emperor who gave them their name, these thermae had been the second-largest in Rome. These highly evocative ruins had been given quite a facelift during the 1980s, with the vegetation that had overrun parts of the buildings being cleared and some illegal structures that had been constructed over the years torn down.

While all that helped, it wasn't what made this the ideal location. Since 1937, when a stage had been installed, the Rome Opera company had used the central part of the complex – the caldarium – to host its events during the summer. The location had plenty of operatic history for the occasion to resonate with lovers of the genre.

Two complete orchestras accompanied the Three Tenors – the Maggio Musicale of Florence and the Orchestra of the Rome Opera House – and such a big ensemble created its own issues. Even transporting them from and to rehearsals became an organisational ordeal.

Only a week before the concert the body charged with protecting the heritage site put the concert into question amid fears that it might result in some permanent damage to the Baths. This created another headache for the organisers as it would have been a nightmare to find another site, not least as construction for the stage scenery was already underway. Fortunately, the fears were ultimately unfounded and permission was given to go ahead.

The biggest hurdle, however, was what to sing. The Indian conductor Zubin Mehta insisted that the three had to sing together because, otherwise, they might as well have held three concerts in separate locations. The problem was that there weren't any operatic works that three tenors could sing together.

To overcome this problem a special score was penned that allowed them to sing a medley that could blend their talents.

This worked far better than anyone could have anticipated. The blend that the magic of the venue brought, along with a focus on more accessible pieces, enthralled not just those who typically attended operas but also those for whom the genre held no fascination.

Not everyone welcomed the success. For some, the repertoire they'd gone for was too populist, as if that threatened to tarnish the elitist, high-brow reputation of classical music, especially as the Three Tenors had started the experience by linking opera with a working-class sport like football. This received short shrift from Luciano

Pavarotti, who retorted, 'I'm sorry to be arrogant but …
the music, like sport, should be for everyone.'

In truth, the snobbish beliefs of an elitist few mattered
little. The impact that the trio achieved by using the
platform of football to engage a whole new audience was
ground-breaking. As the tenor Andrea Bocelli describes,
'As an aficionado football fan and a young opera singer still
trying to figure out my path in life, I remember [the Three
Tenors'] broadcast held me in thrall the entire time.'

Pavarotti would be on stage again the following day,
when, as part of the opening ceremony, he sang once more
the aria 'Nessun Dorma' from Giacomo Puccini's *Turandot*.
This too would in itself come to symbolise the World Cup,
albeit not purely for that performance. In fact, somewhat
coincidentally, the BBC had opted to use that same aria,
sung by the same tenor, for the credits of its daily World
Cup coverage. It proved to be an immediate hit, so much so
that the 1972 recording of Pavarotti singing 'Nessun Dorma'
– the version that the BBC had opted to use for the credits
– even made it to number two in the UK's musical charts.

While for a generation it's impossible not to think of
Italia 90 without hearing 'Nessun Dorma' in their heads,
that it was picked for a TV programme was very fortuitous.
Much of it had to do with a junior BBC sports producer
named Philip Bernie. He heard 'Nessun Dorma' playing
on the radio and was impressed by the aria, particularly the
rousing finale with the extended '*vincerrr … ooo*'.

Weeks later, when Bernie was making a short taster
documentary about Italian football for the draw of the
upcoming World Cup, he recalled that moment. He wanted
to end the documentary with a music montage featuring
Italian midfielder Marco Tardelli's famous celebration after
scoring the goal that sealed the World Cup for Italy against

West Germany in 1982. Bernie was struck by Tardelli's mouth-agape expression of extreme exaltation, with tears streaming down his face and his arms pumping wildly. It was an 'ultra-Italian expression' that he believed married up perfectly with the climax of Pavarotti singing *'vincero'* – I will win. The interplay of opera and football, of passion and emotion, worked brilliantly. It was as if Tardelli was singing the aria himself. Des Lynam, who fronted the BBC's coverage for that World Cup, even went as far as claiming, 'It will be remembered as probably the outstanding theme of any major televised sporting event ever.'

That such high praise seems totally adequate reflects just how momentous this combination of song and football was. What makes it more remarkable is that this wasn't where this convergence ended. Perhaps as if to signal how football was evolving from a game into a pop-culture phenomenon, music is as much part of Italia 90 as the football itself. It's also a reflection of just how ambitious the organisers of that World Cup were that they called on someone like Giorgio Moroder to write the tournament's official theme song.

Two years earlier, Moroder had been asked to write the official theme for the Seoul Olympics and had delivered 'Hand in Hand', a song that features a driving beat and electronic instrumentation that's typical of Moroder's style. Also typical of his style was the inclusion of melodic synthesiser lines and a chorus of female vocals that sing the song's title. Fittingly for the Olympics, the lyrics were about the power of unity and the importance of coming together to face challenges. The song had a positive and uplifting feel, with a catchy melody that's easy to sing along with. It was a memorable and energetic song that showcased Moroder's talents as a composer and producer. Its cultural impact hasn't been a lasting one but it was still a hit at the time, selling in excess of 13 million copies and hitting top spot in the charts of many countries. Italia 90 had to have something like that, if only for the host country to be able to celebrate the life of one of its most successful sons.

Born in South Tyrol, at 15 the young Moroder had picked up a guitar and found that he had a natural talent for it. Between 1959 and 1966 he toured across Europe earning a living as a musician. Eventually he ended up in Berlin, where he started writing music, earning a discreet fame that eventually led him to Monaco and then the US. Once there, he began working with a young Donna Summer, with whom he produced the hit that arguably gave birth to disco music: 'Love to Love You Baby'. He'd be with Summer for the key moments of her career, composing the likes of 'I Feel Love', 'Hot Stuff' and 'No More Tears', as well as hits for other disco divas, something that earned him the title of 'Father of Disco Music'.

His success wasn't limited to the music charts. During this period he also began composing movie soundtracks and scores, including those of *Midnight Express*, *American Gigolo*, *Superman III*, *Scarface* and *The Never Ending Story*. His work on *Midnight Express* earned him an Oscar for best soundtrack, a triumph that he repeated twice more, with his theme songs for *Flashdance* and *Top Gun*. 'Take My Breath Away', the title track from *Top Gun*, which resulted in Moroder's third Oscar, came in 1987, so his popularity was as high as ever when the invitation to write the World Cup song arrived.

Moroder got working on this in Los Angeles, together with his G.M. Project ensemble that was made up of Paul Engemann, Molly Ruffalo and Joe Milner. The first cut was a song with English lyrics – 'To Be Number One' – that was written by the lyricist Tom Whitlock, before working on an Italian version.

Talking about this process a couple of years later, Moroder said:

> Writing an anthem is not easy, and it is very different from writing a song. First of all, an anthem must necessarily be majestic, with a solid musical structure, but at the same time catchy and accessible to everyone.
>
> Given the international scope of the song, it must also have modern and carefully crafted sounds. Our country is not just about melodies and Neapolitan mandolins. The drive towards rock, perhaps with Latin sounds, is very strong.

To help shape that 'Latin sound' Moroder turned to Edoardo Bennato and Gianna Nannini. The two were already incredibly popular in their home country, yet neither was considered a typical Moroder singer. Nannini was a classic rock chick typical of the late 80s, with a harsh, raspy voice and an aura to match. Bennato, too, came from a rock background, although he was more shaped by Bob Dylan's folk rock. Both were defined as *canta-autore* – singer and songwriter – a tag that carries added weight in Italy, which has a rich tradition and where such artists are considered to be a cut above 'mere' pop singers.

Both then were unlikely choices. No one was more surprised at the choice than Bennato himself. He remembered:

> When my friend Franco De Lucia said, 'Look, Caterina Caselli [a legendary Italian singer and music executive, who, among others, discovered Andrea Bocelli] and Gianna Nannini want the lyrics of the song that will be the anthem of the

World Cup from you,' I replied, 'Are you crazy?' I sang and wrote without managers and producers. I was always in opposition. I did everything by myself. I lived surrounded by friends from the courtyard, in the Neapolitan district of Bagnoli.

I was free to ridicule everyone. I even got fired from the record company after [my debut] album and started playing on the street with a harmonica, drum and guitar.

For Bennato that freedom allowed him to sing about uncomfortable subjects, which he did frequently, using irony as a weapon against people in power. This made him a focal point of Italian counter-culture as well as an idol for dissatisfied Italian youths.

Whereas Pavarotti hadn't been troubled by linking his music to football, it wasn't the same for Bennato. Indeed, he was so worried about the negative impact to his reputation that taking part in such a populist event might have, that it almost prevented him from accepting. 'I was certain that I wouldn't be forgiven for writing "Notti Magiche", but Caterina and Gianna convinced me,' he said.

Unusual though it was, the choice was inspired. Bennato wrote the Italian lyrics for the song that they retitled 'Un Estate Italiana' (An Italian Summer) and, within the simple framework that Moroder constructed, they managed to combine words that were quite powerful. Has ever a song touched upon the impact of football as well as this?

> *Quel sogno che comincia da bambino*
> *E che ti porta sempre piu lontano*
> *Non e una favola, e dagli spogliatoi*
> *Escono i ragazzi e siamo noi*

That dream that begins as a child
And takes you further and further away
It's not a fairy tale, and from the locker rooms
The boys come out and it's us

They even managed to echo the triumphant '*vincero*' in their chorus of:

*E negli occhi tuoi*
*Voglia di vincere*
*Un'estate*
*Un'avventura in piu*

And in your eyes
Desire to win
One summer ·
One more adventure

The song made its debut on the night of the draw, and by the time the duo sang it at the opening ceremony it was everywhere. For Bennato, a huge Napoli fan, it also led to a bewildering interaction with one of his heroes. 'During the afternoon as we were going through rehearsals for the opening ceremony, I saw Diego Armando Maradona walking straight towards me from the other side of the pitch,' he said. 'Hey, Edoardo,' he was told when the Argentine reached him. 'Can you present me to Gianna Nannini?'

While that anecdote captures the essence of the Napoli legend, it also shows the cultural significance that 'Un Estate Italiana' held, going beyond the traditional confines of a football song.

Bennato is fond of retelling another story that shows how popular the anthem had become:

In 1991, B.B. King was playing in Pistoia. They asked him if he wanted to duet with me and he replied, 'Bennato? Who is he?' When they told him that I was the one who wrote the World Cup anthem, he agreed, and on stage, we sang 'Signor Censore' together. Later we duetted again in Sardinia and he greeted me saying, 'Hey man, you can play the blues.' I won my World Cup!

All that might not have been possible had official World Cup songs not come into being through an unlikely origin story: a printing press in Chile.

That the South American country won the right to host the World Cup in 1962 is, in itself, a wild story, the brief version of which goes something like this: after two World Cups hosted in Europe, the South American countries successfully argued that it was their turn to hold the competition. Argentina were the favourites, not only because they'd failed in previous bids but as they had the best infrastructure. The Chilean bid committee, however, embarked on an extensive tour, meticulously building personal relationships and support for their claim. Then, in a brilliant move, when the FIFA Congress met in 1956 to make the final decision, they countered Argentina's claim: 'We can start the World Cup tomorrow, we have it all,' with the phrase *'porque no tenemos nada, queremos hacerlo todo'* (because we have nothing, we want to do it all). All their efforts paid off as Chile received more than three times as many votes as Argentina.

That desire to do it all wasn't merely a nice slogan, it reflected the grit of a whole country determined to make the most of the opportunity.

Nothing manifested that more than the story of how 'El Rock del Mundial' came to be. The son of the Los Ramblers' former lead singer Jorge Rojas explains, describing the circumstances that led to the song's creation:

> My father worked with my grandfather in his printing press and, bearing in mind the excitement of the next World Cup, they planned to do business with hats, headbands and stationery related to the event, but it was a very important and expensive investment.
>
> It was there that an uncle told him that seeing that he was a musician, why didn't he write a song dedicated to this occasion. So in three days the lyrics were made and then the music of this anthem, all from a family idea it was not commissioned by the organisation or FIFA, as are the songs today.

The lack of official backing didn't harm it and 'El Rock del Mundial' became an instant hit. To this day, it's still among the best-selling singles in Chilean history, with reportedly over two million copies sold. So popular did it become that presses had to give printing copies of it priority over anything else. Back in 1962 it was also the perfect uplifting tonic that a nation reeling from a powerful earthquake that left thousands dead needed to make the effort necessary to host the world.

With a simple rockabilly tune aimed at getting people dancing, and uncomplicated lyrics with a universal theme, it's easy to see why 'El Rock del Mundial' was eventually adopted by the organising committee and accepted by FIFA. This song, which starts off with the lyrics, 'The 1962 World

Cup is a universal celebration / Of the sport of soccer as a general motto / Celebrating our victories, we will dance rock and roll' is catchy, uplifting and straightforward; it's the template that all World Cup official songs, which became a staple of the competition after 'El Rock del Mundial', still follow to this day.

England had taken to this tradition early, and by 1966 had their own official song for the home World Cup. In reality, official is perhaps stretching it: the FA had merely approved the release of a World Cup song called 'World Cup Willie' by skiffle icon Lonnie Donegan, and it was a hit. From then on it became something of a tradition for there to be an official song whenever the English team made it to a major tournament. Some – 'Back Home' and 'This Time' – became cult classics; others were instantly forgotten.

'All the Way' was decidedly among the latter. The official song for Euro 88 was produced by Stock, Aitken and Waterman – who at the time dominated the English music charts – and featured the usual host of England players in the official video. Much like England that summer, 'All the Way' proved to be a disaster and didn't sell well.

The stink that 'All the Way' raised lasted for a long time. 'When the World Cup 1990 came around there was a distinct lack of enthusiasm on behalf of everybody, I mean players and artists, nobody really wanted to touch it,' David Bloomfield, the FA's press officer in 1990, confirms.

Bloomfield would change all that. A big music fan, he chanced upon a regional TV programme called *Best and Marsh*, which featured George Best and Rodney Marsh talking about great matches. What caught Bloomfield's attention, however, was the show's signature tune, which the end credits revealed was by New Order. This gave

Bloomfield an idea and the following day he called his friend Tony Wilson to see whether New Order would be interested in writing the England song for Italia 90. Wilson not only owned the legendary Manchester music label Factory Records but was also New Order's manager. He was immediately enthusiastic about the idea and accepted, despite the fact that at the time the band was on hiatus.

Fortunately, the band members agreed. As bass player Peter Hook told the *Manchester Evening News*, 'The great thing about New Order is we always used to do things for devilment. If there was something we shouldn't do, we would do it. We flew in the face of doing anything normal and it was a great trait. So we said, "Yes." And of course we were then absolutely terrified as we didn't know what to do.'

They figured it out, however. Expanding on music that band members Stephen Morris and Gillian Gilbert had recorded for a current affairs show, they eventually had the core of the song ready. At that point they turned to Keith Allen, an actor as well as a massive football fan, to help with writing a rap part aimed at giving it a more contemporary feel.

The finishing touches were applied by the players themselves, or at least the handful who actually turned up at the recording studio. The dismal failure of 'All the Way' had convinced many of them to stay away, and those who did go couldn't stay long as they were needed at the opening of a new clothes shop in Middlesbrough.

Even so, that brief interaction was enough for the producers to capture John Barnes's iconic rap. While Barnes's musical ambitions at the time were widely derided, he certainly impressed Hook. 'John Barnes really rose to the occasion,' he said. 'He took it over. He helped Keith Allen write much of the rap section and he nailed the performance within seconds.'

The end result fitted nicely with Bloomfield's original vision:

> My ambition from the very first was to turn out a decent song that could stand or fall on its own merits. If you link it with the football, fine, but it didn't necessarily have to do that. There are all the other examples that, if you didn't listen to them in a football context, it would be totally unbearable, it's torture, but if you link them to football then maybe you can get through the three minutes of it. But with this one I wanted it to be able to stand alone and I think it does.

It certainly does. While it might not have had the chest-thumping quality that made 'Three Lions' so popular, 'World in Motion' is the better song. There's a mellow quality to it that was a shift away from the usual us-against-the-world rhetoric of football songs, something best exemplified by the chorus of:

> Love's got the world in motion
> And I know what we can do
> Love's got the world in motion
> And I can't believe it's true

It was the perfect song for a sport looking to break away from the violence and darkness of its recent past. In a way it foreshadowed what was to come, with football becoming part of pop culture as much as music or films.

The real genius of 'World in Motion' lies in how it manages to be catchy enough to please popular tastes without moving into the realm of cringe; it's a good song. Not many others managed to get that balance right. The USA, for instance, went for a rap piece titled 'Victory' that, despite being produced by hip-hop legend Def Jef, is about as good as you would expect of a rap sung by 20 young, largely white males with no musical talent. Although the song clearly had good intentions, with ideas of self-respect, admiration and strength of character, as well as the ubiquitous anti-drug message, it was simply too earnest. It goes on for three minutes with lyrics such as: 'With dedication, heart and soul you have the tools to achieve your goal,' which is around three minutes more than most people can take of such forced positivity.

The Germans also tried to play it cool. Sort of. They employed the Austrian singer Udo Jürgens, who had won Eurovision for his country in 1966 and was extremely popular in Germany, where he sold more than 100 million records. 'Wir Sind Schon auf dem Brenner' is a typical schlager, the genre that became famous after the Second World War, with its catchy instrumentals and uplifting lyrics. The title and song refer to a German phrase that means 'we are already on the Brenner'. The Brenner is a mountain pass located in the Alps between Italy and Austria and it's a common route for drivers travelling between the two countries. The phrase can be used to indicate that someone is already on their way or in the process of travelling to their destination via the Brenner pass. As with the football played by the national team, the German song was functional more than anything else.

While the Americans and Germans put a lot of effort into their songs, others went with a more DIY attempt.

Costa Rica were among the latter. An eerie introduction – all you hear for the first ten seconds of 'Lo Daremos Todo' is the sound of the wind – eventually giving way to a basic synthesiser-driven tune and the voices of the Costa Rican squad belting out the words as if shouting the national anthem. The end result is that it sounds more like a recruitment theme for a military organisation than a song to celebrate participation at the World Cup.

Other attempts were just as poor, even though they did a brilliant job of foreshadowing what was about to happen. This is the only thing that Sweden got right in this World Cup. The squad sang alongside DJ After Shave in an instantly forgettable ode to Italy and Swedish hopes at the World Cup in a song titled 'Ciao, Ciao Italia'. Sadly for them they were soon saying, rather than singing, ciao to Italy, being one of the first teams to be eliminated, with an abysmal record of played three, lost three.

As with the Swedes, the Dutch also suffered an early exit from the World Cup, amid infighting and big egos clashing with the national federation's management. There were too many players who wanted to run the show and do everything themselves, when, in reality, they'd have been better placed to stick solely to playing. Proof of that lies in the Dutch effort at morale-boosting ahead of the World Cup. 'Het is Fijn in Italie te Zijn' – 'It is Nice to Be in Italy' – was sung by Marco van Basten and Frank Rijkaard. Both were fantastic players but their talents didn't extend to singing. That the accordion trying to give this song a semblance of a melody is whiny and, well, out of tune, doesn't help, but the reality is that nothing could have saved the song from its two singers. Van Basten and Rijkaard are so bad that it's breathtaking how no one stepped in to stop this abomination from being released.

In the history of bad World Cup songs, this surely is the worst.

Thankfully not all songs issued in time for Italia 90 were that bad. Just as every child is beautiful in the eyes of their parents, 'Give it a Lash, Jack' will always be a great song to Irish ears and hearts. Legend has it that it's one of Bono's favourite Irish songs and even if, sadly, that's a myth, it's easy to see why it's a believable one. For this folksy attempt at raising Irish spirits is catchy enough to be enjoyable even for those whose hearts don't flutter at the sight of green shirts.

Regardless of the impact any of the music that came out to celebrate Italia 90 might have had at the time, almost all of it was forgotten as the years rolled by. But football has a way of keeping old ideas alive.

In early June 2021, following an impressive 3-0 win against Turkey in their first match of Euro 2020, as they q made their way back to their hotel the Italian players filmed themselves singing 'Un Estate Italiana' in celebration on their Pullman. It was the first time since Italia 90 that they were competing in a major tournament on home soil, even though on this occasion they weren't the hosts, with the fixtures being spread across Europe. Yet that unique joy that comes from playing in front of your own people on such a big occasion probably inspired the old song's reprise.

It certainly hadn't featured in earlier tournaments. When Italy won the World Cup in 2006, they did so accompanied by the White Stripes' 'Seven Nation Army' (or, to be specific, the 'po-popopo-po-po' chant that echoes the song's beat). That had remained the unofficial Italian anthem in subsequent tournaments, both when they did poorly and when they almost won it all, like at Euro 2012.

So the return of 'Notti Magiche' was quite unexpected. The song had been somewhat tainted by the Italian failure to make it to the final of the home World Cup, as if the mere opening notes of that song were enough to remind them of the heartbreak of seeing Sergio Goycochea eat up Roberto Donadoni and Aldo Serena's penalties to eliminate them from a competition many felt was destined to remain in Italy.

Yet here was the current squad singing that song in a manner that indicated that 30 years was enough to exorcise that particular demon. The Italians weren't expected to go far in the tournament, and the quality of their squad was far inferior to the one that had taken on the world in 1990. Perhaps that was it – with expectations so low there was little to lose by singing 'Un Estate Italiana'.

It caught on, as these small moments of joy tend to, and went viral. By the next match it had become the unofficial Italian anthem of the tournament and from then on it could be heard every time the *Azzurri* played. And they kept playing, beating one rival after another as they mounted one of the most surprising runs to the final of Euro 2020.

At long last, after 31 years, 'Notti Magiche' could come to represent what it had always promised to be: an anthem for nights of Italian magic.

In hindsight, there was an ominous symmetry with Italia 90. Back then the Italians had one of the best teams in the world, while here they started as underdogs. And whereas in Italy they'd always played in stadia where the home support dominated, they were entering the final at Wembley, the home of their opponents.

When the match went to penalties, you could sense what was going to happen. As the home team wilted under pressure, the Italians kept their cool to deliver an unexpected triumph. The redemption of 'Notti Magiche' was complete as it was blasted out during the team's return home as heroes.

The echoes of an Italian summer in 1990 could be heard once more.